Intricate Palette

Working the Ideas of Elliot Eisner

Intricate Palette

Working the Ideas of Elliot Eisner

P. Bruce Uhrmacher

University of Denver

Jonathan Matthews

Carroll College

PEARSON

Merrill
Prentice Hall

Upper Saddle River, New Jersey
Columbus, Ohio

Library of Congress Cataloging-in-Publication Data

Intricate palette: working the ideas of Elliot Eisner / [edited by] P. Bruce Uhrmacher, Jonathan Matthews.
    p. cm.
Includes bibliographical references and index.
ISBN 0-13-112272-X
    1. Eisner, Elliot W. 2. Education—Philosophy. 3. Art in education.
I. Uhrmacher, P. Bruce. II. Matthews, Jonathan.

LB885.E372I58 2005
370'.1—dc22   2004044551

Vice President and Executive Publisher: Jeffery W. Johnston
Executive Editor: Debra A. Stollenwerk
Editorial Assistant: Mary Morrill
Production Editor: Kris Roach
Production Coordination: Thistle Hill
Design Coordinator: Diane C. Lorenzo
Cover Designer: Ali Mohrman
Cover image: Getty One
Production Manager: Susan Hannahs
Director of Marketing: Ann Castel Davis
Marketing Manager: Darcy Betts Prybella
Marketing Coordinator: Tyra Poole

This book was set in Baskerville BT by Integra. It was printed and bound by Phoenix Color Book Group. The cover was printed by Phoenix Color Corp.

Pearson Education Ltd.
Pearson Education Singapore Pte. Ltd.
Pearson Education Canada, Ltd.
Pearson Education—Japan

Pearson Education Australia Pty. Limited
Pearson Education North Asia Ltd.
Pearson Educación de Mexico, S.A. de C.V.
Pearson Education Malaysia Pte. Ltd.

10 9 8 7 6 5 4 3 2 1
ISBN: 0-13-112272-X

*This book is dedicated to all who believe
in the educational power of the arts and
to those who have yet to be convinced.*

EDUCATOR LEARNING CENTER: AN INVALUABLE ONLINE RESOURCE

Merrill Education and the Association for Supervision and Curriculum Development (ASCD) invite you to take advantage of a new online resource, one that provides access to the top research and proven strategies associated with ASCD and Merrill— the Educator Learning Center. At **www.EducatorLearningCenter.com** you will find resources that will

enhance your students' understanding of course topics and of current educational issues, in addition to being invaluable for further research.

How the Educator Learning Center will Help Your Students Become Better Teachers

With the combined resources of Merrill Education and ASCD, you and your students will find a wealth of tools and materials to better prepare them for the classroom.

Research
- More than 600 articles from the ASCD journal *Educational Leadership* discuss everyday issues faced by practicing teachers.
- A direct link on the site to Research Navigator™ gives students access to many of the leading education journals, as well as extensive content detailing the research process.
- Excerpts from Merrill Education texts give your students insights on important topics of instructional methods, diverse populations, assessment, classroom management, technology, and refining classroom practice.

Classroom Practice
- Hundreds of lesson plans and teaching strategies are categorized by content area and age range.
- Case studies and classroom video footage provide virtual field experience for student reflection.
- Computer simulations and other electronic tools keep your students abreast of today's classrooms and current technologies.

Look into the Value of Educator Learning Center Yourself

A four-month subscription to Educator Learning Center is $25 but is **FREE** when used in conjunction with this text. To obtain free passcodes for your students, simply contact your local Merrill/Prentice Hall sales representative, and your representative will give you a special ISBN to give your bookstore when ordering your textbooks. To preview the value of this website to you and your students, please go to **www.EducatorLearningCenter.com** and click on "Demo."

Contents

Foreword

"COUNT ME IN!"

You are about to engage with a superb book that has been inspired by the work of my lifelong friend and colleague, Elliot Eisner. "Lifelong" is only a minor exaggeration in this case; Elliot and I have known each other for more than 50 years. As is the case with many of my closest friends, Elliot and I argue about a lot of things. He thinks about education in terms of the arts; I think about it like some sort of psychologist. (I would have said "social scientist," but I fear that my credentials for the "scientist" descriptor are somewhat tainted.) He gets great pleasure from irritating the "mainstream" of educational scholarship; I like to think of myself as operating within that mainstream, more or less. Once, during a Stanford University School of Education faculty meeting, I sought to find some aspect of educational scholarship about which Elliot and I could both agree and suggested that certainly we agreed that any serious assertion about education had to be accompanied by some sort of "warrant"— a term that John Dewey (an icon for both of us) used regularly. Elliot would have none of it, insisting that *warrant* was a term that dripped of its roots in the sciences and in the law, both antithetical to his sense of truth and beauty.

But we don't argue about everything. We are both Chicagoans who love the astounding collections and ambience of that city's magnificent Art Institute (where Elliot was once a student) and who remain married to women we met while working in Chicago-area synagogues as youth workers or teachers. Indeed, I first met Elliot when he was *my* youth group leader at the Jewish People's Institute on Chicago's Douglas Boulevard on the west side of the city. He met his wife Ellie when he worked as a youth leader at her synagogue on the south side of the city. And he first met my wife Judy when he was youth director at *her* synagogue in the suburbs of north Chicago. West, south, north—when it came to working with young people and earning a living, Elliot had no geographic or directional biases.

The Art Institute of Chicago has long been a kind of second home to Elliot. Back in the "old days," you entered the building and began to ascend a marvelous central staircase, at the top of which hung El Greco's magnificent *Assumption of the Virgin*. I'm certain that painting was a favorite of Elliot's, as it has been for so many of us who spent long hours at the Institute. I recall the painting with particular affection, however, because of how its study influenced my own intellectual and aesthetic development.

Domenico Theotokópoulos, called Ei Greco, Spanish, b. Greece, 1541–1614, The
Assumption of the Virgin, *1577, oil on canvas, 401.4 × 228.7 cm, Gift of
Nancy Atwood Sprague in memory of Albert Arnold Sprague, 1906.99—unframed.
Copyright© The Art Institute of Chicago.*

I think the following anecdote also illustrates a maxim regarding Eisner's
view of the educative power of the arts.

For three full weeks during my first year in the College of the University of Chicago in 1955, I sat with four other students and Professor Harold
Haydon as we studied that one painting. We studied slides of the entire
painting and of its details. We traveled downtown to view the original more
than once. As a student of Talmud, I had experience spending many days
delving ever more deeply into a single passage of sacred text but never
imagined one could do that with a painting. Haydon taught us to look at
that particular work, and in doing so he helped us learn how to look at all
works of art, both visual and in other media. In the process, he also helped
us learn to look and see more generally.

Fast-forward to 1969, and I am now co-teaching Introduction to Clinical
Medicine to a group of 10 first-year medical students at Michigan State University's new medical school. My fellow teachers are a pediatrician and a physiologist. Somehow, I am leading the discussion as one of the students is making
a presentation on the renal system (the urinary tract and associated structures
and functions) as a way of understanding a particular clinical case. I approach

the diagrams he has prepared, and as I cover part of his diagram with my hand, ask: What would happen if this part of the system were absent? I then move to another part of his representation and raise a similar query. After class, my physiologist colleague marvels at how deeply I must understand the physiology to ask such penetrating questions. I then confess that my knowledge of physiology is sorely limited; I was applying to the analysis of the renal system what I had learned to do in analyzing the El Greco painting! I was not transferring content knowledge; I was employing "ways of seeing."

I tell this long story because I find in it a connection to the work of Elliot Eisner. Elliot has long valued the critical importance of the enlightened eye, the ways in which education exercises its influence through informing the human capacity and disposition, not only to look, but to see. For Eisner, the juxtaposition of seeing, knowing (connoisseurship), and criticism form foundations for both learning and scholarship. Ways of seeing, of making sense of the world through one's aesthetic sensibilities, lie at the heart of the process. This is a powerful lesson for all educators, at all levels.

Psychoanalyst Bruno Bettelheim, one of Elliot's University of Chicago mentors, shared Eisner's view of the centrality of ways of seeing. In his classic *The Informed Heart*, Bettelheim observes that psychoanalysis is simultaneously three achievements: a method of psychotherapy, a theory of personality, and a way of seeing and making sense of the world. Although it is typically discussed in terms of its first two functions, Bettelheim argues that in its third role, as a way of seeing, psychoanalysis makes its most profound contribution to human understanding. Not coincidentally, Bettelheim, too, came to education from the arts. His doctorate from Vienna was in art history and aesthetics, not in psychology or education. Eisner and Bettelheim shared a common bond regarding the centrality of the arts in the worlds of education and community. Just as Eisner reflects the impact of his teachers, this volume also illustrates eloquently his influence on others, on both his many remarkable students and his illustrious peers. They have elected to come together to write of the man, his work, and its importance for our community.

What kind of role has Elliot Eisner played in the world of education and education scholarship? Of course, this entire volume is devoted to answering that question, but I shall address it in a more personal manner, via a story that Elliot himself loves to tell.

This one may be Elliot's favorite story. At least, I've heard him tell it many times in many contexts—from faculty meetings to informal gatherings at one of our homes. Whenever he tells it, it fits the occasion, and everyone laughs heartily—especially Elliot. I find in it a number of clues into who Elliot Eisner is, and how he defines himself.

One morning in *The New York Times*, the following advertisement is displayed prominently:

Wanted: a courageous, skilled and knowledgeable person to lead an expedition to a dangerous and hitherto unmapped region of Africa populated by a variety of aggressive and dangerous animals. Successful applicant should

*have substantial experience exploring in wilderness areas of Africa, demon-
strated skill with a variety of weapons, and evidence of personal bravery and
leadership skills.*

    The next morning, bright and early, a small, unprepossessing
Jewish man enters the office and announces, "I've come in response to
the ad." The receptionist ushers him into the office of the expedition's
sponsor.

    "So you are interested in the position we have advertised. How
much experience do you have in Africa?"

    The visitor responds: "I've never been there, and to tell you the
truth, I wouldn't be caught dead there."

    The sponsor is puzzled. "And what kinds of background do you
have with firearms?"

    "Between you and me, they scare me to death. I don't want any-
thing to do with guns of any kind."

    Exasperated, the sponsor continues: "And the evidence of your
personal courage under stress?"

    The visitor laughs: "I'm a coward through and through; my
shadow gives me palpitations."

    "Then why in the world have you come in response to our ad?"

    "I wanted to come first thing this morning and let you know—
regarding your job—*Count me out!*"

Why does Elliot so love that story? First, I think he likes the idea of the
little Jewish guy getting the best of the arrogant and apparently well-heeled
sponsor. But I also think that Elliot has been saying something similar to the
conventional wisdom of educational research for more than 40 years, as
well: Take your paradigms for research and evaluation, for evidence and
inference, your conceptions of criticism and understanding—and "Count
me out." Elliot has followed the advice of my late mother when she taught
me how to slice brisket in our delicatessen: Always cut against the grain. As
Bruno Bettelheim used to advise us, "Get a good fix on the direction in
which your field is currently headed, and then set out in the opposite direction. By the time the field recognizes that it's embarked on the wrong journey, you will already be where they will wish they had gone."

    Elliot has not been satisfied, however, to shout "Count me out" and
remain there. He has consistently proposed, exemplified, and educated for
another way, an alternative route, and a different way of making sense of the
world. He has not isolated himself or his students in a separate universe,
periodically sending artillery shells of critique and disdain to pound away at
the other side. Instead, he has actively engaged those with whom he disagrees, in conferences and in his writings, in faculty meetings and at dinner
parties. In a powerful way, Elliot has exclaimed "Count me in" even as he
has asserted "Count me out." Eisner's perspectives on ways of seeing, on the
educational imagination, on expressive objectives, on the varieties of curriculum, on the teaching and learning of the arts, on qualitative research
methods, and on so many other topics have never been ignored by his peers,

even as they have battled with him about them. It is no accident that he was elected president of the American Educational Research Association, an organization whose members mostly do not share his perspectives about criticism and connoisseurship. Many of us may have disagreed with Eisner, but we could never ignore his powerful ideas.

In reading many of these essays, we also can discern a sense of Elliot Eisner the person. He is a wonderfully warm, generous, supportive, funny, and loyal friend, colleague, and mentor. His warmth pervades everything he does and everyone whose life he touches. I still remember the evening when, upon learning that my daughter-in-law's father came from a family of luggage manufacturers, Elliot's eyes lit up. "Did you make Dresner luggage?" he asked. Upon hearing an affirmative response, Elliot abruptly left our house and headed back home (less than two blocks away). He soon reappeared lugging an ancient suitcase he had retrieved from his garage. "My family used to own a luggage store in Chicago," he exclaimed. "This is an original piece of Dresner luggage!" This exuberant act was characteristic of Eisner the person. Making personal connections, transforming new acquaintances into old friends, Eisner's interpersonal style is a significant ingredient in accounting for the role he has played in the field of education.

I would say of Eisner's work what Immanuel Kant once said about the *Critique of Pure Reason:* "But he who undertakes to judge, or still more, to construct a [philosophical] system ... must satisfy the demands here made, either by adopting my solution, or by thoroughly refuting it and substituting another. To evade it is impossible."

In his writings, Eisner raises fundamental questions about knowing, investigating, and educating. We come together in this volume to acknowledge the centrality of the questions he raises and the compelling character of the arguments and examples he puts forward. We are privileged and empowered when we explore those critical and stimulating views; we must engage with and address them. Eisner's perspectives provide an elegant contrapuntal line that enriches the other melodies of education and its study. His is a counterpoint that harmonizes at some points and introduces provocative dissonances in others. Here is a set of ideas, of ways of seeing, of measured critiques of prevailing views, and of practical approaches to the improvement of education. With respect to our appreciation for Eisner's remarkable contributions to our field, I join with educators all over the world in declaring: "Count me in!"

Lee S. Shulman

President, The Carnegie Foundation for the Advancement of Teaching and Charles E. Ducommon Professor of Education Emeritus, Stanford University

Preface

*T*his book is about many things. It is about ways of thinking about curriculum, about educational evaluation and research, about arts education, and about teaching, teacher education, and school reform. What makes this book unique is that the ways of thinking about these issues are influenced by aesthetic and artistic paradigms. Remarkably, the ways of thinking about these separate areas of educational specialization are inspired by the works and life of a single person, Professor Elliot Eisner (1933–).

No one has been a greater champion of the broad utility of artistic and aesthetic paradigms for educational thought and practice than Elliot Eisner. Eisner's educational importance and influence is a result of his profound understanding of the implications of the aesthetic approach; his visionary, challenging, and appropriate application of this approach in a number of areas; and his rare ability to communicate his ideas with clarity and eloquence.

When we began to contact authors who would help us understand Eisner's ideas and contributions to education, some of them said, "Ahh, you are writing a *festschrift*," a celebration of Elliot's life. Indeed, to some degree we are, but in addition to that we have asked each of the authors to begin with Eisner's ideas—not end there—and to consider the implications and possible extensions of his ideas to the next generation.

The book begins with a chapter that introduces Elliot Eisner's basic ideas and their origins in his experience. The body of the book is composed of four sections that address Eisner's impact on curriculum; arts education; research and evaluation; and school reform, teaching, and teacher education. The fifth section offers reflections on Eisner by Howard Gardner and Maxine Greene. The book ends with an epilogue that provides observations culled from the various chapters. An essential Eisner reading list, selected from his hundreds of works, is also provided.

CURRICULUM

William Schubert writes of philosophical sensibilities and imagination, qualities that Elliot Eisner not only embodies but that he brings out in others. Schubert's autobiographically flavored work reveals how his own trajectory in the curriculum field has been fueled and fostered by Eisner's. In melding theory and autobiography, Schubert argues that "lives" matter. While Eisner is renowned for the power of his works, these works are best understood in the context of his life—as a mentor, a gatekeeper of sorts to the profession, a colleague, and a tireless worker for educational issues that matter most.

Daniel Tanner's chapter recovers John Dewey's observation that four types of impulses animate children. Tanner believes these impulses or functions ought to be lifelong in all of us and that schools could do more to develop them interdependently. The "lenses of art," writes Tanner, "can help curricularists to develop a more holistic conception, vision, and realization of the curriculum field." An arts-mediated perspective would help educators to properly emphasize emergent-generative processes rather than established-convergent ones.

Kieran Egan reminds us that keeping an end in view in the difficult and complex profession of education is no easy task. Eisner, says Egan, has been a keeper of the vision and a critic of the means that have lost sight of their ends. Egan persuades us that the current standards and testing movement is a means that fails to convey us to desirable educational ends, a muddled strategy that is as miseducational as employing the arts in the curriculum for non-arts ends. Egan's chapter explores multiple instances of damagingly deficient means-ends thought and practice. In an educational environment that deludedly works at cross purposes to its best and ultimate ends, Egan argues that we desperately need Elliot Eisner and others with a similar ability to discern the consequences of educational ideas and actions.

James Henderson cites Eisner as a source for many of Henderson's forays into transformative curriculum leadership. In particular—building on Eisner's ideas of criticism, connoisseurship, an expanded notion of literacy, and his general criticism of reductionism—Henderson takes Eisner's ideas into democratic ideals that move away from the Tyler rationale. Eisner has not written specifically about the role of democracy in education, but Henderson finds Eisner to be a good starting place for that kind of thinking.

ARTS EDUCATION

Janice Ross reflects on the implications of Eisner's ideas for dance education in particular and arts education in general. To achieve these ends, she explores the biographical origin and development of key Eisner ideas about cognition and education, tracing them over time from his work as a youngster at Vogue-Wright Studios, his initiation into the New Bauhaus at the Illinois Institute of Technology and the Art Institute of Chicago, his work as a teacher of art to inner-city children, and his intense commitment to the academic life, rooted at the University of Chicago and reaching fullflower at Stanford.

Elizabeth Vallance looks at Eisner's concepts of aesthetic modes of knowing and educational criticism in two different contexts: in art museums, and in the preservice education of elementary classroom teachers. She finds that Eisner's ideas provide a helpful form of assessment for museums and provide to elementary school teachers a consciousness-shifting perspective on what is educationally significant.

John Steers provides an overview of arts education in the United Kingdom and then makes connections between Eisner and the state of the arts in the UK. Once again, the theme of "works and life" comes to the fore. Eisner's influence is not only through his work on the Kettering Project, Discipline-Based Art Education, and his views on art, cognition, and mind, but also through the model he has provided to British arts educators through his life of scholarship, advocacy, service, and mentoring.

Bennett Reimer examines Eisner's ideas for music education by focusing on three categories that Eisner has influenced: the role of the arts in human consciousness, the transfer from arts learnings to non-arts learnings, and the role of Eisner's ideas in the policy arena. Reimer also takes issue with Eisner's critique of standards.

RESEARCH AND EVALUATION

Tom Barone suggests that Eisner has been intellectually courageous on many fronts, but perhaps his most courageous efforts have been in the area of educational research. Barone takes readers through a history of arts-based educational research and then informs us of the progress and setbacks still occurring. Barone ends his piece by suggesting two kinds of efforts one might take to advance this new research genre.

David Flinders highlights three aspects of Eisner's contributions to scholarship: his conceptions of transactive knowledge, educational criticism, and epistemic seeing. The first idea, writes Flinders, provides the basis for rethinking notions of truth, validity, and objectivity. The second provides a genuine alternative to those who want a perspective on education practice inaccessible to educational science. The third provides a language to talk about mind and perception. Flinders ends his piece with questions for future educational researchers to ponder.

Propelled by an essay written by Barone and Eisner about arts-based inquiry, Philip Jackson takes the reader on an intellectual journey in which he explores ways of talking about teaching and schooling. Jackson expresses some reluctance about referring to all aesthetically crafted, critical narratives about schooling as research, emphasizing the importance of the author's intentions and audience.

Denise Pope offers a glimpse of what it is like to be a student in Elliot Eisner's classes. She writes appreciatively of the trenchant wisdom and practical advice that Eisner generously shares with his students. She also discloses some of Eisner's key sayings about qualitative research and discusses implications of his ideas for preparing future researchers.

D. Jean Clandinin's poetic narrative speaks of Eisner and his work in three ways: as an artist painting with words, as the originator of educational connoisseurship, and as an educational connoisseur himself. She tells of the significance of Eisner's work and life not only for herself but also for others who wish to engage in thoughtful and imaginative inquiry. She points out that those who wish to carry on these ideas must engage policy-makers and researchers as well as teachers.

SCHOOL REFORM, TEACHING, AND TEACHER EDUCATION

Sam Intrator's chapter develops Eisner's ideas about aesthetics into an examination of three types of curricula: the aesthetic, anesthetic, and monoaesthetic. This chapter focuses on four features of the aesthetic curriculum, which combine to create for students "an exhilarating intellectual and emotional experience."

Stephen Thornton looks at Eisner's ideas from the vantage point of what a school program would look like if Eisner's school reform project succeeded. Thornton argues that an emphasis on institutional reform has caused important curricular reform issues to suffer from lack of attention. He explores the scope of this problem by examining its impact in his home field of social studies education.

Robert Donmoyer's chapter looks at school reform from an historical perspective. In particular, he focuses on the works of Thorndike and Dewey and then situates Eisner in the Dewey camp. Though the current standards and testing environment may lead one to think that the Dewey/Eisner side has lost the battle for the schools, Donmoyer argues that this vision of education is still vitally important and offers several ideas about what this camp should do if it wants to try and make some headway.

REFLECTIONS

Howard Gardner pays tribute to Eisner by writing that he is one of the "few genuine educators" that Gardner knows, exploring, in the process, the fundamental characteristics of a true educator. In doing so, Gardner also compares his own ideas with Eisner's.

Maxine Greene also pays tribute to Eisner in an interview conducted by the authors. Greene points out the similarities and differences between her ideas and Eisner's. In doing so, she also models for readers the ways in which scholars with congruent ideas sustain and push each other.

The extraordinarily deep and diverse powers of the contributors to this volume and the breadth of ground that they claim Eisner's ideas cover and transform are strong testimony to Eisner's remarkable influence over educational thought and practice. Eisner's work remains immediate, vital, and radically challenging. Given the escalating influence that national standards and testing have over teachers' and children's lives, Eisner's eloquently and passionately expressed ideas may achieve their greatest importance in the coming decades. The editors hope that this volume will serve as an ideal vehicle for comprehending the range and importance of Eisner's work, and that it will lead readers to a reexamination of Eisner's seminal writings, enhanced by a new appreciation of their context and significance.

Acknowledgments

There are a number of people who helped us in preparation for this book whom we wish to thank.

To begin, we thank Debbie Stollenwerk of Merrill/Prentice Hall for her assistance and expertise. She helped make the process of editing this book a joy. Thanks, too, to Mary Morrill, editorial assistant. We also thank Angela Urquhart of Thistle Hill Publishing Services. And we extend gratitude to the many others (whose names we do not know) at Merrill/Prentice Hall and Thistle Hill who assisted us in creating this book.

We interviewed a number of people in our writing of Chapter 1. We wish to thank the following for their time and insights: Ellie Eisner, Elliot Eisner, Benita Flack, Elliot Golub, Jerome Hausman, Larry Mayster, Bill Russell, Lee Shulman, Gail Anderson Uikema, Lani Lattin Duke, and Decker Walker.

Tanya Chamberlain helped us stay in contact with Elliot Eisner when he traveled, and she sent whatever materials we asked for with rapid speed. We appreciate her support.

We also had assistance from University of Denver doctoral students. Christy Moroye assisted us in making various editorial decisions, as did Cassandra Trousas. On short notice, Christy helped us proof the text, and we are appreciative. We also thank Cassie for helping us with the title for this book.

We offer a special thanks to Mary Rudolph, who organized our files, edited manuscripts, typed and retyped various chapters, kept in touch with authors—in short, helped make this book possible.

Elliot Eisner has been supportive and helpful to us throughout the entire process of this book. He has continued to mentor us long after our Stanford days, and we are appreciative for all he has done for us.

Thanks also to all the authors in this book. Consummate professionals that they are, they made our editing tasks easy.

Finally, and most importantly, thanks to our wives and children for the daily love that makes everything else possible. Thank you Stephanie Matthews and Lisa Uhrmacher, Kyle and Connor Matthews, and Arianna and Paul Uhrmacher.

Elliot Eisner speaks about Discipline-Based Art Education to the
Betty Foundation in 1995.
Photo provided by Elliot Eisner.

1

Building His Palette of Scholarship

A Biographical Sketch of Elliot Eisner

P. Bruce Uhrmacher
University of Denver

Jonathan Matthews
Carroll College

*I*t is not possible, in a single chapter, to adequately consider the life and work of a scholar as complex and prolific as Elliot Eisner. In fact, that is the charge of this entire volume, the collective responsibility fulfilled by the assembled authors. Our aim in this chapter is to provide stories and explanations that will help readers begin to know both Eisner the person and his key academic concerns.

Dr. Eisner, the Lee Jacks Professor of Education and Art at Stanford University, holds five honorary degrees, three from universities in the United States, one from De Monfort University in England, and one from the University of Oslo. He has been elected to membership in the Royal Society of Arts in the United Kingdom, the Royal Norwegian Society of Sciences and Letters, and the National Academy of Education in the United States. Eisner has held a number of presidencies in scholarly organizations, including the National Art Education Association, the International Society for Education Through Art, the American Education Research Association, and the John Dewey Society. He has also received numerous awards for his work, including the José Vasconcelos Award from the World Cultural Council, a John Simon Guggenheim Fellowship, and the Palmer O. Johnson Award from the American Educational Research Association. As of 2003, he has delivered more than 700 invited papers, written more than 270 articles, and published 6 books.

Dr. Eisner has been at the forefront of many educational reforms. He has helped reshape the way we think about curriculum development and about themes related to it. He has taught us to recognize the cognitive nature of art. He has been a pioneer in the development of qualitative forms of research and educational evaluation. He has influenced teacher education and school reform.

A few personal stories collected from those who have known Elliot over the years may help you know the person behind the academic ideas. The first is from Jerome Hausman, Director Emeritus of The Ohio State University School of Art and the National Art Education Commission on Research in Art Education. He tells the following tale:

> In New York City, during a brief respite at the National Art Education Association Convention, Eisner, David Ecker (formerly a professor in the Department of Art and Art Professions at New York University), and I went off to Barney's [a high-end clothing store in New York]. With his usual sense of mission, Elliot led the way to the men's suit section. The salesman who tried to help us soon realized that Elliot was a person who would find his own way. Jackets were tried on Ecker with reckless abandon. Each time, Elliot would carefully examine the stitching on the inner portion of the lapel. "That's how you can tell that a suit is well made," Elliot asserted. Even the experienced salesman watching Elliot's means of "evaluation" was puzzled. He turned to me and said, "In my thirty years of selling suits, I have never heard of this!" Oh well, in his thirty years of sales experience he had never encountered anyone like Elliot! (Personal communication, 2003)

Bruce Uhrmacher, a former student of Eisner's (1985–1991), tells another story:

> I was with Elliot in Seattle and we had some time so we wandered downtown near the Pike Place Market. We went into an antique store and Elliot saw a clock across the room. He told me when and where it was made and paused. "That clock is about $450," he said. We went to check. He was right. Next we went into a store that sold Persian carpets. We looked at a few in the front showroom. He walked all around a particular carpet, crouching down to get another view. He ran his hand over it and he even gave it a practiced shake. "Look at that sheen!" He was entranced and the salespeople enjoyed his appreciation.
> "Come with me," a salesman said. We walked through an old office, went outside, up a flight of stairs and into a back warehouse. There they displayed carpets of what I took as museum quality. Elliot repeated his studied observations. They were thrilled to be able to show them to someone who appreciated fine rugs. Elliot was helping them notice aspects of the rugs that even they hadn't seen. I thought this was something that just happened, but as I relayed this story to others who knew Elliot well, I learned that this kind of thing happened to him all the time.[1]

---

[1] Also, see Barone (2002).

Jonathan Matthews, also a student of Eisner's at Stanford (1988–1994), relates this perspective:

> It was at the National Art Education Association's annual conference that I first heard Elliot lecture. A colleague of his had scheduled him and several other prominent art educators to speak in a roundtable session. Unfortunately, this colleague had neglected to confirm arrangements with the roundtable participants. Having just introduced myself to Elliot, I told him that I was interested to hear him speak in the roundtable session that would be taking place in the coming hour.
>
> "What roundtable session?" he asked.
>
> I showed him my program and he shook his head in disbelief. "This never should have been listed. It will have to be canceled." Elliot had an Area Luncheon to attend that conflicted with this unanticipated session. We walked together to the room to post a notice of cancellation but had trouble getting to the door because the hundreds of people who were already waiting there couldn't all fit in the room. Elliot couldn't bring himself to turn away so many people. He hurried back to the luncheon room and persuaded Jerome Hausman (one of the other four members of the advertised roundtable) to join him in trying to make a go of it.
>
> I tape-recorded his words and later transcribed them. My typewriter was giving shape to what seemed a carefully composed, elegant essay ... and yet I knew that this was a surprise talk delivered without the help of notes while sitting on a hard chair in a stiflingly crowded room.

That Eisner would turn out to become a prolific writer and speaker and a leader in the field of education was unexpected by those who knew him as a child and teenager. Larry Mayster, a longtime friend of Elliot's, said, "When Elliot was in high school, his number one priority was soccer; females were number two. Academics weren't even on the list." Elliot's other friends agree, but Benita Flack is quick to point out that art was always a major interest of Elliot's.

As a teenager, Elliot hung out with a group of friends, all boys except for Benita. Together they constructed a clubhouse out of an abandoned basement, fitting the environment with flooring, electricity, and everything else needed to make it a perfect gathering place. Elliot was outgoing, athletic, and considered a nice guy. At that time, Albert Madansky, who would later become the HGB Alexander Professor Emeritus of Business at the University of Chicago, was considered the "genius of the group."

Elliot met Ellie Rose at a Jewish Reform Youth Group in 1952 when she was 15 years old. She was the outgoing president. Elliot was the incoming youth group advisor. It would be three years before they saw each other again. Says Ellie: "Elliot called me out of the blue. I almost said, 'Elliot who?'" For Ellie, who grew up on the south side of Chicago, the 45-minute bus ride to Elliot's childhood home on the west side was a long distance to a very different neighborhood. For Ellie's parents, at least at the onset, but not later, it was a trek "to the wrong side of the tracks." Ellie and Elliot got married January 6, 1957. "We balance one another very well," she says. "Elliot is a type A. I'm the more rational, calmer individual."

EISNER'S DISSERTATION ON CREATIVITY

Eisner will always be remembered for being in the center of various controversial discussions on significant educational issues. Before all that, however, was Eisner's foray into the scholarship of creativity. His dissertation, written at the University of Chicago, developed a typology of creative behaviors found in the visual arts. Arguing that it might be useful to think of various types of creativity rather than creativity as a single behavior, Eisner analyzed four types of creativity: boundary pushing, inventing, boundary breaking, and aesthetic organizing (Eisner, 1962).

Boundary pushing refers to extending the limits of known objects or materials by applying them in unique and novel ways (Eisner, 1964, p. 312). As Eisner points out, the child who uses the eraser of a pencil as a rubber stamp or the adult who first thought of using rubber for the blades of an electric fan are both engaged in boundary pushing, extending the use of an existing object into something new. *Inventing* refers to activities in which known objects and materials are put together to create something new. The *boundary breaker* is one who "questions the very premises upon which current practices in a field of inquiry are based" (1964, p. 313). Alexander Calder, says Eisner, questioned the idea that sculptures must be stable. Rather than having people walk around the sculpture, Calder created pieces in which the object turned while the spectator remained stationary. Finally, *aesthetic organizing* refers to a type of creativity in which something new is not created. Rather, "the producer utilizes component elements in order to produce a product which is quite beautiful or moving or satisfying" (p. 313). Eisner notes that a child may write a story that is not unique, but may be well organized and pleasant to read.

The journal *Instructor* provided Elliot with his own column, entitled "Think With Me About Creativity" (Fall 1962–Spring 1963). In 1965 when Elliot began his work at Stanford University, he dropped the issue of creativity from his palette of scholarship. He'd speak often of imagination, but he did not delve into creativity. By then other ideas captured his thinking. What is interesting to notice, however, is that the seeds of Eisner's commitment to pluralism can be found in his early scholarship. First, he saw four types of creativity rather than just one. Second, his series in *Instructor* reveals his commitment to educational practice as well as to theory. From the start, Eisner would keep his eyes on both.

CURRICULUM

During the 1960s the objectives movement was in full force. Objectives were popular for a number of reasons, and Eisner articulated these most cogently. One of his great strengths is that he is able to articulate both sides of an argument clearly and succinctly. This is one of the reasons, among others, educational practitioners as well as scholars appreciate his work. Superintendent of the Piedmont Unified School District, Gail Anderson Uilkema, a former student of Elliot's, said of him: "When I read his first book, I remember saying to him, 'Elliot, I just realized that you are a painter with words.' He paints a picture that is understandable and usable. Elliot is truly a conceptual artist."

Presenting the argument in favor of objectives, Eisner stated that "they provide the goals toward which the curriculum is aimed … [and] once clearly stated they facilitate the selection and organization of content." Pointing out their problematic qualities, Eisner wrote: "If educational objectives were really useful tools, teachers, I submit, would use them. If they do not, perhaps it is not because there is something wrong with the teachers but because there might be something wrong with the theory" (Eisner, 1967/1985, p. 32). He delineated a number of problems that stem from overreliance on objectives. But Eisner did not stop at critique alone. He created a theoretical and practical alternative for understanding and implementing instruction. In contrast to the highly proscribed behavioral objective, Eisner's concept of *expressive outcome* is the consequence of "curriculum activities that are intentionally planned to provide a fertile field for personal purposing and experience" (Eisner, 1994b, p. 119). In 2003, with the standards movement in full force, Eisner revisited and extended his earlier work (Eisner, 1995) to critique this educational phenomenon.

"Expressive outcomes" hints at the arts-based approach that is at the heart of Eisner's approach to curricular issues. Wary of reductionistic and technical language, Eisner reconceptualizes educational issues using aesthetic metaphors. Terms such as *literacy* (see Eisner, 1998), *rationality* (see Eisner, 1991a, pp. 51–52), and even *concept* (see Eisner, 2002, pp. 21–22), among others, would be infused with new meaning.

Of course, not everyone agrees with Eisner's perspective. In the 1960s James Popham took issue with Eisner's ideas about objectives. Today, a number of educators believe that Eisner isn't giving the standards movement its full due. Bennett Reimer, in this book, argues that Eisner is defining standards too narrowly.

Also significant is the fact that Eisner has initiated and coined *cognitive pluralism* (1994b) as a curriculum ideology. To understand Eisner's thinking about education, one would do well to begin with his understanding of human nature. Fully articulated in *Cognition and Curriculum Reconsidered* (1994a), the basis for his thinking is Deweyan. In short, human beings interact with the environment largely through their senses, which are designed to selectively take in information. From such interactions, one may form concepts. Concept formation, which precedes language, depends upon an image derived from the sensory material. When people want to express themselves, they convert their concepts into a form of representation, which may be linguistic or mathematical, but may also be musical or visual. Each form of representation allows us to express some concepts but not others. Each form reveals and conceals.

During an era obsessed with issues of conformity and standardization, Eisner follows a different path. Influenced by the work of Sir Herbert Read, Eisner argues that education should foster *productive idiosyncrasy* among students, rather than mold all to standard uniformity. In short, he is interested in helping children learn to use their senses to achieve greater degrees of perceptive and expressive differentiation, so that they may formulate concepts and represent them through a variety of forms.

QUALITATIVE EVALUATION AND RESEARCH

Educational and program evaluation was both measurement and science oriented before Eisner set out to help redraw the landscape. According to Eisner, "Evaluators thought of themselves as a species of social scientist (or psychologist), the true experiment was the favored design, and measurement of carefully stated objectives was the favored activity" (1991b, p. 168). In the 1960s, he noted that "at my own institution, Stanford's School of Education, even correlational studies were thought at that time to be merely reconnaissance efforts: real research required the 'true' experiment" (1991b, p. 179). He goes on to state, "Perhaps the primary contribution of my earlier work is its effort to free inquiry from the restrictions of a scientific model, not in order to reject science but to make it possible for scholars to work with other assumptions about the nature of human understanding and the conditions that enlarge it" (pp. 180–181).

Eisner has been one of the strongest critics of scientism, the belief that the scientific method is the only route to worthwhile knowledge. As early as 1972, Eisner was already looking for new ways to assess education. In his characteristic style, he pointed out what was wrong with relying exclusively on quantitative forms of evaluation and research. Unique aspects of children, teachers, and classrooms were being neglected for law-like generalizations. Moreover, understanding derived from metaphor, analogy, and poetic insight—not to mention what other arts might provide in aiding understanding—had no place in scientism. The force of Eisner's arguments critiquing the limitations of the scientific method, plus his reconceptualization of the methods of evaluation and research, have changed the educational landscape forever.

Taking his cue from art criticism, Eisner devised a mode of evaluation and research based on a contextualized perception of what actually takes place in schools and classrooms: educational criticism and connoisseurship. The educational connoisseur is someone who is able to notice what is subtle yet significant. Connoisseurship is, as Eisner would continually stress, "essentially the art of appreciation." Criticism, then, is the art of disclosure, of communicating one's perceptions.

Eisner's criticism and connoisseurship provided an aesthetically crafted form for expressing one's educational insights through words. Still popular today, educational criticism and connoisseurship has not been without its critics. Some are concerned with the elitist notion of connoisseurship itself (Grumet, 1989). Others worry about ascertaining validity from such a literary method (Phillips, 1987).

Through legitimizing an arts-based approach, Eisner created an atmosphere that enabled educational researchers to begin expressing their insights through paintings, plays, and other forms of representation. Because of Eisner's trailblazing, the American Education Research Association now encompasses a special interest group called *arts-based inquiry.*

ART EDUCATION

When Eisner began his work in art education, there were a number of salient ideas that he would expose as erroneous. Some of those included the beliefs that children develop best in art if left to their own resources; adults should not intervene in children's natural development; the major function of art education is to develop children's general creativity through art; what's important in art education is process, not product; children see the world more clearly than adults; teachers should not attempt to evaluate work in art since children's minds are qualitatively different from adults'; teachers should not attempt to talk about art since verbalization usually kills art; and the belief that the best curriculum in art is one that simply provides children with the widest variety of materials for their creative exploration (Eisner, 1973–1974). Each of these beliefs Eisner challenged.

In 1967 Eisner began work on the Kettering Project. Its aim was to develop an effective art curriculum supported by useful instructional materials for children of elementary age. Some assumptions that the project embraced included (a) the most important contribution that can be made by the visual arts to the education of children is that which is indigenous to art (Eisner, 1969, p. 11); (b) artistic learning is very complex, and the curriculum offered should extend beyond the traditional range of art activities; and (c) the curriculum should attend not only to the productive domain but to aesthetic, critical, and historical domains as well (pp. 12–13).

Dwaine Greer, Michael Day, and Stephen Dobbs were among the graduate students who worked on the Kettering Project at Stanford under Eisner. Along with Eisner, all became formulators and communicators of the dominant art education reform movement of the last thirty years, Discipline-Based Art Education (DBAE). In DBAE, students work in the four primary art disciplines: art history, art criticism, aesthetics, and art production. In its desire to improve the quality of arts education, the Getty Education Institute for the Arts provided support for continuing development and dissemination of DBAE. Its director was Lani Lattin Duke. According to Duke:

> I first met Elliot over lunch in a restaurant in Claremont, California, when he was giving a speech there. What struck me about this meeting with Elliot was his democratic posture. I knew he had strong and

well-thought-out points of view about content and what should be taught. But in our conversations he did not promote his approach to the exclusion of others. At the conclusion of that first meeting in Claremont, we asked Elliot if he would be willing to share some of his ideas about different ways in which Getty could get involved with arts education. A week or so later, we received a paper from Elliot laying out options without bias and without recommending any one. The generosity with which he gave of his time and his ideas impressed me, as well as his presentation. As I continued to do my research, and convene small groups of academics and practitioners from the field of arts education, Elliot's paper helped anchor my own thinking and served as an important guidepost. It was a natural inevitability that he would become the intellectual godfather of the Getty's art education program. (Personal communication, 2003)

Eisner has been a member of the advisory board of the Getty Education Institute for the Arts[2] since its inception in 1982 and authored its first general statement on its aims and characteristics. The National Art Education Association embraces Discipline-Based Art Education's powerful approach as an idea and policy for thinking about and organizing curriculum. As a policy or as a model, almost every state embraces the concept, and it is also used in Australia and the United Kingdom. In addition to hundreds of articles and chapters addressing arts-educational issues, Eisner has published two important books focused on his home field: *Educating Artistic Vision* (1972), and *The Arts and the Creation of Mind* (2002).

TEACHING, TEACHER EDUCATION, AND SCHOOL REFORM

In regard to Eisner's own teaching, Decker Walker, a former student and now a colleague of Eisner's at Stanford, reports:

I'd like to say some things about Elliot as a teacher. He's a very demanding person. He gives very few A's. He comments on your paper as though it were sent for publication.

In interaction, in discussion and so on, he's very concerned to give not the right answer but the most adequate answer that reflects all the complexities of the problem.

I think Elliot has two gears. He has the academic warrior gear, a kind of University of Chicago attitude, and when he's in that gear he has very high standards. He understands issues in their complexities and that makes him in some people's minds overbearing, forceful, not a good listener, and an expositor. But when you talk with Elliot over

[2] The Getty Education Institute for the Arts was called the Getty Center for Education in the Arts during its formative years. Many of the important DBAE documents are published under its earlier name.

a walk, in the hall, in less formal settings, he is a wonderful conversationalist. He listens, he responds, he's extremely witty, and he's a very caring person. (Personal communication, 2003)

Hermine Feinstein witnessed both sides of Eisner. She writes about her first meeting with him in an essay entitled "A Letter to Elliot" (1991): "I remember when I met you in the late spring of 1973, [as a prospective doctoral student considering Stanford]. ... The previous week I had interviewed with Mark Luca at U.C. Berkeley, a three-hour collegial conversation with lunch included. My meeting with you was different: twenty minutes, no lunch." During her meeting with Eisner, she was annoyed by the way he alternated between looking at the prospective student and looking out the window and by his daunting grilling of her: "'Getting a Ph.D. from Stanford is not like getting a Masters degree in painting. ... You most likely will not have time to paint. ... Why do you want to come to Stanford? ... What interests you specifically about how people learn to draw and paint? What do you think are the crucial variables? What do you consider to be the similarities and differences among the various arts?'"

"How dare he discount my Masters degree," thought Feinstein. "I did my best to answer. ... My intimidation turned to anger, and I haughtily ended the inquisition with, 'If I knew all those answers, Professor Eisner, I wouldn't be here.' ... I marched out of your office in a white rage. ... I concluded that I respected your ideas; I also concluded that I didn't like you. Over time, the latter changed."

Eisner's no-nonsense quality as a teacher, speaker, and dissertation advisor may be somewhat rooted in his background. Elliot Golub, Eisner's cousin (and concertmaster of The Music of the Baroque orchestra in Chicago), believes that Eisner's vigorous, almost adversarial approach to academic inquiry and debate ultimately grows from their families' dynamics. As he puts it, "From the beginning of time our families have debated things, rooted in the culture of Talmudic scholarship. Talmudic Scholars spend their whole lives debating arcane points. We have a cultural history of saying, 'What does this mean? This may not be what it seems to obviously state.'"

It would be wrong to believe that Eisner's verbal assertiveness betrays malice or ill will toward his educational "adversaries." In fact, the direct opposite of this is the case, according to Golub:

What makes Elliot so special is that he knows how to enjoy things. He can take the greatest pleasure in just small little things, putting things together. Elliot is always looking for the thread that binds things together. He is looking for the visceral meaning, the search for the significant. He enjoys being alive. I think of him as a child, having good ideas. What he imparts to students is this joy, this pleasure: "See what I know and see what pleasure it gives me; you come along and experience this pleasure too." (Personal communication, 2003)

Elliot himself relates that his relatives were engaged intellectually and involved in social matters. "Once a month the whole family would get together for meetings. Dues were paid and the meetings became the center for debate. It was role modeling." For Elliot, the home, not the school, modeled and fueled his intellectual engagement.

In regard to his thinking about issues pertaining to teaching and teacher education, Eisner has focused on the artistry of teaching. Scientism has created a dominant and limited image of schooling. According to Eisner, it has reduced our views of rationality and cognition. It has narrowed our emphasis on what should be studied and how. It has taken our concentration away from students' rich experiences and focused on a narrow set of behaviors. "The history of the curriculum field has been dominated by the aspiration to technologize schooling and to reduce the need for artistry in teaching," wrote Eisner (1994b, p. 368).

He has also noted that the aspiration to create teacher proof materials rests on a mistake. According to Eisner, teachers need materials that stimulate their ingenuity rather than materials to which they are to be subservient (p. 372). A problem for schools, he believes, is that factors influencing schooling may have their source far from the school or school district (p. 374). The school, he argues, must be a growth environment for the teacher if it is to be an optimal growth environment for the student (p. 379). He also believes that much of teacher education ought to be done on-site. There is still a need for colleges and universities, he suggests, but the bulk of preservice education should be done in schools.

In regard to school reform, Eisner has brought three trenchant analyses to the topic. First, from Eisner's perspective, school reform requires paying attention to the ecology of schooling, which includes intentions, curriculum, pedagogy, school structure, and evaluation. These dimensions interact. Change one dimension and all the others change either consciously or unconsciously. It would be prudent to be conscious of the changes. [Eisner would be the first to admit that his analysis is a place to begin one's thinking about change, not a place to end. Issues pertaining to administration and school-community relations are also key constructs that need attending. Arthur Foshay (2000) created the fullest analysis of all the dimensions that warrant attention.]

Eisner's second school reform analysis explains that educational controversies stem from competing values and goals. In 1974, Eisner and Vallance explore "Conflicting Conceptions of Curriculum" in their book of the same title. Later, Eisner would call these various orientations *ideologies*. "Ideologies," he says, "are belief systems that provide the value premises from which decisions about practical educational matters are made" (in Jackson, 1992, p. 302). School reform depends upon understanding a school or district's ideology.

Eisner's third school reform analysis examines the forms of representation being employed in the curriculum.

> Forms of representation are the devices that humans use to make pub-
> lic conceptions that are privately held. They are the vehicles through
> which concepts that are visual, auditory, kinesthetic, olfactory, gusta-
> tory, and tactile are given public status. This public status might take
> the form of words, pictures, music, mathematics, dance, and the like.
> (Eisner 1994a, p. 39)

Eisner's analysis reveals that forms of representation develop different cognitive skills. If students know, for example, that their final products will take the form of collages, they will look for information that may take a visual form. They will use skills that enhance visual presentations, and ulti-mately what they will learn and know will be greatly influenced by the form of representation itself. A literary description of a castle provides some infor-mation. A visual depiction provides other kinds of knowledge. Each form of representation reveals and conceals.[3]

Thus, in his thinking about school reform, Eisner brings a holistic or, as he has termed it, an ecological perspective to the enterprise: Understand the values and mission of the school, pay attention to changes in the educa-tional dimensions, and focus on the forms of representation being cultivated or neglected.

Eisner has summarized his own goals for education in various ways. In 1976, when his children were 16 and 14, Eisner characterized the kind of school he would like as follows:

> The school I would like my children to attend would have a sense
> of intellectual excitement about it. ... When I entered that school
> I would hear a quartet playing in the corner of the building, like
> wafts of freshly baked bread, its aromatic quality would permeate the
> atmosphere. Children would be moving about, some intent on proj-
> ects that had captured their imaginations and therefore their souls.
> The school I would like my children to attend would have an array of
> cozy places, small nooks and crannies in which small children could
> hide. ... The school ... would be a visual delight. Paintings, sculpture,
> prints, and murals would vitalize the spaces. ... The school ... would
> have stage crews building scenery and dance troupes creating chore-
> ography. ... What we have in this school, this place of life, is a center
> of human enterprise, a mixture of energy and imagination, a treat for
> the senses, a celebration of the mind, a realization of the curiosity, the
> power, and the competence of growing young minds. (Eisner 1976,
> pp. 213–215)

---

[3]Eisner has continued his analysis of forms of representation over the years. He has noted that forms of representation have import for issues pertaining to process, content, equity, and cul-ture (Eisner, 1998, p. 51). He has also pointed out that forms of representation stabilize thought (p. 27) and allow a kind of editing so that one may refine his or her thinking. Forms of repre-sentation also provide an opportunity for discovery, and when turned into a product provide the creator a personal signature (p. 27).

IN CONCLUSION

We hope that this brief overview of the ideas and person of Elliot Eisner has whetted your appetite for what follows. The contributors to this volume, in their separate chapters, add chromatic richness and intricacy to our sketch. We've simply and roughly drawn the outlines of a palette that subsequent chapters build into a working form laden with a spectrum of colors, to be used by you to build your own understanding of this complex and influential educator.

REFERENCES

Barone, T. (2002). *Aesthetics, politics, and educational inquiry: Essays and examples*. New York: Peter Lang.

Eisner, E. W. (1962). *The development and use of a typology of creative behavior in the visual arts*. Doctoral dissertation, University of Chicago.

Eisner, E. W. (1964). Creativity in art has many faces. *Chicago Schools Journal, 45* (April), 311–318.

Eisner, E. W. (1969, November). Teaching Art to the Young: A Curriculum Development Project in Art Education.

Eisner, E. W. (1973–1974). Examining some myths in art education. *Studies in Art Education, 15*(2), 7–16.

Eisner, E. W. (Ed.). (1976). *The arts, human development, and education*. Berkeley, CA: McCutchan.

Eisner, E. W. (1985). Educational objectives: Help or hindrance. In *The art of educational evaluation: A personal view* (pp. 29–38). London: Falmer Press. (Original work published 1967)

Eisner, E. W. (1991a). *The enlightened eye: Qualitative inquiry and the enhancement of educational practice*. New York: Macmillan.

Eisner, E. W. (1991b). Taking a second look: Educational connoisseurship revisited. In D. Phillips & M. McLaughlin (Eds.), *Evaluation and Education at Quarter Century, National Society for the Study of Education Yearbook*. Chicago: University of Chicago Press.

Eisner, E. W. (1994a). *Cognition and curriculum reconsidered* (2nd ed.). New York: Teachers College Press.

Eisner, E. W. (1994b). *The educational imagination* (3rd ed.). New York: Macmillan.

Eisner, E. W. (1995). Standards for American schools: Help or hindrance? *Phi Delta Kappan, 76*(10), 758–764.

Eisner, E. W. (1998). *The kind of schools we need: Personal essays*. Heinemann: Portsmouth, NH.

Eisner, E. W. (2002). *The arts and the creation of mind*. New Haven: Yale University Press.

Eisner, E. W., & Vallance, E. (Eds.). (1974). *Conflicting conceptions of curriculum*. Berkeley, CA: McCutchan.

Feinstein, H. (1991). A letter to Elliot. In a Festschrift of articles prepared in honor of Elliot Eisner. Papers delivered at the annual meeting of the National Art Education Association, Atlanta.

Foshay, A. W. (2000). *The curriculum: Purpose, practice, substance*. New York: Teachers College Press.

Grumet, M. (1989). Word worlds: The literary reference of curriculum criticism. *JCT, 9*(1), 7–23.

Jackson, P. (Ed.). (1992). Curriculum ideologies. In *Handbook of Research on Curriculum* (pp. 302–326). New York: Macmillan.

Phillips, D. C. (1987). *Philosophy, science, and social inquiry*. New York: Pergamon Press.

PART 1

Curriculum

2

Sensibility and Imagination

Curriculum Contributions of Elliot W. Eisner

William H. Schubert
University of Illinois, Chicago

I just returned from Professors of Curriculum, which is a group of curriculum scholars with elected membership. It meets in conjunction with the ASCD annual conference. I spoke with a young scholar from Stanford, Elliot Eisner, who is making great strides in the field. He has been talking and writing about the need for those in curriculum to be critics and connoisseurs of educational situations. He has a background in the arts and sees the cultivation of educational imagination as a key to understanding, designing, and improving educational experiences. I spoke with him at length about your dissertation, assuming that you have interests in common that center on the place of imagination in curriculum and teaching, hoping that you would someday share perspectives.

This was the gist (though of course not a quote) of a comment made to me by my doctoral advisor, J. Harlan Shores, in 1974, as I was beginning the dissertation stage of my program. Shores was an exemplary advisor (see Schubert, 1992, 1996). He often went out of his way to provide opportunities for students. He was best known for his classic synoptic text with B. Othanel Smith and William O. Stanley, *Fundamentals of Curriculum Development*, first published in 1950 and revised in 1957 (Smith, Stanley, & Shores, 1950, 1957), which in retrospect reminds me of Eisner's work in *The Educational Imagination*. In the mid-1950s, Shores served as president of the ASCD, and had written several articles in ASCD publications on the need to anticipate possibilities in educational practice, a topic which in retrospect reminds me of educational imagination.

After six years as an elementary school teacher, I concluded that two of the greatest resources a teacher can have are philosophical sensibilities and imagination. As a teacher I thought a great deal about what to teach, why, and how. But I detested writing lesson plans. I thought they trivialized a complex human consideration, and reduced a thoughtful person into a drab and brittle piece of paper. My best teaching, I concluded, evolved in the milieu of interactions with students, caring about them, imagining possible journeys they might lead. Such considerations were inspired by reading philosophers (from Plato, Lao Tsu, Jesus Christ, St. Francis, Spinoza, and Marx to Whitehead, Bergson, James, and Dewey). Along with these, literary figures and artists (e.g., Salinger, Steinbeck, Saint-Exupery, Frost, Albee, Renoir, Kandinsky, Miro, Picasso, Rothko, Chagall, Pollock, and so many more, including popular artists such as Bob Dylan and the Beatles) stimulated my imagination and challenged the assumptions underlying my philosophy. The educational writing that also touched my evolving sensibilities and imagination was in the area of philosophy of education, the subject of my major in Master's work at Indiana University, 1966–67, just after I finished my Bachelor's degree at Manchester College and before I began teaching in Downers Grove, Illinois.

When I embarked on doctoral studies at the University of Illinois at Urbana-Champaign, I wanted to convey this sense of the value of philosophical sensibility and imagination to students I taught as a graduate assistant. I saw my career moving from teaching in public schools to teaching those who would teach in public schools. I tried to bring a sense of the imaginative acquired as an elementary school teacher to pre-service and in-service teachers. Just as I role-played as a prehistoric man, or a believer in Buddhism, or an advocate or opponent of the need to learn how to divide with fractions for my sixth graders, I found myself role-playing different perspectives on teaching and curriculum for students of education. I guess I was being imaginative, challenging philosophical assumptions, and advocating the continuous refinement of both as necessities for educators. In my dissertation I wanted to tell the story of my inquiry into imagination as a basis for curriculum and teaching (Schubert, 1975).

Why am I beginning the chapter this way? After all, the chapter is supposed to be about Elliot, not me. Or is it? Or can it be? When I think of Elliot's influence on curriculum studies, I think of his renowned scholarship and the artistry of his writing and speaking. Clearly, I want to write of that in this piece on his contributions. Too, however, I want to write of another kind of curriculum that Elliot has provided for me and for others in the curriculum field—namely, a curriculum on how to be a curriculum scholar. I want to do this autobiographically, and Eisner's Preface to the first edition of *The Educational Imagination* speaks directly to that matter. Elliot said, "All written works ... that attempt to open some new ground, have an autobiographical character" (Eisner, 1979, p. vii). I hope here to point to some new ground, in at least small ways, while presenting my image of Elliot's contributions. In fact, he had already begun to relate autobiographically the emergence of his educational imagination on the page preceding the Preface, by identifying five teachers who made a difference in his life: "Phil Jackson, Frank Chase, Ben Bloom, Joe Schwab, John Goodlad." Elliot met these scholars during his doctoral studies at the University of Chicago, where he completed the Ph.D. in 1962. While Harlan Shores was my official mentor in doctoral studies, I want to say that

Elliot Eisner has informally mentored me (perhaps without knowing it) for nearly 30 years since doctoral studies. I say this even though I never had a course from him, and if I totaled all of the hours we have spent together in nearly 30 years that we have known each other, it would doubtless amount to less than a day. Our actual encounters have been limited mainly to conversations on the phone, letters, and chats at conferences. Computing the time involved in such transactions, however, doesn't include the main ways scholars get to know one another—poring over writings, attending presentations, listening to tapes (and now, searching the Web). Moreover, all of this tabulating is quantitative; none of it indicates the quality of those interactions, however brief or extensive they might be. Therein lies an illustration of the scarcity of the time on task concept!

Qualitatively, whenever I write, teach, consult, speak, and otherwise share my wares as a curriculum professor, Elliot is present in influence. There he is, in my mind's eye, with others (the philosophers, the artists, the filmmakers, the educators and curriculum theorists) I hold in high regard—looking over my shoulder, offering criticism and inspiration from their positions of connoisseurship. What Elliot has brought to my work in the curriculum field is, I think, a microcosm of what he has brought to the field itself. So, for the remainder of this chapter, I want to recall salient memories of Elliot and the curriculum he has provided for me as I have sought to contribute to curriculum studies.

My method for doing this is to jog my memory by pulling from my file cabinet the folder (over 30 years old by now) labeled "Eisner, Elliot" written in the beautiful calligraphy of Ann Lopez Schubert (my wife). Her aesthetic sensibilities indelibly mark the first decade of my work in the professoriate, since we always worked together during that time. In fact, she heads the list of the cast of characters that guides whatever contributions I might offer to the curriculum field. Over the years, family and illness have moved us beyond working side-by-side, yet the sharing of ideas and practices that grows through new living conditions influence my work brightly on a daily basis. I note Ann's contributions to my own here, because she has known Elliot over the years, as well, and we have learned together of his contributions.

Leafing through the "Eisner, Elliot" file stimulates my memory, a cognitive endeavor that I consider more powerful than is given in most renditions of Bloom's taxonomy (Bloom, 1956). Ann (Lopez, 1993) helped me see theory as embodied, part of one's being, part of one's living practice. I see memory as similarly embodied, a basis of personal theory and repertoire, an idea that I addressed much earlier vis-à-vis teacher education, when I argued that teacher education is, in fact, theory development—developing a living theory (Schubert, 1982).

Today, scholars at the frontiers of literacy and language theory are beginning to realize what Elliot perceived from Dewey, other philosophers, and in-depth experience with the arts. He recognized that the arts vastly augment ways of knowing and should become a new kind of subject matter that educators seldom emphasize. To increase educator realization of this needed perspective, Elliot drew upon respected colleagues to produce Part II of the 1985 Yearbook of the National Society for the Study of Education. Together, Elliot and these colleagues called for teaching and learning diverse ways of knowing—scientific, aesthetic, intuitive, narrative, formal, practical, spiritual, and more (Eisner, 1985a). Showing practical application, in the same year, Elliot presented a volume that demonstrates the value of aesthetic and other ways of knowing applied to dilemmas of educational evaluation (Eisner, 1985b). Almost a decade later, Elliot readdressed the problem of cognition and curriculum. He said that cognition must be seen within the entire landscape of education, as "fostering an individual's ability to construct, diversify, and deepen meaning." This is enabled when "forms of representation are means through which different kinds of meaning can be made" (Eisner, 1994a, p. 86). Further, Elliot points out that "the separation of the mind from the body ... has contributed to a narrow conception of intellect" (p. 87). In his clarion call for educational practices that broaden the forms of representation human beings can embrace, he addresses the cultural, and reminds educators that "students are not only a part of our culture; they are a part of our future and we are a part of theirs" (p. 89). He concludes: "The view of mind and knowledge that I have tried to advance ... is intended to contribute to the reconceptu-alization that is necessary. Reconceptualization, although it is a necessary condition, is not sufficient. In the end, reconceptualization must lead to practical consequences. A challenging agenda remains before us" (p. 89).

While this challenging agenda is offered to schools, worthy recipients indeed, it is also a challenge to curriculum professors. As one curriculum professor, I want to relate how Elliot has challenged me as I have engaged in a continuous reconceptualization of my work over the years. Encounters with Elliot have contributed to the curriculum that is my journey in cur-riculum studies, and that curriculum constitutes the continuously evolving theory within me.

The blank front of my Eisner folder reminds me to recall what occurred before the folder was formed. When Harlan Shores told me of his conversation with Elliot, I thought back to my ponderous set of note cards that Shores recommended I keep on all I read during doctoral studies. I remembered the cards on Elliot Eisner's writings. First there was the one on a 1969 AERA monograph edited by Jim Popham on evaluation. There, Elliot offered his critique of conventional instructional objectives, providing an alternative through expressive objectives. I remember resonating posi-tively with this critique amid the swirl of pressures to conform to behavioral objectives and the rigidity of lesson plans (Eisner, 1969). I recalled, too, *Confronting Curriculum Reform* (Eisner, 1971), wherein Elliot called on an array of scholars to strive for a field grounded empirically in curriculum devel-opment, implementation, and evaluation. Here, empirical did not mean quantitative (with which an equation too often improperly made); instead, its original connotation simply entails deriving knowledge from experience. Knowing something of the conflicting origins of the field, at that time in my career, I realized that curriculum studies emerged from both educational foundations and educational psychology. Elliot, however, wanted to emphasize inquiry unique to the phenomenon of educational experience—not merely borrowed from another field. This harkened back to Dewey's strong argument in *The Sources of a Science of Education* (1929), and surely relates to the formative influence of Elliot's professor, Joseph Schwab's (e.g., 1969) advocacy of practical inquiry, as well as Elliot's Stanford colleagues, Lee Cronbach and Patrick Suppes (1969), who called for disciplined inquiry, both decision- and conclusion-oriented. Building particularly on the influences of Dewey and Schwab, Eisner refined the idea of milieu in a 1967 article in *High School Journal*, a piece I found to be helpful for my dissertation (Schubert, 1975), insofar as teachers must learn to imagine possibilities within the context of their teaching.

Toward the conclusion of my doctoral studies I was impressed with the essays and conceptualization set forth in *Conflicting Conceptions of Curriculum*, designed by Eisner and his former doctoral student Elizabeth (Beau) Vallance (Eisner & Vallance, 1974). This book, published by McCutchan, set forth one of the first conceptualizations of curriculum orientations: curriculum as the development of cognitive processes, curriculum as technology, curriculum as consummatory experience or self-actualization, curriculum for social reconstruction or relevance, and curriculum as academic rationalism. Key articles and their authors were offered as illustrative of each of the five orientations to show diversity within each grouping. I recall that we used this book for several years in introductory graduate-level curriculum courses when I began my career at the University of Illinois at Chicago (UIC). Much later I recall my colleague Herb Walberg (who published many books with McCutchan) and John McCutchan (the publisher) contacting me to see if I would be willing to join in authoring another edition of *Conflicting Conceptions of Curriculum*. It was noted that the volume was the best seller in the McCutchan line. While I was flattered at the invitation and considered it seriously, I knew that the reason the book sold so well was that Eisner and Vallance designed it; a revision that changed the editorship would not provide what was desired. In any case, Eisner had gone on to develop new conceptualizations of the curriculum field. Noteworthy among them are the six curriculum ideologies that he developed in the third edition of *The Educational Imagination* (1994b): religious orthodoxy, rational humanism, progressivism, critical theory, reconceptualism, and cognitive pluralism.

At this writing I understand that the fourth edition is about to be published, and I await the modified categories that Eisner will use there to depict orientations to the field. The point is not whether a new edition gets it right, but that Eisner (beginning with Eisner & Vallance, 1974) spurred curriculum scholars to think about how to characterize perspectives that abound in the field in a given period. Prior to Eisner's conceptualization, categories had been appropriated from authors in philosophy of education (e.g., essentialism, perennialism, progressivism, and reconstructivism). The use of such categories in curriculum, however, derived categories from other sub-areas of education, not from curriculum experience itself. So before Eisner, the only hint I can find of categories unique to curriculum discourse is in Smith, Stanley, and Shores (1957, pp. 229–424) when they elaborated on three patterns of curriculum organization: subject, activity, and core. Yet, this scheme pertains to organization alone, not to the larger notion of perspective on the whole of curriculum studies. In 1975, shortly after the appearance of the Eisner and Vallance book, William Pinar (1975) characterized curriculum traditionalists, conceptual traditionalists, and reconceptualists, and six years later Giroux, Penna, and Pinar (1981) designed a reader of key articles in each of Pinar's categories. Many others built category schemes to portray the emergent field of curriculum studies, but a full treatment of curriculum category schemes is beyond the scope of this chapter. Since this chapter is partly autobiographical, I note that when we researched *Curriculum Books: The First Eighty Years* (Schubert & Lopez Schubert, 1980), we began to see three recurrent orientations in each decade of the 20th century, and eventually named them *intellectual traditionalist, social behaviorist*, and *experientialist*. We referred to the categories as guest commentators, a literary device which I used to criticize each of the chapters in my synoptic text, *Curriculum: Perspective, Paradigm, and Possibility* (Schubert, 1986/1997). In researching *Curriculum Books: The First Hundred Years* (Schubert, Lopez Schubert, Thomas, & Carroll, 2002) we identified one additional category (critical reconstructionist), explored a separatist category to denote scholars who are original enough to defy classification, and also explored a conciliarist category to denote those who select willy-nilly from many different viewpoints without regard for inconsistency of selection. Finally, I am at work on a yet unnamed existential/Socratic-ironic/postmodern/literary commentator.

That I now feel comfortable role-playing each of these voices, known to my students as *guest speakers*, is due in no small measure to the freedom of representation that Elliot Eisner has provided the field. Referring to the language of another great advocate of the artistic imagination, Maxine Greene (e.g., 1995, 2001), I have felt encouraged, even challenged, to be perspectival. Together, though not always in agreement on the political or ideological dimensions of imagination, Greene and Eisner have contributed much to convince gatekeepers of the legitimacy of aesthetic inquiry, especially as former presidents of the American Educational Research Association (Greene 1981–82, and Eisner 1992–93). Their presidential addresses were each a tour de force to bring about new conceptualizations of educational research and therefore novel forms of curriculum inquiry. Both have significant sections in the second edition of the AERA-sponsored book, *Complementary Methods for Research in Education* (Jaeger, 1998). See the Barone and Eisner (1998) section on arts-based research and Greene's (1998) section on philosophic research.

The first edition of the *Complementary Methods* book (Jaeger, 1988) had little or no emphasis on the arts as a basis of educational research, except more incidentally in articles by Robert Stake on case studies and by Harry Walcott on ethnography. The most careful development of arts-based research is Elliot's *The Enlightened Eye* (Eisner, 1991a), wherein he exquisitely develops the intellectual underpinnings of qualitative research and also shows how it can enhance educational practice. I strongly recommend this book for my students who do qualitative dissertations.

Elliot had been working on gaining acceptance for arts-based inquiry for many years, and the road was paved with obstacles. When I first attended AERA in 1975, Division B (Curriculum Studies) was called "Curriculum and Objectives," giving the ethos of behavioral objectives. One of my first encounters with Elliot occurred in 1979, when I continued on a quest I had begun shortly after graduate school. I decided to organize AERA symposia of scholars I held in high regard. I wanted to see what happened when I got them together. In preparation for the 1980 Annual Meeting in Boston, I invited Elliot (along with Maxine Greene, Michael Apple, and Mario Fantini) to discuss the "Expanding Domain of Curriculum Inquiry." In the "Eisner, Elliot" folder I found a typed copy of Elliot's paper for that session, entitled "On the Differences Between Scientific and Artistic Approaches to Qualitative Research." I had forgotten that I used the same paper after it was published in *Educational Researcher* (Eisner, 1981) as a major reading in curriculum and research courses for many years. In these AERA symposia I had the opportunity to interact with my bookshelf. The authors who I had not known personally were now becoming my friends. When my book, *Curriculum Books: The First Eighty Years*, was published in 1980, I was thrilled to receive an unsolicited note from Elliot Eisner. I just found the letter, dated February 23, 1981, which I quote here not to toot my own horn but to illustrate the inspiration that can be provided for a beginning scholar when a senior scholar of great reputation takes time to send a letter. Elliot wrote:

> Just a brief note to tell you that I think you've done an admirable job in pulling together the literature in the field of curriculum. I now know where to direct my students in helping them get on top of what scholars in the field have had to say about curriculum theory and curriculum planning.

We continued to exchange letters, and then in 1981 as AERA vice president, Elliot assigned me to the Division B committee to determine who should receive the newly (1979) instituted Lifetime Achievement Award. Later, in 1983, Elliot called to ask if I would chair the Division B program. Pleasant surprise that it was, I scarcely realized how much work was involved in this wonderful (though thankfully once in lifetime) experience. Fortunately for me, Ann was able to co-chair the job. This meant that we received all proposals for about 40 program slots, read them all (for papers and symposia), selected reviewers, mailed proposals to reviewers, determined acceptances based on reviewer ratings, and designed sessions (which meant placing papers together in sessions and selecting chairs and discussants). There were no sections or subtopics within Division B in those days, so no section chairs to help with the duties. We were the co-designers of the Division B (Curriculum Studies) program. In a large sense, Elliot had provided us with the opportunity to work on a unique curriculum design project, a kind of portrayal of research and theory developments in the curriculum field for a year. That, too, is curriculum, but not the kind one usually considers.

Elliot's address to Division B (traditionally done in the second year of the vice presidency) was entitled "Can Educational Research Inform Educational Practice?" I concluded my introduction of him by saying, "One of the greatest values of Elliot's work resides in his ability to stimulate the imagination of educators (both scholars and practitioners) to see problems through different lenses, to entertain new possibilities, and to create fresh perspectives for the direction of their work." I also noted, among his publications, a then recent issue of *Educational Leadership* (in January of 1983). In it Eisner (along with Bob Donmoyer, Tom Barone, and Madeleine Grumet, among others) wrote on the contributions of art to curriculum and teaching.

Moved by the quality of the articles, especially Elliot's (1983) piece on the art and craft of teaching, Ann and I wrote a short letter of appreciation which appeared subsequently in *Educational Leadership* (Lopez & Schubert, 1983), saying that the January articles "facilitate educational leadership that rightly puts art and the quest for goodness at center stage and relegates the technical and procedural to an assisting role." There is a sense in which seeing teaching as an art and craft engages teachers, educational leaders, researchers, and students in a continuous search (call it research, if you will) that informs educational practice. It makes good practice conjoined with good research. It does what Elliot called for in his vice presidential address, later published in *Phi Delta Kappan* (Eisner, 1984). He concluded by reiterating "the need to create a critical language for describing educational practice" (noting that it is not intended to replace relevant scientific language), saying, "We need not one but two eyes through which to see and understand what concerns us. ... We will have to design our own ship and sail it into the waters we seek to map. For the language of criticism we need, the philosophical and political space must be provided for new forms of disclosure to be developed" (1984, pp. 451–452). To me, this means making the critical disclosure integrated with the art and craft of teaching. This is the next dimension of union of theory, research, and practice, a union so deep that it is seamless.

"The seamless coat of learning," an aesthetic image from Whitehead (1929, p. 11), moves us back to autobiography. When one tries to capture classroom experience autobiographically through artistic rendition—be it story or visual art or other—there is wholeness. The aesthetic, interpretive portrayals of Tom Barone (one of Elliot's former students) bring together educational experience from many venues. In the mid-1980s, when writing the chapter on curriculum evaluation for *Curriculum: Perspective, Paradigm, and Possibility* (Schubert, 1986/1997, pp. 275–276), I selected a passage from Barone's piece from Eisner's *The Educational Imagination* (1979, pp. 240–245) as one of the best extant pieces of criticism. Today, I recommend that students read Barone's *Touching Eternity* (2001) and theory that situates educational criticism and literary nonfiction, such as Barone's *Aesthetics, Politics, and Educational Inquiry: Essays and Examples* (2000). In fact, much of what we find in what has come to be called arts-based educational research (for which there is now a Special Interest Group in AERA) depicts the seamless character of educational experience. Lived educational experience in the hands of a thoughtful critic/connoisseur like Barone can enable one to see both unity and diversity in such productive concepts as Elliot's implicit, explicit, and null curriculum. This is keenly evident in the choice Elliot made when George Willis and I asked him to write the lead article in a book for which we asked members of the curriculum field to identify and write about the influence of a work of art, a genre, or several works on the way they see curriculum and teaching (Willis & Schubert, 2000). Elliot chose to use a brush of broad stroke and paint a portrait of the impact of arts on his early life experience, calling it "What the Arts Taught Me About Education" (Eisner, 1991b). He brilliantly and succinctly summarized what the arts taught him about education as follows:

> What, then, have I learned from the arts that has influenced the way I think about education? I have learned that knowledge cannot be reduced to what can be said. I have learned that the process of working on a problem yields its own intrinsically valuable rewards and that these rewards are as important as the outcomes. I have learned that goals are not stable targets at which you aim, but directions towards which you travel. I have learned that no part of a composition, whether in a painting or in a school, is independent of the whole in which it participates. I have learned that scientific modes of knowledge are not the only ones that inform and develop human cognition. I have learned that, as constructive activity, science as well as the fine arts are artistically created structures. I have learned these lessons and more. Not a bad intellectual legacy, I think. And not a bad foundation on which to build better schools for both children and teachers. (p. 47)

This seamless learning experience over many years is, I believe, illustrative of the autobiographical character of educational experience that goes far beyond school. When I teach about curriculum, I find students receptive to Eisner's explicit curriculum, implicit (which I associate with the oft-used hidden curriculum), and null curriculum (that which is not taught or is given short shrift). Over the years, too, I have increased in my

fervor to add yet another, what I have variously called the outside curriculum or the non-school curriculum or the out-of-school curriculum (see
Schubert, 1981; Schubert, 1986/1997, pp. 107–115; Schubert & Melnick,
1987). I see in Eisner a great faith in the possibility of schools, which
I would like to share, but I am not convinced it is warranted. If I could snap
my fingers or work diligently to have schools like the ones Elliot calls for
in *The Kind of Schools We Need* (Eisner, 1998), I would do so, but I am not
always convinced that schools are the places to expect the best education to
prosper. We may need to imagine entirely new kinds of places for education. If I might return to another kind of two-eyed image, I increasingly
conclude that we need to look at how persons as autobiographies grow and
develop. This means keeping one eye on the non-school and the other on
school. Where do the greatest possibilities for growth reside? The answer to
that question is where we should turn our curricular imagination most
fully. We learn and grow in families, homes, friendships, communities,
cultures, hobbies, jobs, travels, non-school organizations (from church,
health care centers, and scouts to sports, arts groups, and gangs), and
increasingly the mass media. We can hardly deny that today some of
the most powerful teachers and curriculum directors are those who
design and enact movies, television programs, popular music, radio broad-
casting, computer games, comics, advertisements, videogames, Web sites,
and more.

I think in summing up another autobiographical statement, this one
published in a volume called *Reflections* (1991c), Elliot powerfully characterizes what experience with the arts can provide:

> Finally, if the arts celebrate anything, they celebrate sensibility and
> imagination. By sensibility I mean that sheer pleasure of experiencing
> the qualitative world. By imagination I mean the ability to take leave
> from the immediate and the immediately practical and to allow oneself
> to consider what might be. Without attention to sensibility, the world
> itself is dimly known. It is sensibility that makes subtle the vivid. It is
> sensibility that makes possible what we normally regard as perceptivity.
> Indeed, sensibility is the first road to consciousness, and its refinement
> is an important human achievement. We give little attention to the
> development of the sensibilities in school. Imagination allows us to free
> ourselves from the press of the immediate, the practical, and the literal.
> It is through the imagination that the ability to read is possible, and it is
> through the imagination that new possibilities emerge. The arts put a
> premium on both. My educational passion is to make a genuine and
> significant place for such features of human capacity within our
> schools. (p. 144)

Why not stop with the word *capacity*, and passionately desire this development of sensibility and imagination anywhere? Why should we hope for
it to develop under the surveillance of state and corporate institutions?
How, I wonder, did Elliot Eisner's own great sensibilities and imaginative

capacities derive? A major contribution of Elliot to the curriculum field is unleashing the capacity for wonder. I wonder, then, if Elliot's education in the arts was principally derived from a school-based education.

In an activity I often use in teaching educators, I ask them to imagine (or to construct) a pathway, and name that pathway with an interest or a skill or value that they are each glad to have. Then, on the pathway, I ask them to label milestones (episodes of significant influence) from birth to present. I ask them to tell stories in pairs or in small groups. As they listen to the stories of one another, I encourage them to identify qualities of powerful learning that they perceive in those stories. I am astounded by the fact that rarely is a powerful milestone (apart from a negative one) identified from school experience. Most powerful learning experiences seem to occur outside of school. I have not done a systematic research of this, but pedagogically I have conducted the experience for two decades, which might amount to some level of connoisseurship.

I have seen Elliot in action as a connoisseur, and it is amazing to see the breadth and depth of his critical eye. I recall an episode when we both spoke at a Pi Lambda Theta Biennial Council and Leadership Conference held at the posh Ambassador West Hotel, near Chicago's Magnificent Mile on August 4, 1995. I gave participants an elaborate welcome to Chicago, my hometown, and talked about mentorship (a theme of their conference) in many different and unlikely dimensions of life experience—from parents, to friends, to aspects of mass media, to Elliot Eisner as a mentoring senior colleague in the field. Elliot gave his usual brilliant oration, and afterward suggested we walk and talk for the afternoon. We ate at a lovely café, called Albert's, where Elliot knew about wines, pastries, and other gourmet delectables. We walked and talked our way to Marshall Field's, Saks Fifth Avenue, Neiman Marcus, Tiffany's, and more. While discussing curriculum theory, Elliot pointed out suits of even greater aesthetic qualities than those by Armani, explained criteria for determining fine diamonds, and critically assessed art and architecture that adorned the streets, sidewalks, and store aisles of our journey. While some of Elliot's connoisseurship may well have come from the University of Chicago, the Illinois Institute of Technology, the School of the Art Institute of Chicago, or more recently Stanford, I will bet that more of his milestone experiences came from a host of enriching environs outside of school. That is not to put down school. Instead, it is to recognize that one kind of extension of the legacy of Elliot Eisner is to ask how we can imaginatively perceive curricula informally embodied in non-school educational experiences. To put all of our hopeful educational eggs in the basket of one institution is something we should avoid. We should not abandon school; we should work and hope for its possibility to enhance sensibility and imagination wherever this can be done, realizing that curriculum is greater than school alone. How can we learn from venues of educational experience outside of school and simultaneously help them grow? Or, said like the admonition of Gandalf (the sage wizard in the movie, *The Lord of the Rings: The Fellow-ship of the Ring*), in conversation with young Frodo:

Frodo: I wish the ring had never come to me. I wish none of this had happened.

Gandalf: So do all who live to see such times, but that is not for them to decide. All you have to decide is what to do with the time that is given to you.

What a great (and timely) variation on the fundamental curriculum question, "What's worthwhile (to know, experience, do, be, become, need, overcome, contribute, share)?" Moreover, think of how many have now considered it, via Gandalf, given the popularity of the movie, as compared with that of any curriculum book!

Tapping the popular arts for my teaching of curriculum, I often encourage students to depict their responses to curriculum literature through film and many other art forms, even via advertising. On October 25, 1983, I wrote to Elliot, saying, "In a class that I teach on curriculum design I have students select a curriculum book to advertise to the rest of their classmates." (I sent him two illustrations of ads for *The Educational Imagination*.) On November 2, Elliot wrote back, saying, "Thank you very much for sending me the two advertisements. I especially loved the illustrated piece. It was really interesting for me to see that the authors quoted the e. e. cummings quotation. The actual quotation states 'I would rather learn from one bird how to sing' and as a student wrote 'I would rather learn from one cloud how to dream.' It works almost as well!" In commenting on my students' work, Elliot was engaging in the art and craft of teaching; he was providing a bit of curriculum for me and for my students. Again we can see the theme of being a curriculum for those less senior in the field.

Just this year, Elliot was invited to deliver a rare second John Dewey Society Lecture. His first, in 1979, led to the first edition of *Cognition and Curriculum* (Eisner, 1982). Delivered in New Orleans in 2002, his second JDS Lecture was recently published in the *Journal of Curriculum and Supervision* (Eisner, 2002). Therein he declares, "Imagination is no mere ornament; nor is art. Together they can liberate us from our indurated habits" (Eisner, 2002, p. 348). To pedagogically nudge educators to move past indurated habits, I attempt to personally engage students and others in curriculum considerations by focusing on their experiences with the arts. I ask them to identify a work of art (e.g., music, theatre, film, visual art, literature) that had powerful impact on their outlook. Sometimes I designate "high art" and sometimes, popular arts. In any case, we then ask: What is it about this work of art that reached you so deeply and profoundly? What did the artist/author do to reach you? How can we see the artist as a teacher or curriculum developer and the work itself as a curriculum? What qualities of teaching did the artist or work embody? When we identify the qualities that brought powerful impact, we then consider how to bring similar qualities to our own educational situations. How can we emulate the contributions of these artists, these powerful educators?

During the past several years, I have begun to use many more works of art and literature in my courses on curriculum. I increasingly contend that the arts reach more deeply into curriculum matters than many works that intentionally set out to be about curriculum. To build on excellent works of art and literature is a goal worth pursuing as we engage future teachers, curriculum leaders, researchers, scholars, teacher educators, and the public. One way to build on great works of art, especially fiction, is to create fictional characters and situations out of our own educational experience. As my colleague, Bernardo Gallegos, and I have often discussed in this era of increasingly difficult human subject review guidelines, maybe fiction is an answer, not just a way past the surveillance of Institutional Review Boards who try to detect possible harm to individuals and to university reputations. We see fiction as a way to more honestly depict the realities and possibilities that exist, warts and all, without hurting anyone who is the focus (or subject?) of research. Although the idea of fictional theses has been tried on a limited basis (see Kilbourne, 1999), we want to explore the advantages of fiction over domination implicit in the whole idea of research subjects. After all, almost any image of research subject carries with it a sizable implication of subjugation. Doing fiction as connoisseurs and critics of lived experience needs to be explored more fully as a valuable form of research.

In addition to creating fiction that portrays educational insight, I also emphasize that existing fiction (and other artistic portrayals) needs to be interpreted for the insight it offers to educational issues, even if the fiction writers do not purport to be addressing schools or education. We need to work diligently to make the case that most good art is, in fact, about education in the broad sense of how human beings grow from life's journeys. Those journeys need to be recognized as curricula, and well worth the time and effort of curricular inquiry. I am currently exploring courses in which graduate students study novels, poetry, and film to glean educational insights, even though the artists who created works studied would be unlikely to recognize the educational dimensions of their work. Clearly, Elliot Eisner realizes the importance of educational insight embedded in arts of all kinds, as well as in the outside curriculum. Even in a book primarily about schooling (Eisner, 1998), he says of the arts:

> Their location is not limited to galleries, concert halls, and theatres. Their home can be found whenever humans choose to have attentive and vital intercourse with life itself. This is, perhaps, the largest lesson that the arts in education can teach, the lesson that life itself can be led as a work of art. (p. 56)

This lesson is evident in the artistically oriented curriculum scholars who studied with Elliot: Decker Walker, Gail McCutcheon, Elizabeth Vallance,

Robert Donmoyer, Tom Barone, James Henderson, Stephen Thornton, David Flinders, Bruce Uhrmacher, and many more. These are individuals I have come to know and respect. What they have gained from Elliot as their mentor is well characterized by Barone (1996), when he said:

> Through the pedagogical efforts of Elliot Eisner—embodied in his writings, in his service activities, in his presentations at zillions of podia, in untold numbers of teachable moments—members of the educational profession were persuaded to see subject matter that they never expected to see, to experience chance intrusions about which they would soon begin to exercise judgment. Thanks to the pedagogy of Elliot Eisner, the field of education has acquired greater character. So many of its members, I mean, are now more fully alive. (p. 116)

Elliot's students, former students, and colleagues in the field who have grown to know Elliot over the years (I am but one example) symbolize the many who have encountered this artistry of ideas, which Tom Barone expresses. We have come away inspired to imagine new forms of curriculum, teaching, and human growth. That is indeed a legacy of sensibility and imagination!

REFERENCES

Barone, T. E. (1996). From the classrooms of Stanford to the alleys of Amsterdam: Elliot Eisner as pedagogue. In C. Kridel, R. Bullough, Jr., & P. Shaker (Eds.), *Teachers and mentors: Profiles of distinguished 20th century professors of education* (pp. 105–116). New York: Garland.

Barone, T. E. (2000). *Aesthetics, politics, and educational inquiry: Essays and examples*. New York: Peter Lang.

Barone, T. E. (2001). *Touching eternity: The enduring outcomes of teaching*. New York: Teachers College Press.

Barone, T. E., & Eisner, E. W. (1998). Arts-based educational research. In R. M. Jaeger (Ed.), *Complementary methods for research in education* (pp. 73–116). Washington, DC: American Educational Research Association.

Bloom, B. S. (Ed.). (1956). *Taxonomy of educational objectives: Cognitive domain*. Chicago: David McKay Press.

Cronbach, L. J., & Suppes, P. (1969). *Research for tomorrow's schools: Disciplined inquiry for education*. New York: Macmillan.

Dewey, J. (1929). *The sources of a science of education*. New York: Liveright.

Eisner, E. W. (1967). Curriculum theory and the concept of educational milieu. *High School Journal, 51* (December), 132–146.

Eisner, E. W. (1969). Instructional and expressive objectives: Their formulation and use in curriculum. In W. J. Popham, *Instructional objectives*. Chicago: American Educational Research Association Monograph Series on Curriculum and Evaluation and Rand McNally.

Eisner, E. W. (1971). *Confronting curriculum reform*. Boston: Little, Brown.

Eisner, E. W. (1979). *The educational imagination: On the design and evaluation of school programs*. New York: Macmillan.

Eisner, E. W. (1981). On the differences between scientific and artistic approaches to qualitative research. *Educational Researcher, 10*(4), 5–9.

Eisner, E. W. (1982). *Cognition and curriculum.* New York: Teachers College Press.

Eisner, E. W. (1983). The art and craft of teaching. *Educational Leadership, 40*(4), 4–13.

Eisner, E. W. (1984). Can educational research inform educational practice? *Phi Delta Kappan, 65*(7), 447–452.

Eisner, E. W. (Ed.). (1985a). *Teaching and learning the ways of knowing.* Eighty-fourth Yearbook of the National Society for the Study of Education, Part II. Chicago: University of Chicago Press.

Eisner, E. W. (1985b). *The art of educational evaluation: A personal view.* London: Falmer Press.

Eisner, E. W. (1991a). *The enlightened eye: Qualitative inquiry and the enhancement of educational practice.* New York: Macmillan.

Eisner, E. W. (1991b). What the arts taught me about education. In G. Willis & W. H. Schubert (Eds.), *Reflections from the heart of educational inquiry* (pp. 34–48). Albany: SUNY Press.

Eisner, E. W. (1991c). My educational passions. In D. L. Burleson (Ed.), *Reflections: Personal essays by 33 distinguished educators* (pp. 136–145). Bloomington, IN: Phi Delta Kappa Educational Foundation.

Eisner, E. W. (1994a). *Cognition and curriculum reconsidered.* New York: Teachers College Press.

Eisner, E. W. (1994b). *The educational imagination: On the design and evaluation of school programs.* (3rd ed.). New York: Macmillan.

Eisner, E. W. (1998). *The kind of schools we need: Personal essays.* Portsmouth, NH: Heinemann.

Eisner, E. W. (2002). What can education learn from the arts about the practice of education? *Journal of Curriculum & Supervision, 18*(1), 4–16.

Eisner, E. W., & Vallance, E. (Eds.). (1974). *Conflicting conceptions of curriculum.* Berkeley, CA: McCutchan.

Giroux, H. A., Penna, A. N., & Pinar, W. F. (Eds.). (1981). *Curriculum and instruction.* Berkeley, CA: McCutchan.

Greene, M. (1995). *Releasing the imagination: Essays on education, the arts, and social change.* San Francisco: Jossey-Bass.

Greene, M. (1998). Philosophic inquiry methods in education. In R. M. Jaeger (Ed.), *Complementary methods for research in education* (pp. 189–323). Washington, DC: American Educational Research Association.

Greene, M. (2001). *Variations on a blue guitar: The Lincoln Center Institute lectures on aesthetic education.* New York: Teachers College Press.

Jaeger, R. (Ed.). (1988). *Complementary methods for research in education.* Washington, DC: American Educational Research Association.

Jaeger, R. (Ed.). (1998). *Complementary methods for research in education* (2nd ed.). Washington, DC: American Educational Research Association.

Kilbourne, B. (1999). Fictional theses. *Educational Researcher, 28*(9), 27–32.

Lopez, A. L. (1993). *Exploring possibilities for urban curriculum and teaching in three urban contexts.* Unpublished doctoral dissertation, University of Illinois, Chicago.

Lopez, A. L., & Schubert, W. H. (1983). Art at center stage. *Educational Leadership, 40*(5), 74.

Pinar, W. F. (Ed.). (1975). *Curriculum theorizing: The reconceptualists.* Berkeley, CA: McCutchan.

Schubert, W. H. (1975). *Imaginative projection: A method of curriculum invention.* Unpublished doctoral dissertation, University of Illinois, Urbana-Champaign.

Schubert, W. H. (1981). Knowledge about out-of-school curriculum. *Educational Forum, 45*(2), 185–199.

Schubert, W. H. (1982). Teacher education as theory development. *Educational Considerations, 9*(2), 8–13.

Schubert, W. H. (1992). On mentorship: Examples from J. Harlan Shores and others through lenses provided by James B. Macdonald. *JCT: An Interdisciplinary Journal of Curriculum Studies, 9*(4), 47–69.

Schubert, W. H. (1996). The longevity of a good mentor: J. Harlan Shores. In C. Kridel, R. V. Bullough, Jr., & P. Shaker (Eds.), *Teachers and mentors* (pp. 185–194). Hamden, CT: Garland.

Schubert, W. H. (1997). *Curriculum: Perspective, paradigm, and possibility.* New York: Macmillan. (Original work published 1986).

Schubert, W. H., & Lopez Schubert, A. L. (1980). *Curriculum books: The first eighty years.* Lanham, MD: University Press of America.

Schubert, W. H., Lopez Schubert, A. L., Thomas, T. P., & Carroll, W. M. (2002). *Curriculum books: The first hundred years.* New York: Peter Lang.

Schubert, W. H., & Melnick, C. R. (1987). Study of the "outside curriculum" of student lives. *Journal of Curriculum & Supervision, 2*(2), 200–202.

Schwab, J. J. (1969). The practical: A language for curriculum. *School Review, 78,* 1–23.

Smith, B. O., Stanley, W. O., & Shores, J. H. (1950). *Fundamentals of curriculum development.* Yonkers-on-the-Hudson, NY: World Book.

Smith, B. O., Stanley, W. O., & Shores, J. H. (1957). *Fundamentals of curriculum development.* New York: Harcourt, Brace, and World.

Whitehead, A. N. (1929). *The aims of education.* New York: Macmillan.

Willis, G. H., & Schubert, W. H. (Eds.). (2000). *Reflections from the heart of educational inquiry: Understanding curriculum and teaching through the arts.* Albany: SUNY Press. (Troy, NY: Educators International Press, Classics in Education 2000 reprint of the 1991 edition.)

3

The Mind's Eye

Daniel Tanner
Rutgers University

As a doctoral student, many years ago, I had occasion to visit Ms. Jacobson's fifth grade classroom in an inner-city school with an enrollment composed of predominantly minority, at-risk children. Upon my arrival at mid-morning, I found that the class had just gone outdoors for recess with their teacher. I had some 20 minutes to kill, so I sat down at one of the tables in the back of the room to do some paperwork of my own. However, my eyes were drawn repeatedly to the continuous panorama of vivid murals-in-the-making, which extended on brown parchment paper around the walls of the sides and back of the room. The murals depicted epochal periods and events, from prehistoric to modern times. Neatly grouped on the floor below each mural were jars of paint and clean brushes on sheets of newspaper. Below the first mural, depicting cave men and prehistoric creatures, I noticed that one jar was still open, containing a wet brush. The color of the paint was an earthy brown. The section of the mural directly above revealed a small, unfinished area of rich earth begging to be filled in to complete the landscape. The temptation was irresistible. I picked up the brush, carefully wiping the excess paint on the lid of the jar, and began painting, being careful not to change any features of the children's work. Then I heard them coming up the stairs, returning to their classroom. A sudden rush of wrongdoing came over me, and I quickly placed the brush back into the paint jar and went to the front of the room to greet Ms. Jacobson.

On my return to the office, back on campus late that afternoon, a phone message was waiting for me, requesting that I call Ms. Jacobson. When I telephoned her the next morning, she informed me in a warm and amused tone of voice that the children wanted to see me about my painting. As a conciliatory move, I bought a bushel of beautiful apples on campus for $1.75—a federally subsidized price at a time of a huge apple surplus—and brought the apples to the school. I made a short speech of apology, saying that I hoped I didn't mess up their mural the previous day. One little boy,

33

apparently the spokesperson for the class, stood up, and, after thanking me for the apples, said, "It's all right, Dr. Tanner. You can come to our class any-time and we'll teach you how to paint." The children and I joined together in good-natured laughter. Ms. Jacobson later told me that my face was almost as red as the apples.

Much more recently—in fact only a few years ago—one of my graduate students brought a tape recording to my class, Curriculum and Instruction, of her third graders' reactions to the California Achievement Test that they had taken the previous day. At her request, I approved of her playing the recording to the class. The third graders were asked to express "How I felt when taking the test." The children's statements were framed typically as efforts to please the teacher. "The test was hard, but it was good for my brain," said one child, as others declared in turn: "It made me think." "It made me nervous, but I learned a lot." "I could feel my brain straining." "It must help Ms. McGreevey find out what we need to learn." And so on. After hearing the entire recording, and at the end of our class discussion, an idea came to me. I posed a question to the teacher, Sharon McGreevey: "What if you had asked your third graders to take out their crayons and drawing paper to draw pictures of how they felt when taking the test?" Sharon thought it was a great idea, and proceeded to do so the very next day.

ART AS AUTHENTIC EXPRESSION

When Sharon brought the 22 children's drawings to our curriculum class back on campus, and passed the drawings around the class, it was obvious that she was still astonished and even seemed a bit upset at the results. Some of the drawings made me think of the Norwegian artist Edvard Munch (1863–1944), and his haunting paintings, especially *The Scream*—the mask-like face with bulging mouth and eyes, framed in swirling purple background of land and sky.

It is well known that Munch's painting reflected his childhood terrors and tragedy from losing family to the plague of tuberculosis. Now, I am not likening the childhood terrors of Munch to the fears of 8-year-olds facing up to a national standardized test. But the test is perceived as a verdict on the educational worth of their young lives. Most of the children's drawings bore dramatic captions: "I feel sad and miserable." "I felt scared." "I don't want to think." "O God help me." "Sad!!!!!!!!!!!!" "I felt like I was going to drop dead." One drawing showed an apple falling from a child's head. The apple was labeled "teacher," and the caption: "F–" and "My life is gone!"—with a gravestone engraved with the child's name, "Timmy." On the ground at the base of the gravestone was another apple, bearing the caption "And worse—Parents!" Some of the other drawings surrounded the child's face with repeated cries of "Help." Others filled the background with unhappy faces of classmates surrounding the face of the child who had created the draw-ing. Only two paintings had smiling faces, but one, with a threatening splotchy background, was dark purple. In the other, encapsulated in the child's head, were nonsense scribbles depicting thoughts, a lightbulb above the head, and the caption "I needed a lot of brain work."

Sharon McGreevey is an outstanding teacher. She appropriately looks to the enthusiasm and optimism that so characteristically energize her 22 8-year-olds as the positive and binding force for her class. She strives to build upon this enthusiasm and optimism in all lessons. She never evaluates or measures a child in terms of limitations. She seeks to treat every learning experience in terms of possibilities and good reason.

Ms. McGreevey had been well aware of the anxiety created with the administration of tests to the children near the close of each school year. And so she explains to the children that the tests are used simply to help each and every member of the class to improve in their studies. She avoids, as much as she is able, treating the test as an all-important event. To relieve the children's anxiety, she follows up the test each year with a brief and casually led discussion. So this year it came as a shock to her when she looked at the children's drawings. Yet her children know full well the impact of the state-mandated tests administered to their fourth grade schoolmates each year—tests that evaluate the worth of each child, their class, their teacher, and the school. Clearly these high-stakes tests impact the school curriculum very directly and carry the message to all students of every age that the so-called academic subjects, the subjects most easily measured by standardized tests, are what really count. But Ms. McGreevey refuses to prep her children by teaching for the test and taking valuable time from real learning. She knows that her most important mission is to instill in children the enjoyment of learning.

THE IMAGINATION AND THE IMAGINARY

The experiences recounted above from Ms. McGreevey's and Ms. Jacobson's classes are indeed very different. Yet they reveal some provocative implications. In Ms. McGreevey's class, the artwork revealed the expression of children's authentic feelings, whereas the oral statements of the same children reflected the children's efforts to please the teacher, even if it meant masking their real feelings. The visual arts in many elementary schools are thought of as means for stimulating the imagination of children, with imagination being conceived as an imaginary state removed from reality. "Unfortunately," wrote John Dewey, "it is too customary to identify the imagination with the imaginary, rather than with a warm and intimate taking in of the full scope of a situation" (1916, p. 236).

The children's drawings in Ms. McGreevey's class intimately embraced the full scope of the situation, whereas their oral statements had avoided this by redirecting their thoughts to verbalizing what they perceived as responses that would meet the expectations of their teacher and would serve to please their teacher. The oral statements terminated any possible further inquiry. The artwork opened up a disturbing situation begging investigation and melioration.

FOURFOLD CURRICULUM FUNCTIONS

Looking back, a few years after my incident with Ms. Jacobson's fifth graders, I had occasion to reread John Dewey's *The School and Society* (1900, rev. 1915) and *The Child and the Curriculum* (1902). In *The Child and the Curriculum* Dewey noted, from his observations of children in his laboratory school at the University of Chicago, that children are moved by fourfold instincts or impulses—social, constructive, investigative, and expressive/artistic. These instincts or impulses, as Dewey called them, have enormously profound implications for cognitive and social development and growth throughout life. Indeed, we might term them as the fourfold curricular functions for developmental education.

Ms. Jacobson's classroom, even when empty of children, conveyed to me an atmosphere of action in which I had an irresistible urge to "join in" with the painting of the children's mural. The expressive/artistic impulse or function, which had been latent in me as an adult, somehow was awakened so as to impel me to artistic expression through the dynamic environment of a fifth grade classroom. In effect, the fourfold functions—social, constructive, investigative, and expressive/artistic—should be lifelong in all of us. Unfortunately, they are not. Hence the school experience for many of us may be the last time and place for any organized or systematic artistic expression through social, constructive, and investigative engagement.

From the mural work in Ms. Jacobson's classroom, I could envision the social engagement of the children in their cooperative planning and investigative activity into the historic time frames to be depicted, and their constructive engagement in transforming material resources into visual artistic expression.

However, the fourfold functions are not always stimulated to grow and develop throughout life. With regard to the formal studies in school, the investigative may be confined to abstract knowledge, the social to competitive test-score comparisons, and the constructive and artistic diminished and labeled "nonessentials" of the curriculum. Whereas the fourfold functions should present opportunities for strengthening curriculum unity, they become diminished and encapsulated into separate and increasingly isolated subjects.

The isolation of the various subjects from one another only serves to mitigate the possibilities for realizing the interdependence of knowledge and developing the mind's eye through practical applications and the uses of the imagination in solving real problems. The school subjects and disciplines of knowledge do not exist as discrete and independent entities in the real world. The worth of any one area of knowledge in the curriculum should be determined by what it contributes to other areas of knowledge for growth in the life of the learner.

The point is that none of the fourfold functions should be conceived in isolation. The expressive function should be carried out in a context of vital

FIGURE 1
Fourfold Curriculum Functions for
Developmental Education

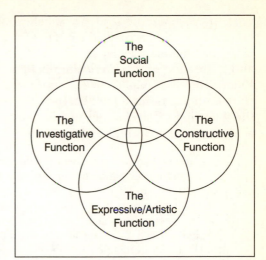

social interaction, constructive work with materials and techniques, and investigative activity into contrasting art forms and themes. The vital interdependence of the fourfold functions is shown in Figure 1. No function can be met and fulfilled in isolation from the other functions. Whether in vocation or avocation—indeed, in many an emergent situation—individuals find themselves making a sketch or diagram, or engaging in producing an art form for recreation. Dewey wisely viewed recreation as "re-creation." In Dewey's words:

> Recreation, as the word indicates, is recuperation of energy. No demand of human nature is more urgent or less to be escaped. The idea that the need can be suppressed is absolutely fallacious. ... Education has no more serious responsibility than making adequate provision for enjoyment of recreative leisure; not only for the sake of immediate health, but still more, if possible, for the sake of its lasting effect upon habits of mind. (1916, p. 205)

THE MIND'S EYE

The fourfold functions illustrated in Figure 1, taken together in vital interdependence, are necessary for developing the mind's eye. The dramatic account of the scientific race for DNA reveals that in working with many models, the scientists rejected various ungainly three-dimensional models on aesthetic grounds in the belief that nature seeks symmetry, leading to their structural conceptualization of the double helix (Watson, 1968). In a sense, the scientists were "playing" with different possible models to the extent that their work was "permeated with the play attitude"—an infusion that is "art—in quality if not in conventional designation" (Dewey, 1916, p. 206).

At this point the reader may believe that the focus of this chapter is on art education, but actually the intent of the author is to reveal how the lenses of art can help curricularists to develop a more holistic conception, vision, and realization of the curriculum field and the advancement of education. Elliot Eisner has made and continues to make some of the most significant contributions to this effort. In *The Educational Imagination* (1994), he writes the following with reference to expressive outcomes as the consequences of activities in all areas of the curriculum:

> It would be erroneous to assume that some fields, such as the fine arts, have a monopoly on the use of expressive activities. This is not the case. Any activity—indeed, at their very best, activities that are engaged in to court surprise, to cultivate discovery, to find new forms of experience— are expressive in character. Nothing in the sciences, the home or mechanical arts or in social relationships prohibits or diminishes the possibilities of engaging in expressive activities and in the process of achieving expressive outcomes. The education problem is to be suffi- ciently imaginative in the design of educational programs so that such outcomes will occur and their educational value will be high. ... Such outcomes are not the exclusive domains of the arts. (pp. 120–121)

With regard to artistry in the process of teaching any subject or in any field, Eisner explains that

> Artistry is important because teachers who function artistically in the classroom not only provide children with important sources of artistic experience, they also provide a climate that welcomes exploration and risk-taking and cultivates the disposition to play. To be able to play with ideas is to feel free to throw them into new combinations, to experiment, and even to "fail." (1994, p. 162)

LEARNING AS AN EMERGENT-GENERATIVE PROCESS

The "failure" that Eisner refers to is not an end point, but a means to gaining further insight into possibilities for solving a problem. Mistakes, errors, or failures can be fruitful as turning points in all activity, whether investigative, constructive, expressive/artistic, or social. No creative activity or accomplish- ment has been conducted and attained without fruitful mistakes.

Unfortunately, the implicit, if not the explicit, message conveyed to students in the conventional classroom is to avoid mistakes. The instruc- tion is error-oriented rather than idea-oriented. It is no wonder, then, that when students are writing a theme, or engaging in answering a question in class, their use of written or oral language becomes almost mechanical and constricted in order to avoid mistakes. The teaching-learning process is treated as an established-convergent process—a process whereby emphasis is given primarily to specificity and predictability of learning outcomes. In other words, success is measured by the extent to which the students avoid mistakes in meeting the required learning specifications or outcomes. Correct answers are typically memorized and then regurgitated on the test. No wonder then that what is memorized for the test is quickly forgotten. Yet teachers are encouraged to engage in aligning the curriculum to the test or teaching to the test. This process mitigates the opportunities and possibilities of designing the curriculum so as to stimulate the learner in the desire to go on learning. Emphasis is given to learning as an established-convergent process, as opposed to an emergent-generative process.

In life, many seemingly established-convergent situations have a way of becoming emergent-generative situations. Take, for example, the "simple" task of following a given recipe from instructions on an index card. One can predict that the outcomes or results will differ greatly by virtue of differences in individual experience, tastes, imagination, and creative inclinations. Uniformity of outcome is necessary in a factory product, such as Wonder bread or a McDonald's hamburger. Established-convergent learning is concerned with specificity and predictability. Emergent-generative learning is concerned with possibility. Much lip service is given to the need to develop higher-order thinking, while problem solutions are being taught routinely as established-convergent situations in the absence or genuine hypothetical thinking. In other words,

> ... the pupil who is investigating significant problems and is allowed to learn through mistakes will be better equipped to deal intelligently with future problems. The whole notion of hypothetical thinking is based on the recognition that the solutions to problems are not always self-evident and that solutions often are derived by pursuing divergent paths. Longer-term projects in the classroom, seminar, laboratory, shop, and studio environments—designed to stimulate pupils to think divergently in formulating and investigating problems—can provide opportunities for valuable kinds of collateral learnings and can serve to enhance the pupil's desire and capability for continued learning. (Tanner & Tanner, 1995, p. 293)

The entire educative process is defeated if the school neglects to cultivate in the student the desire to go on learning. This requires the productive engagement of the student's interests, emotions, motives, and capabilities. And this cannot be done by external imposition. The best chance for developing this desire in the student is by creating a rich and stimulating learning environment that opens the curriculum in terms of possibilities for the good person leading the good life in the good society.

THE CURRICULUM THAT ISN'T THERE

Elliot Eisner wisely avoids unproductive disputation regarding the hidden curriculum of the school, and adds the "null" curriculum as one of the three curricula that all schools teach. I have discussed in some detail various aspects of the explicit and implicit curriculum, but not what Eisner terms the "null" curriculum. "When we look at school curricula with an eye toward the full range of intellectual processes that human beings can exercise," observes Eisner, "it quickly becomes apparent that only a slender range of those processes is emphasized" (1994, p. 99). Eisner continues in defining the null curriculum as

> ... the options students are not afforded, the perspectives they may never know about, much less be able to use, the concepts and skills that are not part of their intellectual repertoire. Surely, in the deliberations that constitute the course of living, their absence will have important consequences on the kind of life that students can choose to lead. (1994, p. 107)

The most serious curriculum problem is equal access to a full and rich curriculum. On the surface, schools may appear to offer a similar curriculum of basic subjects and traditional academic subjects coupled with some elective options in the middle school and beyond. However, as discussed earlier, traditional schools and those serving a high proportion of at-risk students tend to gear the curriculum to facts and skills in an error-oriented curriculum, whereas schools serving more advantaged students are more likely to follow an idea-oriented curriculum. Worksheets and workbooks proliferate in the former; theme writing, library work, projects, seminars, studio work, student portfolios, and field experience may be commonly available in the latter—coupled with elective options for enrichment, exploration, special interests, and, in the high school, specialization. Access to counseling, health services, and student activity programs also differs widely, not to mention differences in learning resources and quality of faculty and facilities.

Even within the same school the curriculum for lower achievers may be error-oriented, whereas the curriculum for other students may be rich and diversified in comparison. In many schools, teaching to the test may prevail, with the external tests driving the curriculum and with little or no attention given to curriculum design and articulation for a general education core. The problem is not curriculum diversity, but disparity among diverse student populations. American democracy hinges on access to a full and rich curriculum for all children and youth.

TOWARD CURRICULUM RENEWAL

The key word or slogan in school blaming and in national educational policy reports over a span of more than two decades has been "reform." The term *reform* implies the need for correction or removal of faults, malpractice, abuses, or misconduct. The term or slogan itself is abusive and unproductive with regard to the public schools. Instead of building on best practices as developed through research and demonstrated success, or what may be regarded as the best available evidence, the tone is one of attack and negativism. Instead of moving constructively in addressing educational problems, the call is for diverting public education funds to building another kind of school so as to divide the cosmopolitan school population by special interests. Prescriptions for reform typically are couched in terms indicative of industrial production, factory output, product, and efficiency.

It would seem that any responsible public group, commission, or agency calling for school reform should be under a moral obligation to provide the financial support to bring about the needed improvements based upon the best available evidence. Instead, the schools have been battered by a pandemic of external testing that has come to drive the curriculum. External testing fixes the blame on the public schools and serves to distract the public from recognizing the need for increased and more equitable school financing in instituting improvements.

Like life itself, all institutions, and especially the public schools of a free society, require constant renewal. And the means of renewal is problem solving. In effect, curriculum development should be a problem-solving process (Giles, McCutchen, & Zechiel, 1942; Tanner & Tanner, 1995). The very design and function of the curriculum must be harmonious with the nature and needs of the learner and with the principles of American democracy (Tanner & Tanner, 1995, pp. 232–234).

No program for educational renewal, improvement, innovation, or reform can succeed if the design and function of the curriculum violates the nature of the learner and the democratic prospect. This is the most fundamental principle for curriculum development. In the field of biology there is the principle that structure determines function. In architecture the principle is form follows function. Much of the curriculum in form and structure is dysfunctional. The curriculum for general education suffers from segmentation of studies and isolation from the life of the learner. The subject matter lacks practicality and generalizability. "It's only academic" is an expression in real life when referring to an idea lacking practicality and generalizability. But in school the practical and generalizable criteria for knowledge do not seem to apply to the academic subject matters which, nevertheless, are prioritized as essentials to the neglect of the "nonessentials."

The arts truly are essentials. They help us to see, to create a more harmonious environment, and to engage in the act of re-creation. In high school I remember a spring day when my friend Whitney and I were standing alone on the school terrace on a hilltop overlooking some fields and woods. "How many shades of green do you see?" asked Whitney. I was taken aback by the question, partly because Whitney never struck me as "the poetic type," but also because it had never occurred to me to even ponder such an idea. And so I began to see the countless shades of green emerging with nature's renewal each spring.

REFERENCES

Dewey, J. (1900, 1915). *The school and society*. Chicago: University of Chicago Press.

Dewey, J. (1902). *The child and the curriculum*. Chicago: University of Chicago Press.

Dewey, J. (1916). *Democracy and education*. New York: Macmillan.

Eisner, E. W. (1994). *The educational imagination: On the design and evaluation of school programs* (3rd ed.). New York: Macmillan.

Giles, H. W., McCutchen, S. P., & Zechiel, A. N. (1942). *Exploring the curriculum*. New York: Harper.

Tanner, D., & Tanner, L. (1995). *Curriculum development: Theory into practice* (3rd ed.). New York: Macmillan.

Watson, J. D. (1968). *The double helix*. New York: Atheneum Press.

4

The Curriculum as a Mind-Altering Device

Kieran Egan
Simon Fraser University

*W*orkers in any complex institution have to engage with a variety of means to achieve the institution's end, whether it be making refrigerators or educating children. In the great enterprise of public education and in its institutions the means that lead toward the end of educated human experience include, among much else, designing systems of schooling, methods of instruction, and a curriculum. Each of these means toward the end of education is in itself extremely complex. Designing adequate methods of instruction entails engaging with a series of further complex means to that end. To design adequate methods of instruction, one has to understand the nature of children's learning, their stages of development, how they are motivated to learn, and so on. And each of these in turn becomes an end toward the achievement of which there is a series of further means. So, for example, understanding children's stages of development is a topic of great complexity, about which there are a number of competing theories. Better articulating each of these theories, or testing their reliability, becomes an end for a range of further means—like developing methods of critical inquiry and skills as an empirical researcher, and these ends generate further means…. Well, you get the picture; indeed, you have known this particular picture all along. It is the picture that helps explain why the study of education is both so fascinating and so frustrating. It is also a kind of thinking that has come into education from areas like planning to build refrigerators, and we might, as we go along, come to wonder whether it is always a good way to think about education. For now though, we can recognize a fairly commonsense way in which we can recognize certain actions taken because they are good means to particular ends. As with any form of language, it has certain uses, so let us see what we can do with it.

One of Murphy's laws is that means replace ends. That is, for most of us, most of the time, our desire to contribute toward some particular end requires us to engage with the means to achieving that end and, given the rather dim creatures we mostly are—"the bulk of mankind is as well quali-fied for flying as thinking," as Jonathan Swift so considerately put it—the means we engage with soon displace in our minds the end we are supposed to be serving.

This might be no bad thing, of course. By playing a small role in a complex enterprise we aid the achievement of the general end of the enterprise. Scientific exploration relies on thousands of people working industriously on detailed parts that are means toward some more general end. But, sometimes, the means pursued, while derived from an image of the overall end, can come not only to displace the end in the mind of the individual contributor, but can also turn out to be antithetical toward achieving the end. "The Law of Unintended Consequences" is the genus of which a species is "Means Displace Ends."

Another similar species is evident when the means toward the overall end conflict with one another. Consider the case where the overall end is the economic betterment of an undeveloped region and the means are seen as generating power, providing irrigation, and controlling the flooding endemic to the area. It is decided that the overall end will be achieved by building a dam that will deploy these three means at the same time. The Law of Unintended Consequences can lead, in this species, to a situation such as that described by Arundhati Roy in *The Cost of Living* (1999):

> The government claims the Sardar Sarovar project will produce 1450 megawatts of power. The thing about multipurpose dams like the Sardar Sarovar is that their "purposes" (irrigation, power pro-duction, and flood control) conflict with one another. Irrigation uses up the water you need to produce power. Flood control requires you to keep the reservoir empty during the monsoon months to deal with an anticipated surfeit of water. And if there is no surfeit, you are left with an empty dam. And this defeats the purpose of irrigation which is to store the monsoon water. It is like the conundrum of trying to ford a river with a fox, a chicken and a bag of grain. The result of these mutually conflicting aims, studies say, is that when the Sardar Sarovar Projects are completed and the scheme is fully func-tional, it will end up producing only 3% of the power its planners say it will. About 50 megawatts. And if you take into account the power needed to pump water through its vast network of canals, the Sardar Sarovar Projects will end up consuming more electricity than they produce. (p. 129)

When the enterprise in which we are engaged, such as education, is not only complex but is value-saturated at every turn, the "law" whereby means displace ends is of constant concern, as is the discovery of conflicting means. Unintended consequences abound. What is the protection against this constant danger? Well, one solution is to keep vividly in mind the ulti-mate end, and constantly calibrate the means so that they are always serving that end. Easy to write, of course, but much less easy to do. We so readily become absorbed in the means to the means to the means to the end, that we find it very hard to keep calibrating the details of our daily activities in light of some grand end. Indeed, most of us clearly have a very hard time even articulating what the end of education is—so what hope do we have that our chosen means are actually means to that somewhat amorphous, vaguely held, and commonly contentious end?

In addition—as if that wasn't enough—the intricacies of the particular means in which we might become expert, sometimes, carry echoes of other ends that influenced the development of those means. For example, it seems sometimes the case that research methodologies derived from psychology are used on educational phenomena in ways that might produce knowledge of some psychological interest, but that pass by the educational problem they were supposed to be serving.

The curriculum is the most obvious of the means to help us attain the end of educated experience. To be able to design a valuable curriculum, obviously enough, one needs to have a clear image of what the educated experience is like that forms the end of the activities of schooling. But, oddly enough, most people seem happy to leave articulating what this educational end is like to others; as though one could securely engage with some means to an end while not being clear about what the end is; as though, in some cases, one could treat education as a technical enterprise rather than as a value-saturated one; as though one doesn't need to have a precise sense of the quality of educated human experience in order to con-tribute toward its attainment by others. And, of course—one problem with my choice of means-end language, which we'll come to later—there is a nig-gling sense that educated experience as an end should be tied up more immediately in the means of bringing it about.

Elliot Eisner, among his many accomplishments, has consistently, dur-ing his career, pointed out means that have lost sight of their ends. He is one of those rare people who seems constantly to have in mind a vivid sense of the end of our great enterprise, and who has the flexibility of mind to be able to calibrate his varied activities and contributions so that they constantly serve the overall aim. He has also consistently been a considerate guide, whose own sensitivity and intricate understanding of education have enabled him to help others see how easy it can be to become disconnected from, or partially separated from, the proper end of educational work. Most of us are inclined to stray in the warrens of methodology, the caves of theory, the mazes of practice, and there have been few voices during the past decades as reliable as Elliot Eisner's to call us back to our central purpose. These have not been decades in which we can point to great successes in professional educational work, but Elliot Eisner has been one of those who have made contributions that would be outstanding in any time. Now I want to explore the kinds of issues raised here and look at just a few of his strik-ing contributions to calling us back to educational sanity by calibrating means to end.

THE MIND-ALTERING DEVICE

The phrase "curriculum as a mind-altering device" is taken from Elliot's Eisner's recent *The Arts and the Creation of Mind* (2002). It pointedly identifies
the curriculum as the school's main device for transforming children's
minds from uneducated to educated. Now, that is a sentence likely to make
some people bristle. Maybe they think it is teaching that deserves such
recognition rather than the curriculum. The kinds of curriculum wars that
enveloped education for decades find echoes in the current wars between
those who promote curriculum as a primary focus for influencing the students' minds and those who want to reduce the role of curriculum and raise
instead spontaneous discovery or see the interaction between student and
teacher as much more important than anything in the curriculum. Well, of
course these are fruitless and ultimately pointless arguments. Elliot Eisner
has more than once patiently clarified that while the curriculum is "an
agenda for the development of the mind" (2002, p. 148), that agenda needs
to be mediated to be brought into effect. Once one recognizes this, the supposed distinction, along with the battle lines that have been drawn along it,
simply melt away. What we have is a more synoptic vision of the role that
curriculum and teaching together play.

But let us take a moment to look at the way the curriculum wars have
built up battle lines within curriculum. Most adults in Western societies, and
probably the majority of teachers, if asked to say what should constitute the
curriculum would list the set of knowledge, skills, and values that would best
equip a student to fit into and contribute to current society. According to this
view, becoming educated means learning whatever is needed to fit into society as it is, or is likely to become. If children will need computing skills and
good literacy and numeracy, then those are the items that will be prominent
in the curriculum. If history is a part of the curriculum, for example, it will
be because it is thought important that students understand how their current society and current world conditions came about.

Second is the common view that to educate someone you must teach
particular kinds of knowledge—regardless of their utility and relevance to
current social needs—in order to shape the mind to perceive the truth. We call
this the academic curriculum, because it was mainly Plato's idea, and the
school he set up was in a small park on the outskirts of Athens, sacred to the
hero Academus. (It did all right as schools go, surviving for about 900 years
until dissolved by the emperor Justinian.) The academic curriculum is made
up of those privileged kinds of knowledge that can show the truth about
things. History, to use the same example, will be in an academic curriculum so
that students will come to understand how and why the world has changed,
our own society's role in this being of no particular importance.

Third is the view that to build an adequate curriculum you need to
understand students' individual capacities and facilitate their fullest development. Each student is different, has particular potentials, and should be

given the opportunity to develop them as fully as possible. Schooling, then, should not be a business of pushing predetermined curricula on students, but rather students' own interests and needs should be allowed to shape the curriculum. Students should be allowed to explore the world of knowledge at their own pace and in the style best suited to their individual ways of learning, because by giving them this opportunity they will learn much more than by any forceful methods. The history learned in this curriculum would be selected according to how well it could support the students' individual intellectual and psychological development; its relevance to the student's needs would be crucial.

Nearly everyone assumes that these three views are of value, and that an adequate curriculum will incorporate all three of them. There will be inevitable tensions resulting from the competing claims these three emphases make on the limited time for completion of students' curricula, but educational administrators are there to maintain a balance among these competing claims—inevitable in a democracy. But this sense of three rather distinct ends for the curriculum makes it difficult for anyone to calibrate the means they are involved in with some overarching end. Now the degree to which we might be involved in an enterprise that bears, at least on the surface, an uncomfortable resemblance to constructing multipurpose dams is a concern for another place. But let me mention a problem that follows having distinct ends which resist easy coordination.

Consider this peculiarity (adapted from Egan, 2001): Let us say you are a movie fan and enjoy going out to a cinema frequently. But now the government imposes a new requirement on citizens. In future it will be compulsory to attend the cinema once a week. As you come out of the cinema in future, you will be required to take a test on the movie you have just seen. You will be asked the color of the villain's car in the chase scene, or the adequacy of the motivation of the leading woman's sister, or the gist of the alien's speech before it transmogrified, or the name of the brother-in-law's pet dog, and so on. Your score on the test will determine your salary for the next week. Then you will face another test and another salary adjustment.

Consider for a moment how such tests and their consequence would likely influence your watching movies. At the very least, they would change what was carefree entertainment into anxiety. You would also spend a lot of effort watching movies trying to second-guess the kinds of questions you are likely to be asked and the focus of your attention would be shifted to fit your expectations of the test.

In such a weird world, the wealthiest class in the society would soon be made up of those with a facility for memorizing the kinds of details asked for on the tests. But this absurd scenario is not *that* far from the situation we have created in schools. The end of satisfaction in learning about the world has been displaced by means that have somehow become largely disconnected from it. Because we aim to use schooling to determine the kinds of jobs and life chances students should have, we have increasingly allowed the need to assess students' abilities for this social-sorting end to displace the alternative end of pleasurable discovery of the wonders of the world. Tough-minded folk tell us that this is just one of those inevitable tensions of democratic societies and their schools. It just so happens that the need to assess how well students are learning, and how well teachers and schools are performing, trumps some alternative ends for the curriculum. Assessment is assumed to be one means toward the end of more adequate education.

One small problem with acceptance of inevitable tensions is brought out by the cinema example. The things assessed are not particularly good indices of what we want to know about students and their learning. It isn't just that the juggernaut of assessment is a means to an end that displaces other educational ends, and seems not well calibrated to any overarching end, but that the kind of assessment tools we have available just aren't well designed to support the kind of learning other educational ends require.

Part of the difficulty of pointing this out to the proponents of the forms of testing so prominent today is that they are the beneficiaries of those forms. The techniques are designed to select for rewards and glittering prizes those with a particular intellectual facility. Such tests entail self-fulfilling prophecies. Like the cinema example—the wealthy class is quickly made up from those who benefit from such tests, and the tests will seem to them self-evidently successful in selecting the meritorious. It is far from clear, however, that the life tasks and the jobs in our society are best served by the selection of that particular intellectual facility any more than many other intellectual qualities that have become devalued by the very means of assessment we choose to deploy.

Well, if this seems a somewhat familiar argument, it is so because Elliot Eisner has fought a consistent battle on behalf of modes of evaluation that are more adequate to our educational ends and are well calibrated to those ends. He has pointed out that the curriculum "constitutes that array of activities that give direction to the cognitive capacities of individuals" (2002, p. 148). The influence of assessment techniques, too casually used from an immature social science, have a disproportionate and devastating impact on the cognitive capacities that are directed for development by curricula that are calibrated toward the tests rather than to the more complex end of education. If the curriculum is "an agenda for the development of the mind" (2002, p. 148), we have cause to worry that the agenda is being hijacked by inappropriate assessment techniques.

Again, "assessment" has increasingly become a word much preferred to "evaluation." "Evaluation" carries within it some sense of judgments about quality and appropriateness. It carries precisely the notions that are wrapped up in "connoisseurship," and is guided by calibration with the end of education. Assessment tends to be an activity separate from teaching and the curriculum; it comes later to deliver a judgment on how adequately they have been performed. "Evaluative activity goes on concurrently with both curriculum and teaching. ... Thus, both teaching and evaluation interpenetrate curriculum. They are part of an inseparable whole" (2002, p. 150). But to see it this way, of course, one needs to see how all three are tied up as coherent and consistent means towards an educational end. Typical assessment serves one end that competes with, and displaces, others.

For years, Elliot Eisner has been arguing that a significant part of the problem with our assessment procedures is that "operationalism and measurement have focused so heavily on behavior that the quality of students' experiences has been generally ignored or seriously neglected" (1985, p. 361). There is a whole range of educational values that such tests do not assess. It is easy to see a misfit between test and purpose in the cinema example above, but it seems many people have difficulty recognizing a similar disjunction in education. The canons of empirical methodologies "have too often determined what shall be studied and what shall be regarded as important in education" (1985, p. 359).

The immaturity of the social sciences from which the methodologies of assessment come infect education and the concern with the quality of students' experiences with a double disability. Vygotsky pointed out the problem with regard to the psychology of his day, and it is hard not to see his observation as precisely relevant to education's situation vis-à-vis psychology today:

> A concept that is used deliberately, not blindly, in the science for which it was created, where it originated, developed and was carried to its ultimate expression, is *blind*, leads nowhere, when transposed to another science. Such blind transpositions, of the biogenetic principle, the experimental and mathematical method from the natural sciences, created the appearance of science in psychology which in reality concealed a total impotence in the face of studied facts. (Vygotsky, 1997, p. 280)

That impotence seems to many of us, who have long been students of Elliot Eisner's work, to have been demonstrated in transposition from psychology to education of sets of assessment procedures that are insensitive to the educational context in which they are supposed to work. As he pointed out, education has suffered from much the same "scientific" assumptions about the efficacy of assessment in leading to improved educational practice from the failure of the 19th century systems of "payments by results," to Franklin Bobbit's 700+ measurable objectives, to the 1960s "behavioral objectives" movement, to today's "standards" approach. When observing this sorry record, Eisner encourages us to constantly ask: "But what of the students' experiences?" (1985, p. 362). After this long and dismal history, he notes, "What is particularly disconcerting with respect to standards-based reform is the way it distracts us from looking really deeply at our education system" (2002, p. 172). It helps those who wish to avoid the task of explicitly connecting this means to the end of education. Some forms of educational research seem like "avoidance activities": dealing with detailed technical issues diverse from the harder business of dealing with values and qualities of experience.

THE ARTS IN THE CURRICULUM

It is hardly coincidental that Elliot Eisner has frequently used the arts and their educational importance as the launching pad for his critique of curricula driven by the kinds of assessment techniques that seem currently pervasive. The arts exemplify matters of great educational worth, evident to anyone who holds other than a crudely utilitarian conception of education. Teaching the arts adequately requires sensitivity, improvisation, and an ability to respond well to the unpredictable. These are not capacities encouraged by standards-based assessment. One of the ironies that he has to face currently follows the astonishing-to-some discovery that a curriculum rich in the arts leads to improved academic performance generally. Who would have thought it?

The irony of course lies in the breathless enthusiasm now being evinced for enlarging arts programs by those whose end is improving academic performance in other areas of the curriculum. That is, the educational value of the arts is not being recognized, except as a means to some other end. The arts are to become means to better math scores. It is no wonder Elliot Eisner characterizes all this as "hoopla" (2002, p. 172). Those who may be congratulating him for his prescience in seeing the academic value of the arts continue to fail to recognize the point he has been making about the centrality of the arts to education. One feels that many of those now enthusiastic about increasing time for the arts would be doing the same for skipping rope if there turned out to be a positive correlation between time spent skipping and math scores. This results from thinking about schooling that lacks any adequate conception of education or mind.

That is, the value of the arts in education has to do with their being a constituent of the end, not a means. The form of means-ends talk has its uses, but breaks down at points such as these. Continuing to use means-ends conceptions encourages us to think of the arts as utilitarian. That's one way of seeing it. The other is to continue with means-ends language as we have above, and say that the problem is that proponents of the arts for their academic utility have displaced the proper end of education with a utilitarian one. Either way, what we have is incomprehension of the role of the arts in the constitution of mind. The role of engaging with the arts is not efficiency at something else; one doesn't, as Eisner says in his recent book, try to eat a great meal efficiently, or make love efficiently, so why should we be striving for inappropriate kinds of efficiency in education? Any sense of the arts' role in human experience should dispel such ideas.

But what is relatively easy to recognize about the arts, or at least easy to those who have long been readers of Elliot Eisner's work, seems to many people much less obviously applicable to other areas of the curriculum. Consider the three ideas mentioned above with relation to the arts. The first idea leads to a conception of the role of arts as something ornamental, a frill, of some entertainment value perhaps, but not serious, not a core area of the curriculum. It is an idea descended from a time when arts were seen as more appropriate for women, while males were encouraged to pursue the hard, tough subjects that would equip them to run things. The second idea leads to a conception of the arts as indeed important for "refining" the student. But the arts were thought of in terms of a hierarchy of artistic works of value, and the students' task was to learn the criteria of judgment that gave us that hierarchy and learn to "appreciate" the best works in the right way. The student, in this view, was to be a consumer of others' work, and maybe some small number of students who demonstrated great native ability in one art or another might be encouraged to become a producer of art in one of the given traditions. The third idea leads to a conception of the arts as primarily for self-gratification; individual students might "express" themselves any way they want, with no attention to public standards. (For a quite different and much richer account of visions and versions of arts education, see Eisner, 2002, chapter 2.)

That is to characterize each view somewhat extremely, of course. And, undeniably, there is *something* to be said for some aspect of each of these views. But I think it is fair to say that most of the art work one sees in schools is driven by one or another, or some unclear mix, of these three views. What Elliot Eisner has given us, over a number of his books, is a more generous conception of the mind and a more generous conception of the role of the arts in making the mind. The result is a conception that transcends these views, and shows a place for the arts in the curriculum that is central, because it is centrally tied up with the prime educational end of a more abundant mind. To adapt a phrase used by Alex Kozulin about the power of poetry in education: It serves as a "super-tool" among the mind's array of cognitive tools (1998, chapter 6). Elliot Eisner's sophisticated sense of the integration and "interpenetration" of areas of the curriculum shows how the arts are not to be seen as one chunk dealt with at some distinct time in the day, but they have to be taught, and thought of, as interpenetrating the whole curriculum. They are the super-tools that enable students to enlarge their understanding of the world in general.

IN CONCLUSION

I have played a little close to the wire in the above chapter, being perhaps a little less cautious than I ought to have been, and heeding too casually Elliot Eisner's warning about the metaphors and images one deploys in talking about education (see Eisner, 1985, pp. 354–357). Using a language of means-ends tempts one to think in ways that he has consistently suggested impoverishes educational practice. He offers us consistently a more generous and synoptic conception of education, in which interpenetration might be taken as a richer metaphor than the one I started with. My choice, of course, was hardly unintended. Means-ends thinking has a place, if one is careful about keeping it within its proper bounds. But it is also illustrative of forms of thinking that have given us, over the years, an image of education as a technical enterprise, the solution to whose problems can be solved by technical means.

Despite his heroic battle against the technologizing of education, we see its results all around us. But without Eisner's strong and clear voice, how much worse might the situation be? It is hard to see any significant issue addressed in education without some reference to his name and works. They are a weapon, to choose another bad but serviceable metaphor, against the easy and lazy activities within education that continue to wreak havoc in our classrooms. He proposes to us that we see education as an art, not as an insecure social science; or rather, as he would prefer not to be exclusive in that way, he invites us to see education as an art that draws on all areas of human inquiry for its resources.

"What is important in any field," he writes, "is a value, the result of a judgment, the product not only of visionary minds and persuasive arguments, but of social forces that create conditions that make certain aims congenial to the times" (2002, p. 25). We are fortunate indeed to have among us someone like Elliot Eisner who recognizes the centrality of value in education, who has consistently used sound judgment and demonstrated to us how we might try to do the same, who is indeed one of the visionary minds in education today and who has produced over the years an important body of persuasive arguments, and who is sensitive to the social forces that shape our thinking but is able also to recognize those forces for what they are, and to transcend them.

REFERENCES

Egan, K. (2001). Why education is so difficult and contentious. *Teachers College Record, 103*(6), 923–941.

Eisner, E. W. (1985). *The educational imagination* (2nd ed.). New York: Macmillan.

Eisner, E. W. (2002). *The arts and the creation of mind*. New Haven: Yale University Press.

Kozulin, A. (1998). *Cognitive tools: A sociocultural approach to education*. Cambridge: Harvard University Press.

Roy, A. (1999). *The cost of living*. New York: Modern Library.

Vygotsky, L. S. (1997). *The collected works of L. S. Vygotsky* (Vol. 3). Edited by R. W. Rieber & J. Wollock. New York: Plenum.

5

--- ❦ ---

Standing on Elliot Eisner's Shoulders

James G. Henderson
Kent State University

*M*ichael Apple, a prominent scholar in the curriculum field, was interviewed for a recent text on the history of curriculum studies in the United States. In this interview, he states that he sees himself as "standing on the shoulders of Counts and Rugg and Dewey and numbers of other folks from the 1920s, like Du Bois, who were socialist educators and antiracist educators" (Marshall, Sears, & Schubert, 2000, p. 103). I also see myself as standing on the shoulders of other curriculum scholars, and I include in that group Elliot Eisner, who served as my doctoral advisor many years ago. Hence the title of my chapter. The metaphor of "standing on someone's shoulders" connotes a deep sense of respect, and my high regard for Eisner's work centers on what I consider to be two interrelated benchmarks of quality curriculum scholarship: *interdisciplinary breadth* and *humanistic depth*.

Klein (1990) describes interdisciplinarity as "a means of solving problems and answering questions that cannot be satisfactorily addressed using single methods or approaches" (p. 196). Pinar, Reynolds, Slattery, and Taubman (1995) present a textual analysis of curriculum studies in this interdisciplinary spirit. They begin their study with a discussion of the parameters of curriculum work: "The general field of curriculum ... [is] the field interested in the relationships among the school subjects as well as issues within the individual school subjects themselves and with the relationships between the curriculum and the world" (Pinar et al., 1995, p. 6). They then end their lengthy examination with the following statement:

> What you know now is that curriculum is a highly symbolic concept. It is what the older generation chooses to tell the younger generation. So understood, curriculum is intensely historical, political, racial, gendered, phenomenological, autobiographical, aesthetic, theological, and international. Curriculum becomes the site on which the generations struggle to define themselves and the world. Curriculum is an extraordinarily complicated conversation. (pp. 847–848)

As an initiate into disciplined curriculum studies in the mid–1970s and under Elliot Eisner's guidance, I learned to work from this broad inter-disciplinary perspective. I still have vivid memories of informal evening meetings where Elliot and his students discussed the curriculum ideas that served as the basis for his text, *The Educational Imagination*, which is now in its third edition (Eisner, 1994b). Eisner ends this book with a series of final points, including this statement: "The dominant image of schooling in America has been the factory and the dominant image of teaching and learning the assembly line. These images misconceive and underestimate the complexities of teaching and neglect the differences between education and training" (p. 361). In a more recent address, Eisner (1996) challenges educational researchers to avoid simplistic epistemologies and to embrace methodological pluralism:

> Artistry does not reduce complexity, it has a tendency to increase com-plexity by recognizing subtlety and emphasizing individuality. It does not search for the one best method. ... Artistic performance in teaching is a quality of work we ought to cherish and try to foster. Conceiving of teaching at its best as an art does not require us to give up the scientific sources that are helpful in its pursuit. It does remind us that science does not tell the whole story and that the quintessence of performance, *even in the conduct of science itself*, is found in its artfulness. (pp. 18–19) [Eisner's emphasis]

Interdisciplinary breadth in curriculum work is closely linked to *humanistic depth*, as succinctly captured in Huebner's (1966/1999) ironic comment:

> Think of it—there standing before the educator is a being partially hid-den in the cloud of unknowing. For centuries the poet has sung of his near infinitudes; the theologian has preached of his depravity and hinted of his participation in the divine; the philosopher has struggled to encompass him in his systems, only to have him repeatedly escape; the novelist and dramatist have captured his fleeting moments of pain and purity in never-to-be-forgotten esthetic forms; and the man engaged in curriculum has the temerity to reduce this being to a single term—"learner." (p. 103)

Eisner's persistent and incisive criticism of educational reductionism in its many guises is carefully balanced by his compelling humanistic arguments; and certainly, one of the best developed and far-reaching of these arguments is his 1979 John Dewey lecture in which he states:

> The educational agenda that I have described is one built upon a broad conception of mind, a multiple conception of meaning, and the ambi-tion to create genuinely educative and equitable schools. Educational equity is not likely without a range of opportunities for conception and representation, opportunities that are wide enough to satisfy the diver-sity of talents of those who come to school and who share their future with us. (Eisner, 1994a, p. 89)

My introduction to curriculum studies occurred at the historical point in the field where leading curriculum scholars were establishing critical distance from a linear, "modernist" curriculum rationality, symbolized by Tyler's (1949) four-part rationale that was, and still is, the dominant "institutional text" in educational settings (Pinar et al., 1995). These critiques, spurred on by Schwab's (1978) sophisticated analysis of the "eclectic arts" of curriculum deliberation, took many forms, and Eisner contributed to this critical turning of the field in important and positive ways. Unfortunately, many self-identified "postmodern" critical projects in the curriculum field have thrown the *baby* of interdisciplinary breadth and humanistic depth out with the *bathwater* of "vulgar pragmatism" (Cherryholmes, 1988), modern "methodization" (Doll, 2002), and "tranquilized democracy" (Novak, 2002). Eisner, however, has never succumbed to this temptation and professional limitation, and that is why I think he has worthy "shoulders" to stand upon.

I will provide an accounting of Elliot Eisner's critical and constructive contributions to the curriculum field in a way that is consistent with the organizing theme of this book. A central aim of my own career as a curriculum scholar has been the creation of a constructive alternative to the Tyler rationale. I will begin by describing my current progress in realizing this professional goal, and I will then discuss how this scholarship is an example of "working the ideas of Elliot Eisner."

TRANSFORMATIVE CURRICULUM LEADERSHIP

Through collaboration with two university colleagues and a group of progressive educational practitioners in northeast Ohio, I have refined a conception of curriculum-based educational reform. It is a multifaceted decision-making process containing eight interrelated dimensions. The individual dimensions of the reform work are presented in Table 1. These dimensions are displayed as separate categories for discussion purposes only. It should be kept in mind that, at the point of practice, all eight dimensions are deeply embedded in one another. This conception of educational reform is called *transformative curriculum leadership* because the goal is to "elevate" curriculum judgments through the facilitation of deep-seated personal, interpersonal, and cultural changes (Henderson & Hawthorne, 2000).

Building a Democratic Platform is the first dimension in Table 1. Informed by Schwab's (1978) "practical" essays, Walker (1971) identifies "platform" building as a key feature of curriculum deliberations:

> The curriculum developer does not begin with a blank slate. He [*sic*] could not begin without some notion of what is possible and desirable educationally. The system of beliefs and values that the curriculum developer brings to his task and that guides the development of the curriculum is what I call the curriculum's *platform*. The word "platform" is meant to suggest both a political platform and something to

TABLE 1
Transformative Curriculum Leadership

Dimension	Decision-Making Process
Building a Democratic Platform	Creating a curriculum platform that provides a coherent standpoint for facilitating a balanced "3S" education, referring to "deep" subject matter understanding integrated with democratic self and social learning. The intent is to position curriculum work as a *democratic wisdom challenge.*
Building Inquiry Capacity	Determining how to build the necessary "inquiry capacity" to practice democratic curriculum wisdom. Several guides for this decision-making have been created.
Creative Designing	Creating unit designs informed by the platform decision-making. This is the enactment of a *visionary design* process that links the platform construction with student learning assessment before moving to instructional planning.
Artistic, Reflective Teaching	Artistically teaching the unit. This is action inquiry embedded in a creative reflection-in-practice and reflection-on-practice.
Comprehensive Evaluation	Enacting a holistic formative and summative evaluation of the preceding dimensions.
Building a Work Culture	Practicing organizational development that nurtures a supportive work culture. This work has three interrelated components: trust building, critical assessment, and collaborative problem solving.
Cultivating Public Understanding	Practicing community development that cultivates public awareness and appreciation. This work focuses on creating an authentic public "space" for democratic education.
Establishing a Network	Building a support system of transformative curriculum leaders by identifying interested curriculum stakeholders, supporting their transformative leadership efforts, and creating networking opportunities.

stand on. The platform includes an idea of what is and a vision of what ought to be, and these guide the curriculum developer in determining what he should do to realize his vision. (p. 52) [author's emphasis]

The platform construction positions curriculum workers in the democratic "HERE-AND-NOW" (Dewey, 1939/1989). They must carefully consider how the educational services they are providing are, in very concrete ways, instances of democratic living. They must think about curriculum as a challenge to practice wise judgments (Henderson & Kesson, 2004).[1] Dewey's (1938/1963) *Experience and Education* informs the notion of "3S" learning, which refers to the integration of deep subject matter understanding with democratic self and social learning. Wiggins and McTighe (1998/2001) present a concise analysis of subject matter understanding, while Greene's (1988) discussion of the "dialectic of freedom" provides valuable insight into democratic self and social learning.

Through years of research, I have found that the quality of the platform deliberations I have outlined is highly dependent on the inquiry capacities of individual educators. This is, of course, a central point in Dewey's work. Throughout his career he continuously noted that a sophisticated "logic of inquiry" was embedded in problem solving from a democratic point of view (Burke, 1994; Jackson, 2002). Over the years, my collaborators and I have created a number of "inquiry artistry" maps (Henderson, 2001; Henderson & Hawthorne, 2000; Henderson & Kesson, 2004) to guide the necessary inquiry growth, and all of these maps are informed by Schwab's (1978) concept of "eclectic artistry" as refined by Eisner's (1994b) insights into the *educational imagination*.

The creative designing is a particular application of Wiggins and McTighe's (1998/2001) "backward design" process, which involves three steps: clarify the "3S" student learning, determine the acceptable evidence for inferring that this learning is occurring, and plan appropriate instruction. I call it "visionary design" to stress the progressive, forward-looking nature of the curriculum deliberations, thus underscoring the historical fact that democratic self and social learning is rarely facilitated in today's educational settings.

The enactment of this visionary design work requires a democratic educational artistry embedded in what Schon (1983) characterizes as "reflection-in-practice" and "reflection-on-practice." In other words, the teaching must, necessarily, be the practice of a creative inquiry, well articulated by Eisner (1996):

The problematic situations the teacher confronts are often ill structured. Conferring order while being open to chance and to the "happy accidents" that may emerge in the course of one's work are also an

---

[1]Wisdom is defined in the *Oxford English Dictionary* as "the capacity of judging rightly in matters relating to life and conduct; soundness of judgment in the choice of means and ends; sometimes, less strictly, sound sense, especially in practical affairs."

important part of artistry in teaching. Artistry requires a willingness
to shift destination in flight when greater gains or a more satisfying
journey is likely. (p. 16)

This type of reform work also necessitates a very comprehensive
type of formative and summative evaluation, and this is due to the highly
embedded nature of the eight decision-making dimensions. Furthermore, though individual educators may be able to practice many of these
dimensions on their own, their efforts will forever be "at risk" without a
supportive work culture (Fullan & Hargreaves, 1996; Sarason, 1990).
This is why organizational development—with its interrelated trust building, critical assessment, and collaborative action phases (Schmuck &
Runkel, 1985)—is so important. Work on the organizational culture naturally requires community development efforts for a simple reason.
Cultural change is impossible without the cultivation of a broad political
base (Lieberman, 1995; Sergiovanni, 1992, 2000).

This highly collaborative and visionary curriculum decision-making is a
form of educational leadership that focuses on deep-seated personal, interpersonal, and cultural changes. Working in this way places an enormous
stress on individuals; so if these leaders do not find ways to support one
another, they will, most likely, be unable to persist in their transformative
efforts. Therefore, networking is also an essential feature of this "ecological"
reform effort.

The educational practitioners who have helped conceptualize transformative curriculum leadership have provided narratives on this work
in a number of publications that I have already cited. A common feature
of all of these narratives is the tentative and initial nature of their work.
This, of course, is not surprising to anyone who understands the current
test-driven policy environment of American education. In very basic
terms, transformative curriculum leadership is still more a hope than a
reality and more a theory than a practice. In Eisner's language, it is an
exercise in "educational imagination."

STANDING ON EISNER'S SHOULDERS

I now turn to a comparative analysis of transformative curriculum leadership (TCL) with the Tyler rationale that it is designed to replace, and my discussion draws heavily on the critical, humanistic "tools" that Eisner has
created throughout his very productive career.

Though deliberation over educational "purposes" is a central feature
of Tyler's decision-making approach, the normative basis of this work is left
too open-ended. It is a form of liberal discourse that lacks critical imagination. The platform building in the TCL process is a specific application of
Eisner's (1994b) argument that "connoisseurship" and "criticism" are central to educational artistry:

> Effective criticism, within the arts or in education, is not an act indepen-
> dent of the powers of perception. The ability to see, to perceive what is
> subtle, complex, and important, is its first necessary condition. The act of
> knowledgeable perception is, in the arts, referred to as connoisseurship.
> To be a connoisseur is to know how to look, to see, and to appreciate.
> Connoisseurship, generally defined, is the art of perception. It is essential
> to criticism because without the ability to perceive what is subtle and
> important, criticism is likely to be superficial or even empty. The major
> distinction between connoisseurship and criticism is this: connoisseurship
> is the art of appreciation, criticism is the art of disclosure. (p. 215)

The platform building challenges educators to cultivate their *connoisseurship* and *critical* capacities with reference to the "democratic good life." In
order to transform courses of study into democratic experiences, educators
must be able to deeply perceive and publicly render the subtle interplay
between specific subject matter understanding and democratic self and
social learning. The degree to which they do not develop the necessary *connoisseurship* and *critical* capacities is the degree to which their curriculum
purposes will be limited. The Tyler rationale lacks insight into this matter.

Tyler's deliberations over educational purposes are too easily reduced
to a listing of narrow performance objectives. His rationale lacks a robust
interdisciplinary and humanistic "logic of inquiry." He leaves too much to
chance. His rationale does not foreground the challenge of educational
artistry, elegantly captured by Eisner (1994b):

> Teaching can be done as badly as anything else. It can be wooden,
> mechanical, mindless, and wholly unimaginative. But when it is sensi-
> tive, intelligent, and creative—those qualities that confer upon it the status
> of an art—it should, in my view, not be regarded as it so often is by some,
> as an expression of unfathomable talent or luck but as an example of
> humans exercising the highest level of their intelligence. (p. 156)

The Tyler rationale does encourage balanced "3S" learning—the integration of subject matter, self, and social learning. In effect, it does encourage a comprehensive approach to education. Unfortunately, the rationale's
weak humanistic underpinnings permit an easy adaptation to a test-driven
educational meritocracy, resulting in the impairment, if not outright loss, of
subject matter understanding integrated with democratic self and social
learning. Eisner's (1994a) argument for a more diversified approach to "literacy" in education is a central feature of the platform building process, thus
infusing a deep sensitivity for personal equity into the educational decision-
making. Eisner explains:

> A practice [of "multiliteracy"] will of course increase the difficulty of
> making comparisons among the performances of students. But
> whether the comparative ranking of students is in the long-term best
> interests of either the students or the society is something that one can
> certainly argue. In the context of education, the creation of conditions

that lead to self-realization is, I believe, a primary aim. If the means through which such realization can occur makes comparative assessments more difficult, so be it. Education is not a horse race. Speed is not the ultimate virtue. What people can become through an educationally caring community is. (p. 86)

Unlike the TCL process, the Tyler rationale does not deliberately establish a place for teaching artistry. Eisner's *The Educational Imagination* is instructive on this point. His concern for the use of problem-solving objectives and expressive activities requires him to include a chapter on the art of teaching. In effect, his book is an argument for curriculum-based pedagogy. The TCL process also integrates curriculum and teaching artistry. This is an educational "enactment" approach that stands in contrast to curriculum "implementation" strategies. Implementation denotes top-down reform: teachers and their students being asked to implement a prescribed change agenda. The idea of enactment, however, conveys a sense of responsible power sharing. Snyder, Bolin, and Zumwalt (1992) explain:

> From the enactment perspective, curriculum is viewed as the educational experiences jointly created by student and teacher. The externally created curricular materials and programmed instructional strategies ... are seen as tools for students and teacher to use as they construct the enacted experience in the classroom. (p. 418)

Due to its lack of attention to teaching artistry, the Tyler rationale is readily adapted to "power over" educational mandates. The consequence is the separation of curriculum and teaching decision-making, often resulting in bureaucratic, textbook-driven, shallow educational services (Sergiovanni, 2000).

Finally, the Tyler rationale lacks a comprehensive "ecological" sensibility. Its problem-solving focus is too narrowly conceived, thus further revealing its lack of interdisciplinary breadth. A consistent theme in Eisner's scholarship is the importance of a broad approach to educational reform. For example, he writes:

> The reform of education not only requires deeper and more comprehensive analysis of schools; it must also attend to the dimensions of schooling that must be collectively addressed. ... Applied to schools, it means that the school as a whole must be addressed: . . . the intentions that give direction to the enterprise, the structure that supports it, the curriculum that provides its content, the teaching with which that content is mediated, and the evaluation system that enables us to monitor and improve its operation. ... To approach the reform of schools ecologically or, as others put it, systemically, requires, at the very least, attention to intentions—what aims really matter in the educational enterprise as a whole? (Eisner, 1994a, pp. 10–11)

The TCL process promotes this ecological sensitivity. It encourages Pinar et al.'s (1995) multitextual curriculum "conversation" through the careful integration of curriculum, professional, organizational, and community development practices.

IN CONCLUSION

The TCL decision-making process could not have been created without Eisner's insights into educational artistry. His critical and creative ideas, reflecting both an interdisciplinary breadth and humanistic depth, are central to the conception of transformative curriculum leadership. It is for this reason that I feel Eisner provides "shoulders" to stand on.

Elliot Eisner's work provides hope for a better educational future for all societies espousing democratic ideals. His scholarship is based on a deep faith in educators' ability to enact the artistry of their professional calling, and I end this chapter by giving him the last word. He concludes *The Educational Imagination* as follows:

> The last major point I wish to emphasize here is the need for an ecological orientation to school reform, one that does justice to the complexities of the enterprise. It is the mark of a sophisticated educator to understand this complexity and to avoid the panaceas, nostrums, oversimplifications, and slogans that are often found in the public press. We need to provide responsible leadership that embraces the possibilities of education and is willing to explore the alternative routes that can be traveled to achieve them. If this book has made those possibilities more vivid and if it has provided a sense of what it may take to realize them in our schools, the effort will have been worth it. (Eisner, 1994b, p. 384)

REFERENCES

Burke, T. (1994). *Dewey's new logic: A reply to Russell*. Chicago: University of Chicago Press.

Cherryholmes, C. H. (1988). *Power and criticism: Poststructural investigations in education*. New York: Teachers College Press.

Dewey, J. (1963). *Experience and education*. New York: Macmillan. (Original work published 1938)

Dewey, J. (1989). *Freedom and culture*. Buffalo, NY: Prometheus. (Original work published 1939)

Doll, W. E. (2002). Ghosts and the curriculum. In W. E. Doll & N. Gough (Eds.), *Curriculum visions* (pp. 23–70). New York: Peter Lang.

Eisner, E. W. (1994a). *Cognition and curriculum reconsidered* (2nd ed.). New York: Teachers College Press.

Eisner, E. W. (1994b). *The educational imagination: On the design and evaluation of school programs* (3rd ed.). New York: Macmillan.

Eisner, E. W. (1996). Is the "art of teaching" a metaphor? In M. Kompf, W. R. Bond, D. Dworet, & R. T. Boak (Eds.), *Changing research and practice: Teachers' professionalism, identities and knowledge* (pp. 9–19). Washington, DC: Falmer Press.

Fullan, M., & Hargreaves, A. (1996). *What's worth fighting for in your school?* New York: Teachers College Press.

Greene, M. (1988). *The dialectic of freedom*. New York: Teachers College Press.

Henderson, J. G. (2001). *Reflective teaching: Professional artistry through inquiry* (3rd ed.). Upper Saddle River, NJ: Merrill/Prentice Hall.

Henderson, J. G., & Hawthorne, R. D. (2000). *Transformative curriculum leadership* (2nd ed). Upper Saddle River, NJ: Merrill/Prentice Hall.

Henderson, J. G., & Kesson, K. R. (2004). *Curriculum wisdom: Educational decisions in democratic societies*. Upper Saddle River, NJ: Merrill/Prentice Hall.

Huebner, D. E. (1999). Curricular language and classroom meanings. In V. Hillis (Ed.), *The lure of the transcendent: Collected essays by Dwayne E. Huebner* (pp. 101–117). Mahwah, NJ: Erlbaum. (Original work published 1966)

Jackson, P. W. (2002). *John Dewey and the philosopher's task*. New York: Teachers College Press.

Klein, J. T. (1990). *Interdisciplinarity: History, theory, and practice*. Detroit: Wayne State University Press.

Lieberman, A. (Ed.). (1995). *The work of restructuring schools: Building from the ground up*. New York: Teachers College Press.

Marshall, J. D., Sears, J. T., & Schubert, W. H. (2000). *Turning points in curriculum: A contemporary American memoir*. Upper Saddle River, NJ: Merrill/Prentice Hall.

Novak, B. (2002). Humanizing democracy: Matthew Arnold's nineteenth-century call for a common, higher, educative pursuit of happiness and its relevance to twenty-first-century democratic life. *American Educational Research Journal*, *39*(3), 593–637.

Pinar, W. F., Reynolds, W. M., Slattery, P., & Taubman, P. M. (1995). *Understanding curriculum: An introduction to the study of historical and contemporary curriculum discourses*. New York: Peter Lang.

Sarason, S. B. (1990). *The predictable failure of educational reform: Can we change course before it's too late?* San Francisco: Jossey-Bass.

Schmuck, R., & Runkel, P. (1985). *The handbook of organization development in schools* (3rd ed.). Prospect Heights, IL: Waveland.

Schon, D. A. (1983). *The reflective practitioner: How professionals think in action*. New York: Basic Books.

Schwab, J. J. (1978). *Science, curriculum, and liberal education: Selected essays*. Edited by I. Westbury & N. J. Wilkof. Chicago: University of Chicago Press.

Sergiovanni, T. J. (1992). *Moral leadership: Getting to the heart of school reform*. San Francisco: Jossey-Bass.

Sergiovanni, T. J. (2000). *The lifeworld of leadership: Creating culture, community, and personal meaning in our schools*. San Francisco: Jossey-Bass.

Snyder, J., Bolin, F., & Zumwalt, K. (1992). Curriculum implementation. In P. W. Jackson (Ed.), *Handbook of research on curriculum* (pp. 402–435). New York: Macmillan.

Tyler, R. W. (1949). *Basic principles of curriculum and instruction*. Chicago: University of Chicago Press.

Walker, D. F. (1971). A naturalistic model for curriculum development. *School Review*, *80*, 51–65.

Wiggins, G., & McTighe, J. (2001). *Understanding by design* (special ed.). Upper Saddle River, NJ: Merrill/Prentice Hall. (Original work published 1998)

PART 2

❧

Arts Education

6

The Importance of Being Artist

Reflections on Elliot Eisner

Janice Ross
Stanford University

If you do not change your mind about something when you confront a picture you have not seen before, you are either a stubborn fool, or the painting is not very good.

—Robert Rauschenberg (1966)

*E*lliot Eisner's customary way to introduce himself to a class of new students is to describe himself as an artist. He was, of course, a painter before he was formally an arts educator. Yet one imagines that for him these two ways of being in the world—as an artist and as an arts educator—have always been intertwined. For nearly 50 years, he has been steadfast in his probing of these two outlooks to yield new insights, to use one of his own pithy phrases. In turn, he has taken these insights, freighted with his intimate knowledge and passion for art, and developed them into fresh and compelling models of the ways in which the arts enhance human understanding.

One of the most influential theories Eisner has developed is that of the arts as a paradigm for nondiscursive forms of knowledge. He has spent a substantial portion of his career explaining the unique capacities the arts have for fostering the cultural and artistic development of the individual. Eisner has been a theorist of philosophical arguments about aesthetic matters and a poetic analyst of the practical implications of those ideas for broad areas of education. He bases this on a conception of human nature rooted in premises about the nature of mind. "Mind," he insists, "is a cultural achievement. The kinds of minds that children come to own are profoundly influenced by the kinds of experiences they are able to secure in the course of their lives" (Eisner, 1992b, p. 2). His career has been devoted to making the arts part of that set of experiences.

This chapter focuses on the way in which this insight of Eisner's in itself may well have been a product of *his* specific early experiences as an artist and student. These observations are drawn from remarks he made in lectures delivered internationally between 1992 and 1996. A gifted orator, these talks reveal Eisner's ideas with unusual accessibility and clarity at the same time as they disclose his skill at taking art education theory and popularizing it into an educational policy imperative. "The mind is the product of opportunity," he said as a starting premise for his insistence on the importance of the arts in school (Eisner, 1992b, p. 3). The mind that has been Eisner's most immediate model is, of course, his own. The historical and theoretical aspects of Eisner's experiences (educational and aesthetic) that contributed to the development of *his* mind subsequently played out in his reenvisioning of arts education.

In his early years, while trying to make a living as a fledgling artist, Eisner took a job with Vogue-Wright Studios, the company that illustrated the Sears Roebuck and Montgomery Ward catalogs. Eisner's tasks were to bring the catalog artists the items of clothing they were to draw and to change the water in their water containers. In between, he could work on his own drawings of the clothing as an exercise. "It wasn't much of a job," he said later, with some understatement. "I somehow felt that this work as a commercial artist was not all that it was cracked up to be. The artists themselves were eager to get off the board and to do something else. The work was routine and fragmented. Each was a specialist. One was a specialist in drawing hands and heads, another in backgrounds, a third in laying washes, a fourth in making drawings of figures, a fifth in creating texture and so forth. It was kind of an assembly line" (Eisner, 1995). This was an approach to production—whether it be a catalog or one's personal knowledge—that Eisner would come to vigorously oppose, not only in the art studio but in America's classrooms as well.

Eisner left the Vogue-Wright Studios after a year and a half, sensing that not only wasn't this art—it wasn't even good design. This approach to drawing eviscerated what made the arts meaningful and engaging. It drained him along with his craft. Eisner would effectively spend the rest of his career reclaiming what he felt had been taken out of art in the Vogue-Wright Studios, and arguing for its incorporation into the mainstream of American education. Along the way he articulated a rationale for why it needed to be put back in. In the process, Eisner became instrumental in defining the field of contemporary art education.

Eisner just as readily knew what wasn't education as what wasn't art. He insisted (and, of course, still insists) that education that was uninformed by the values of the arts was missing something critical. With rare insight and articulateness, he named these values as art's championing of surprise, its attention to sensorial experience, and its engagement of nonverbal and visual means to express understanding and meaning. Most importantly, for artists, he understood what the allure, the magic, and the satisfactions of the *work* in the work of art were, and he had a rare eloquence for articulating this. What *they* felt and thought, *he* said. When he spoke, Eisner could rouse an audience of teachers, administrators, policy-makers and students to passion and activism for the arts in education. He could inspire educational administrators to think differently about the arts, and he could move artists to care about the educational facets and consequences of what they were doing. His ideas, which this essay will explore, were persuasive, and his gifts as a writer and orator effectively made them unassailable. (Eisner knows his subject so well that he speaks, indeed he seems to *think*, in whole paragraphs, without notes.) His discussion of the complex and subtle aspects of the mind that are developed and refined through aesthetic curricula offered a bold reconception of the ends of education.

A primary mentor for Eisner was the writing of John Dewey, particularly Dewey's *Art as Experience* (1934), which has been the cornerstone of Eisner's thinking, writing, and conceptualizing about the arts for the majority of his career. "Ah, what I would have given to have written this book," he once remarked in regard to Dewey's theorizing about the nature of our encounters with art in *Art as Experience*. He admired the expansiveness of Dewey's vision, the clarity of his prose, and the efficiency of his analysis of how the mind metabolizes aesthetic experiences. Eisner emerged as one of education's major interpreters of Dewey's aesthetic theories. He explored them for their broader educational utility, and at the same time he insistently highlighted Dewey's use of the arts as a paradigm for the critical learning that traditionally has been ignored by education. Perhaps Eisner was subconsciously tracing his own intellectual path, in which art validated *his* mind.

Eisner's own narrative of his childhood suggests that the elementary school years for him were about the discovery of how encounters with the arts nurtured his heart, his mind, and his humanity. Art classes were where he received acknowledgment and where he was "seen" as an individual, where, uniquely among his school subjects, he consistently joined the elite of "A" students. It was where his heart sang. Art was also where the young Eisner was bold. As a 9-year-old, after he drew a large American flag in colored chalk on the chalkboard in his classroom, his proud teacher sent him to another classroom to reproduce the flag there. Eisner mistakenly drew this "commissioned" chalk flag in the wrong classroom and later recounted that he "didn't feel a tinge of embarrassment" (Eisner, 1995). In the moment of making art, his identity was secure. A motivating force in his life as an educator was discovering how to make this same life raft of individuality through the creation of images available to every child in America's public schools.

Eisner began by probing what it was in the arts that made for this unique capacity. His first job in art education was teaching low-income, African-American boys in the American Boys Commonwealth (ABC), an after-school boys' club in the Chicago neighborhood where Eisner grew up. His students were 7 to 14 years old and his classroom goal, as he later described it, was "to learn from them something about art that would be useful to me as a painter and student of the visual arts" (Eisner, 1995). This is a curiously revealing statement, for in putting himself in the role of a student *of* his art students, Eisner was also trying to sample, through his students, what art might have to teach. He was also allowing that just as meanings in a finished work of art do not always disclose themselves immediately, so too the kind of cognitive growth that working in art prompts is not easily perceivable. The director of the American Boys Commonwealth alerted Eisner to pay attention to the psychological importance of the experiences he was having with his students. It was here that Eisner's orientation began to shift from art to art education.

Eisner was ripe to be excited by education; indeed, in his work in art he steadfastly situated himself on the margins of the fine art professional world and on the cusp of social growth. Repeatedly he gravitated toward the pockets where the social justifications were most immediate and the cultural implications most tangible. From the start, Eisner saw schools as a platform from which to effect social change. This was a moral value he had acquired at a young age as a Jewish American raised in the postwar era: "The fit between education and my background as a youngster growing up in a family with strong social concerns was a good one" (Eisner, 1995, p. 6). He used this social concern to push art education into cultural responsibility as well. "I do not believe that the school's primary focus ought to merely replicate the cultural experience that is provided by the family or the society," he has said. "The school has a special responsibility. That responsibility is to go beyond what it is that ordinary experience in everyday living is likely to foster. ... In short, schools ought not to be factories for cultural reproduction. They ought to be places in which student growth makes it possible for the culture at large to grow" (Eisner, 1992b, p. 15).

"The cultural and artistic development of the individual is significantly influenced by the kind of place that a school is," Eisner cautions. While he allows that all cultural institutions, as well as the family and society at large, are significant forces that foster the cultural and artistic development of the individual, Eisner emphasizes the school because he sees it as providing an intentionally structured and planned agenda that the family and the culture at large do not (Eisner, 1992b, p. 4). Education is a way to draft blueprints for the architecture of cognitive growth.

"Building educational programs in which different sensory modalities are used for the construction or recovery of meaning is one way, in general, of enriching mind," he observes (Eisner, 1992b, p. 8). "Educational equity is increased when the curricula that are provided in schools have sufficient diversity to be inclusive rather than exclusive" (p. 8). He was attempting a curriculum overhaul that was more artistically ambitious than any attempted before.

It is critical that Eisner initially came to art education through the pleasure of his own art experience. This was an enjoyment that was enhanced by this awareness that through art one could work to make the world a better place. It is equally important that as Eisner passed through art as a personal activity to art as an educational medium, he was propelled by two things: a quest to share this pleasure, and a need to understand its mechanics. His subsequent work has continued to be motivated by these two impulses and by his belief in the capacity, indeed the mandate, for education to be an agent for social and cultural transformation. From his first encounter with education as a field, Eisner was as excited about it as a discipline as he had been about painting as a fine art. He noted that educational problems appealed to him because they are "theoretically interesting, intellectually challenging, socially relevant and addressed value issues" that he cared about (Eisner, 1995, p. 6). These were some of the aspects of art that the Vogue-Wright Studios had forgotten, or, more likely, never knew. They were also the aspects of art that were being highlighted by two generative forces in postwar American culture of the time: the legendary German design school, the Bauhaus, and the philosophy of John Dewey.

In the autumn of 1954 Eisner enrolled in the Institute of Design in Chicago. This school—founded by the German designer Laszlo Moholy-Nagy in 1933 under its original name, the New Bauhaus—had grand aspirations of training what Moholy-Nagy called "art engineers." "We don't want to add to the art proletariat that already exists ... we don't want to teach what is called *pure art*," Moholy-Nagy had said in his opening lecture at the school. He framed art instead as the means by which scientific discovery could be reconciled with human needs and desires, emphasizing the importance of collaboration between students and teachers and between artists and industry (Otwell, 1997). The phrase *art engineer* itself encapsulates the marriage of the aesthetic with the utilitarian and practical that Eisner would aim for educationally through policy and curriculum reform. He made the term *art educator* a similarly provocative symbol.

From 1954 to 1955 Eisner had firsthand experience with the Bauhaus's education and aesthetic. He was a student at the Institute of Design, and although Laszlo Moholy-Nagy had died eight years before Eisner enrolled, the vision of this legendary Bauhaus designer was still vividly in motion at the school. In particular, Moholy-Nagy held firmly to his belief that good design and the ideals of modern art could change people's lives. In his most influential book, *Vision in Motion*, published in 1947 and a book that Eisner knew well, Moholy-Nagy laments the way in which art was being reduced to a mere technical skill, into a simple repeated task that requires no thought and little skill. The way out, he posits, is a new method of education that values intellect and emotion equally. Whether or not Eisner encountered these ideas in a persuasive way during his year at the Institute of Design, he most certainly was exposed to the school's radical Bauhaus aesthetic that valued craft and fine arts equally. As an arts educator, Eisner has always been highly ecumenical in admiring good design equally in fine arts and in well-fashioned crafts, and across a wide range of cultures and media.

Eisner once listed his three primary criteria for the development of school educational programs, and the model he described—a program of practical and emotional relevance and logic—would have delighted Moholy-Nagy. Yet these criteria were distinctly Eisnerian in their cultural inclusiveness and focus on the developmental impact of arts experience on students. "First, the works students encounter, whether ideational or material, should represent the most significant achievements within a wide array of cultures. ... Second, the selection of content for an educational program must be sensitive not only to what is excellent within a culture, but what is likely to be meaningful to the individuals being served by the program. ... A third consideration ... is the importance of diversifying the forms of representation that are employed in the educational program. The wider the variety of forms, the wider the forms of meaning and the more likely that a wider range of aptitudes will be tapped" (Eisner, 1992b). The quintessential argument for bringing the arts into the schools is the diversity of forms of knowledge they make possible.

Just as with his experiences at the ABC club, the Institute of Design was a pivotal influence at the right moment in Eisner's evolving schemata. In 1955 Eisner earned his master's degree in art education from the Illinois Institute of Technology, the school awarding degrees for the Institute of Design students. This was a period in America when the influence of a number of key Bauhaus expatriates was just being set in American culture. Many of Moholy-Nagy's counterparts—especially Josef Albers at Black Mountain College and Walter Gropius at Harvard—would similarly inspire the next generation of American artists to carry the Bauhaus influence into American arts and culture. Eisner's experience at the Institute of Design, while limited to just this single year of direct study, would help blaze a path into mainstream American education for the Bauhaus aesthetic and its provocations of an educational system that related artists, craftsmen, and industrial processes. The Bauhaus exposure offered an important model for Eisner of how the arts and social relevance could be married, and how art experience could be richly educative while flourishing in the realm of the practical and socially functional. Armed with this belief, Eisner went back and discovered new areas in the arts from which to argue for their educational centrality. "Curriculum is a mind altering device," he is fond of saying in underscoring art as cognitively formative.

One of Eisner's foundational beliefs is that experiences shape one's anticipatory schemata, allowing one to bracket phenomena so that they become defined and cognitively palpable (Eisner, 1991). This is an extension of ideas Dewey raises in his *Art as Experience* (Dewey, 1934), and one that Eisner has propelled from speculative theory into educational wisdom. The arts, of course, can also physicalize what is in those brackets, yet for Eisner his goal has never been to create more professional artists, but rather to franchise that behavior and way of thinking across the nation's schools, plowing it back into an opportunity for transformation for as broad as possible a band of America's youth. In the process, Eisner has become a messianic force in the policy-making world of arts education. He has always spoken and written about the arts in the plural—embracing visual, performing, and literary art forms with equal enthusiasm—even if his immediate personal experience is centered in painting, and, as a percipient, music. Eisner's aesthetic theories illuminate all the mainstream modernist arts equally, particularly his theory of connoisseurship, which looks at the cognitive processes of practicing artists as well as arts critics and audiences.

The implications of this inclusion of the arena of aesthetic perception as something arts education can teach have been profound. Eisner's insistence that the arts are vehicles through which understanding is enlarged has elevated the practice of aesthetic apprehension into a cognitive skill every bit as desired and challenging as art making. His source of this insight was likely a combination of his own close reading of Dewey, as well as his interrogation of his private mind as he accumulated, enjoyed, and reflected on his own impressive and sizable personal art collection. His first "collection" was that of the Art Institute of Chicago. "The Art Institute became a central element in my life and indeed in my education. I became friends with Giotto, Duccio, with El Greco, Cezanne, and Matisse, as well as with the splendid Tang and Song images and ceramic vessels and pottery horses that the Art Institute owned" (Eisner, 1995). He recounted that when he was in high school, his heart would rise whenever he entered the Art Institute of Chicago ... the friends that he had known so many years were all hanging on the walls there.

He would later come to call the intense emotion this relationship to art inspired "connoisseurship." He defined the term *connoisseurship* as "the ability to read the situation one pays attention to," unpacking Dewey's observation that "the aim of criticism is the re-education of perception" (Dewey, 1934, p. 324). In his model of arts education, Eisner brought arts critics into the classroom (albeit conceptually) for the first time consistently in public education. Most ingenuously, he then turned this enlightened gaze on the classroom itself, promoting educational researchers to join the company of astute appraisers and connoisseurs of the art of teaching. He enshrined the fundamental characteristics of perception and appreciation and showed how they were important educational and artistic values and practices.

Modeling in his own research and writing what he advocated for the field of education at large, Eisner continued identifying and defining the pervasiveness of art-honed skills in every meaningful aspect of school life. He distilled this into a compelling argument for the centrality of arts-bred insight and behaviors in human knowledge. Curiously, this is not a radical assumption, but rather a methodological mapping of the critical points in our lives when we bump up against the practices known as aesthetic. He delights in reminding students of the pervasiveness of art forms at key

life moments—weddings and funerals—when discursive forms yield to
forms more aesthetically and symbolically narrative, such as music, dance,
and poetry.

For those in dance education, customarily one of the most neglected
corners of arts education, Eisner's influence has been particularly significant.
He has created compelling arguments for valuing the physical and locating in
the body and its senses the means through which individuals' sensibilities and
imaginations are enlarged. "Art is not only a way of creating images," he says,
"it is a way of creating our lives and satisfying our quest for meaning."
Repeatedly he takes an art truth and ratchets it up into an educational
truism. The result for the reader or listener is a double pleasure: There is the
satisfaction of recognition, of seeing a small point one knows to be true
affirmed, and then enlarged into a much bigger social truth that carries with
it a similar profundity. "The senses play a fundamental role in the creation of
consciousness and are a means through which our own development is
fostered," he says (Eisner, 1998b).

Eisner illuminated, amplified, and extended nascent 20th century
cultural ideas, and in so doing redefined the field of arts education, making
it an important destination for artists who never imagined they would find
arts education as rewarding and intellectually rich as the arts themselves.
When he arrived on the scene, the field of arts education had been rooted
too long in the practical. He showed how its theoretical and aesthetic dimensions could also be brought to life and the definition of the practical
enlarged. "Our schools should be more concerned with how to make a life
rather than how to make a living," he once proclaimed (Eisner, 1997).
Indeed, it is his unwavering focus on this constructivist approach to living
and mind that has made his life and his work such a respected and emulated
model for 20th century artists and arts educators.

Eisner seems to have gathered for himself a critical set of conceptions
about the importance of *being artist*. Reading Dewey gave him the theoretical permission to focus on the primacy of experience as an educational
value. Experience is a quality the arts have in abundance. Eisner made the
art experience plural. He found varieties of experiences. He knew how to
keep the discussion of arts education alive as cultural values shifted from
emphasizing social utility to expertise and, most recently, to cognitive
skills. Eisner was always steadily there, tugging art to the forefront. Even
when the discussions elided the arts, as for example they seemed to do in
regard to standards, he simply refocused on a new target and deplored the
narrowness of the term *standards*. He demonstrated the illogic of standards
as an educational end by pointing out their absence in the world of art
(Eisner, 1992a).

One of Eisner's favorite ways to close the introductory remarks for his
first-day-of-class lecture is to caution students that his courses do not enable
one to apply ideas in formulaic ways or to tie them into neat packages. He
wants to stir things up. "I hope that you have each encountered ideas that

will challenge and intrigue you for the rest of your lives," he says (Eisner, 1998a). It is a wish that enshrines an essential characteristic of Eisner's vision of the reflective mind as a continual work in progress.

REFERENCES

Dewey, J. (1934). *Art as experience*. New York: Capricorn Books.

Eisner, E. W. (1991). *The enlightened eye: Qualitative inquiry and the enhancement of educational practice*. New York: Macmillan.

Eisner, E. W. (1992a). *Do American schools need standards?* Macie K. Southall Distinguished Lecture, Peabody College, Vanderbilt University, Nashville, Tennessee.

Eisner, E. W. (1992b, March). *The role of education in the cultural and artistic development of the individual*. Paper presented at the UNESCO International Conference, Geneva, Switzerland.

Eisner, E. W. (1995). Fly me to the moon on gossamer wings: My journey through academia. In Ralph Raunft (Ed.), *The autobiographical lectures of some prominent art educators* (pp. 282–289). Reston, VA: The National Art Education Association.

Eisner, E. W. (1997). Quote on a 1997 poster published by the Getty Institute for Education in the Arts, Los Angeles.

Eisner, E. W. (1998a). Comments on his first-day-of-class handout from Education 213 (Aesthetic Foundations of Education), Stanford University, Stanford, California.

Eisner, E. W. (1998b, September). Remarks upon receiving the Harold McGraw, Jr., Prize in Education, National Art Education Association, unpublished.

Moholy-Nagy, Laszlo. (1947). *Vision in motion*. Chicago: P. Theobald.

Otwell, A. (1997). Moholy-Nagy and Chicago. Web posting.

Rauchenberg, R. (1966). Quoted in R. Kostelanez, *The theatre of mixed means*, from an essay ("The Artist Speaks") that originally appeared in *Art in America, 54* (May/June 1966).

7

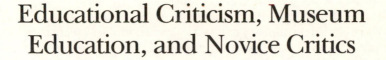

Educational Criticism, Museum Education, and Novice Critics

Elizabeth Vallance
University of Northern Illinois

The aim of criticism is the re-education of perception of works of art.
—John Dewey (1934)

The task of a critic is to perform a mysterious feat well: to transform the qualities of a painting, play, novel, poem, classroom or school, or act of teaching and learning into a public form that illuminates, interprets, and appraises the qualities that have been experienced. ... Thus every act of criticism is a reconstruction. The reconstruction takes the form of an argued narrative, supported by evidence that is never incontestable.
—Elliot Eisner (1991)

One way to assess the impact of Eisner's concepts of aesthetic modes of knowing and educational criticism is to explore them through educational contexts lying outside the realm of K-12 schooling for which they were initially developed. I shall be looking at two such contexts, art museum education and the preservice education of elementary classroom teachers who seek to use art in their teaching, which in different ways test the concept of educational criticism. This chapter explores how criticism can (and does, perhaps inadvertently) work as an approach to assessment, in the first setting, and how art-novice future teachers can use criticism, in the second example. The comparison should expand our understanding of the potential for the role of criticism as both a goal and an assessment tool for art education.

Two enduring models of curriculum theory pertain here and shape the discussion. The first is Joseph Schwab's (1969, 1971, 1973) concept of the four "commonplaces" of curriculum, common dimensions along which any curriculum can vary, components of any educational encounter. They are: the milieu or setting (the school or classroom, in traditional curriculum theory), the subject matter of the curriculum (history, math, art), the teacher (trained and certified, for K-12 public education), and the students (in traditional curriculum theory, neighborhood children with known characteristics and demographic profiles). Schwab's commonplaces have been applied to non-K-12 settings before (Soren, 1992; Vallance, 1979, 1995a, 1995b), and the formulation works; it's quite impossible to prove Schwab wrong.

Here is a brief summary of how the commonplaces seem to apply to art museum education and to an undergraduate course on campus. Art museum education programs, though never offering a "curriculum" in the traditional sense of the word, are fairly contained, since one appeal of museum education is the milieu itself: Students of all ages and art backgrounds come to interact with a collection housed in a finite, usually lovely, space, and this special milieu and quite visible subject matter are dominant constants of a museum's education program. The "teachers" in this program are maximally diverse: They include the teaching professionals and volunteer docents, curators who lecture and teach, the interpretive materials such as extended labels and audio tours, and the unseen presence of the curators' selection and arrangement of the objects on view in the galleries. Thus, in an art museum, the milieu and subject matter are the chief reasons people come (though shopping and eating also come into play); the teachers include a wide range of people, programs, and interpretive materials; and the students are a wild card, a voluntary body of visitors coming and going in a pattern the staff can never fully know. On the other hand, a more traditional curriculum is the art course for elementary education undergraduates: The milieu is the standard university campus and classroom (augmented by art museums and other locales where students are sent for assignments); the subject matter is set by the course description in the catalog but varies with each instructor who teaches it; instructors are university professors selected according to published criteria guaranteeing some constancy of background and expertise; and the students are degree-seeking students who have elected the course. Here, the commonplaces are very much the same as those in K-12—the chief difference being that the students come from a wider geographical area, are of a wider range of age and backgrounds, have exercised more choice in being there, and are taking other courses whose content and sequence we can't regularly know. These students are not as free-ranging as museum visitors, but they do make other curricular choices we cannot fully guide.

A second useful formulation of curriculum thinking, by Dwayne Huebner (1966), was offered the same year as Schwab's. Huebner posited five ways of valuing educational encounters, which he called "rationales." They are these, paraphrased for the purposes of the cases I shall be exploring here:

1) The technical rationale is the perspective we apply in assessing whether an educational approach "worked" in some acceptably measurable sense: Did attendance at museum gallery talks increase, and did parents bring children back for succeeding family programs? Were graduates of the art course for elementary teachers able to effectively incorporate art in teaching fourth grade social studies? This is the perspective that the public is perhaps most accustomed to using, and its endurance is reflected in the continuing reliance on test scores for making judgments about school quality.

2) It is through the political rationale that we assess the political efficacy of educational content or educational change, judged for its likely or demonstrated impact on relationships of power and equity in the relevant community. Thus, an art museum might seek to schedule a particular traveling exhibition because of its relevance to an important segment of the community, or it might place high value on large popular family festivals that attract satisfied crowds, stimulating membership and influencing future votes for tax support. More subtly, there is a political dimension to academic departments' ongoing competition for students electing courses among several choices. The language of the political rationale is as endemic to our discourse on educational choices as the technical rationale is, though it is usually couched in subtler terms than "politics," phrased in terms of responsibility to community or the need to complement a museum's permanent collection.

3) The scientific rationale is the one that educational researchers routinely apply in studying how learning happens: We assess variations on extended labels in an art museum to understand which label formats work best with which audiences of visitors, and we couch our arguments for academic curriculum change in language reflecting "best practices" and successful models for professional preparation. Educational policy-makers rely on the knowledge produced through the scientific rationale to propose changes to school and non-school settings that might ultimately also have technical and/or political values.

4) Less familiar in discourse about K-12 schooling is Huebner's ethical rationale, which is the perspective through which we assess the goodness and fairness of the dynamics among the players: a teacher's respect for students, a principal's respect for and support of faculty. In this perspective, we can ask (and often do, in focus groups), for example, whether the museum's atmosphere is a welcoming one that respects all levels of knowledge about art, or whether the museum has an elitist image. Does this place feel like an ethically comfortable environment where learning can happen in many ways? Does the course on art for elementary education majors respect these students' admitted fears of art? We have long known that these issues are real in classrooms, and it is fair to say that the evolution in classroom management approaches owes much to careful thought about ethical (not to mention legal) ways of intervening with students. Also, it can be argued that Deweyan progressive education, various conceptions of education focusing on the "whole child," and much of the open-schooling and other reforms of the 1960s were strongly rooted in ethical considerations. But ethics are tricky, and less easy to pin down and judge than are variations that can be understood in technical, political, or scientific terms: We see that this is true in the discussions about how to rebuild at the World Trade Center site, where

immediate technical considerations of recapturing the office space confronted the ethical issues of how best to honor the memory of what happened
there. In schooling, we address ethics in philosophy, curriculum, and history
of education courses and in in-service workshops, but we lack regularly accessible ways of weighing ethical concerns.

5) Finally—and also less familiar than Huebner's first three rationales
for valuing educational encounters—the aesthetic rationale would assess an
educational moment for how well it holds together as a whole, as a coherent
moment with a clear and satisfying structure—in short, how strong it is as a
work of art. While public discourse often applies a kind of aesthetic rationale
in many domains—in responding to proposed designs of new civic buildings, for instance—we have not always had a reliable framework or language
with which to view education in aesthetic terms. Every teacher knows, at
the end of the day, whether a lesson was "good" or not in aesthetic terms: We
know if our teaching moment (hour, week, semester, etc.) had a clear beginning, middle, and end, and whether it held together with a unity and
unique identity that set it apart from other parts of life in the same period.
Yet, despite the low profile of the aesthetic rationale in accepted research
methodology, it may be the aesthetic dimensions of our professional choices
that "students"—in classrooms or as museum visitors—respond to and
remember most strongly, for the "visitor experience" studied by many contemporary researchers (Falk & Dierking, 1992; Hein, 1998) can be characterized, in Dewey's terms, as an aesthetic one.

We had not always had a language for talking in aesthetic terms in a way
that was at all reliable: This is the area where Eisner's work has had the greatest impact. Though responsible educators seek to understand the full impact
of the programs they create, traditional educational research methodologies
skirt these issues, favoring rationales that can be addressed by replicable
research and measurement. Elliot Eisner's concepts of aesthetic ways of
knowing and educational criticism together fill a major void that Huebner's
schema helps us to see, righting an imbalance that our societal emphasis on
technical, political, and scientific success both reflects and exacerbates. They
open up the possibility, explored eloquently by Sara Lawrence-Lightfoot and
Jessica Hoffmann Davis (1997), of creating "portraits" of educational
moments that document the essence of these experiences through means
other than statistics.

Eisner argues that although "science is thought to provide the most
direct route to knowledge" (1985, p. 24), other modes of presenting what we
know are at least equally powerful. He cites a passage from Barbara Tuchman's *The Guns of August*, describing the 1910 funeral of Edward VII of
England, a passage that is effective because the writing is vivid, "designed to
elicit images of scarlet and blue and purple and of the plumed helmets and
the gold braid. The writing evokes the scene Tuchman wishes the reader to
see. We are able to participate vicariously in events that occurred when we

were not yet born" (1985, pp. 24–25). It is the ability to create form—in this case, literary writing, but images, dance movements, abstract theories, excellent arguments, and elegant mathematical formulas also qualify—that allows for the vicarious participation in moments not directly available to us, and it is this kind of form that colors the way we know the world. We know much of the world through the visions, or forms—visual images and other formulations of knowledge—that other knowers have presented to us: "Both artist and scientist create forms through which the world is viewed" (Eisner, 1985, p. 26). These vicarious structures, when done well, have positive and appealing aesthetic qualities that contribute to their persuasiveness.

But aesthetic forms do not always communicate easily to novices; the effectiveness for the viewer of aesthetic forms such as dance or sculpture depends on the viewer's "cultivated abilities" (Eisner, 1985, p. 25) to see and hear the aesthetic qualities of the form. Of course, the same can be said of any communication, but aesthetic forms, going beyond a simple laying out of facts, provide a sense of vicarious participation through the use of elements and principles unique to their traditions and not all equally well taught in school: Most of us can read expository prose well enough, but "reading" a work of art may call on skills we don't all have. In Eisner's example, the rhythms of Tuchman's lovely prose can connect us to a sense of the pageantry of an event neither she nor we could ever have seen. Likewise, a great painting that opens us to a lush world of texture and light from centuries ago, or a magnificent mask that suggests rituals of community celebration on another continent, can work for the same reasons. But in each case, the work will be most effective for those who are most attuned to the nuances that contribute to the quality of the form, because not all aesthetic forms speak easily for themselves on first encounter. An aesthetically powerful form can take us there only if we can understand its language: This is why art museums have education programs. We need "the ability to read the forms that aesthetic qualities convey" (Eisner, 1985, p. 35).

Artists and others who create forms that work in aesthetically strong ways are (slightly bending a point Eisner makes about "the aesthetic" itself) "motivated by our need to lead a stimulating life. ... These processes are intended to yield ... the delights of exploration. The aesthetic is also inherent in our need to make sense of experience. This sense-making is located in the choices we make in our effort to create order" (Eisner, 1985, p. 30). Both scientists and artists are makers of order. We respond to orderly forms on the basis of their "rightness," but our being able to determine their aesthetic rightness depends on our own ability to respond to these forms: Critics do this, and by writing criticism, they try to teach the rest of us to do it as well. Likewise, if educators are attuned to aesthetic modes of knowing, they can go beyond technical assessment to both experience a learning situation vicariously *and* be able to convey that experience to others who need to understand the impact of the programs they create. They can do this through the use of criticism.

Creating, noticing, and communicating about aesthetically vivid moments in life—educational or otherwise—depend on our ability to recognize aesthetic experiences from among all the experiences and sensory stimulation of our days. John Dewey's concept of aesthetic experience is crucial here, and it informs Eisner's concept of educational criticism. Dewey argues (1934/1958; summarized in Jackson, 1998) that an aesthetic experience can be framed from the data of everyday life when it has unity, completeness, and uniqueness, and thus can be noticed, remembered, and enjoyed as a complete whole, distinct from everything around it. Thus, we could say that a framed painting hanging on a museum wall is the ultimate embodiment of an aesthetic experience: The artist noticed the view (or, if abstract, perhaps the emotion) she depicts, and made aesthetic choices as she rendered it into paint on canvas; the painting was then framed and placed on view as an aesthetic form available to a museum visitor. Whether any given visitor notices and/or responds to it depends in turn on that visitor's familiarity with aesthetic form—depends, in Eisner's terms, on connoisseurship and the ability to see and appreciate nuances of quality and aesthetic choice (Eisner, 1991), abilities that both K-12 art education and museum education seek to develop. The less clearly "aesthetic" situation of an excellent lesson or semester depends equally on the artist's (teacher's) and viewer's (student's) ability to read the aesthetic qualities of that sort of moment.

The process of reading the aesthetic quality of schooling is what Eisner calls educational criticism, and, like the best art criticism, it guides us to see more clearly the thing we are studying. In *The Enlightened Eye* (1991), Eisner outlines the four dimensions of educational criticism, largely paralleling the traditional steps of art criticism. He calls them *description, interpretation, evaluation*, and *thematics*, presented not as a process but more as a kind of map of what educational criticism should include.

Description, he says, "enables readers to visualize what a place or process is like" (Eisner, 1991, p. 89), helping the reader to see the school or classroom as the critic sees it. Any piece of art criticism has to do this in order to engage the reader, and readers depend on clear vivid descriptions to help imagine themselves seeing—vicariously participating in—that movie, attending that art exhibition, reading that novel, or listening to that recording of Brahms's second piano concerto. A vivid description that conveys the essence and quality of the experience is essential to informed judgments about it; it conveys more than test scores or attendance figures can.

Interpretation attempts to explain the meaning of what we see and experience. In interpreting a painting, a critic may read the symbolic content for us, or put the painting and its style into a historical context that helps us see its role and importance. In educational criticism, interpretation frequently "requires putting what has been described in a context in which its antecedent factors can be identified. It also means illuminating the potential consequences of practices observed and providing reasons that account for what has been seen" (Eisner, 1991, p. 95).

Interpretation allows for understanding in ways that social science theory, seeking generalizable rules and thus needing to narrow down the variables to manageable dimensions, cannot fully do without losing some descriptive richness.

Evaluation is judgment, a normative enterprise of appraising against what Dewey calls "criteria in judgment, so that criticism does not fall in the field of mere impressionism" (Dewey, 1934/1958): These criteria are not predetermined standards, but emerge out of our experience of what constitutes quality in artistic form. Evaluation in educational criticism requires that we be attuned not only to outside standards and norms (on which educational measurement relies) but also to qualitative changes in student experience as evidenced in, for example, portfolios.

Finally, the educational critic creates what Eisner calls "thematics"— what other critics have called "analysis"—generalizations about recurring meanings and pervasive qualities in the lesson or curriculum. A pervasive quality of a painting may be a particular color, or the dominance of hard-edge lines; a theme of a curricular unit on any subject may be the ethical quality of caring and mutual respect evident among teacher and students. The validity of a piece of educational criticism that includes all four dimensions is then assured through three sources of evidence: structural corroboration (the mustering of supporting evidence including other types of data), a concept explored eloquently by Pepper (1945); consensual validation, "a consensus won from readers who are persuaded by what the critic has had to say, not by consensus among several critics" (Eisner, 1991, p. 113); and referential adequacy, the extent to which a reader can locate the qualities addressed by the critic in the subject matter itself.

Huebner's five "rationales," predating Eisner's early arguments for aesthetic modes of knowing and educational criticism by a decade or more, provide a framework for assessing the importance of the ensuing decades of qualitative studies of education. The line of thinking so eloquently argued by Eisner, and now followed by many, has changed the options we have for understanding what happens in schools. Thanks to the efforts of Eisner, and of other researchers including Robert Stake, Louis Smith, Philip Jackson, Gail McCutcheon, Madeleine Grumet, Michael Connelly, Jean Clandinin, Douglas Boughton, Sara Lawrence-Lightfoot, and others, we now accept such non-strictly-quantitative methodologies as ethnography, autobiography, qualitative case studies, and other nonexperimental approaches as valid ways of knowing what happens in school. We have expanded what is acceptable under a more broadly defined "scientific" rationale: The new methodologies are not "scientific" in the sense of working with variables that can be replicated toward generalizability, but we can now more broadly define what is acceptable for understanding how learning happens. Even more broadly, by assuming an aesthetic rationale, we have discovered ways to portray more directly, through criticism, the vicarious experience of being in classrooms. This sets the stage for exploring how criticism fits the task of assessing museum programs, and how art novices can be taught to see the world through critical eyes.

CRITICISM AND THE MUSEUM SETTING

The Saint Louis Art Museum is a tax-supported, free public art museum with a comprehensive collection of American and European painting, sculpture, and decorative arts, as well as Native American, Asian, ancient Mediterranean and Egyptian, African, Oceanic, and pre-Columbian objects. Its education programs cover a wide range of formats (drop-in Gallery Talks, lectures, films, family festivals and performances, as well as classes, school and public tours, teacher workshops, teacher resource materials, sequential-visit programs with schools, and a variety of special programs), variously targeted to young children, school groups, the adult general public, senior citizens, and scholars. Education programs at the museum account for as much as a third of all visitors each year. Educators on the staff teach most education programs, but curatorial staff and guest lecturers enrich the mix. The "teaching" of the museum also includes the art itself and the interpretive materials available in the galleries.

The case of art museum education as a candidate for educational criticism review is fairly clear, perhaps even more so than for K-12 schooling, for many reasons. First, of course, the very subject of the "curriculum," loose though it is (Vallance, 1995b), is art itself; its ultimate goal can be said to be the teaching of criticism, the reeducating of visitors' perception. Secondly, those doing the teaching—educators, curators, editors—are themselves committed to conveying the aesthetic qualities of their subject to visitor-students who are likely art novices but interested in learning. The various teachers in this setting are committed to the language of aesthetics in their very teaching. Thirdly, because art museum education occurs largely within a milieu that itself guides students' experiences through effective signage and labeling, the milieu becomes a legitimate subject of criticism and is generally a powerful part of the visitors' experience. Educational criticism in this setting can address not only the subject as embodied in the artwork but also the educational/aesthetic messages conveyed by the building. Finally, art museum visitors enter the building with a clear expectation of having some aesthetic experience, generally that of responding positively to at least a few of the artworks on view. Focus group data (J. Paul Getty Trust, 1991), indicate that museum visitors are also quite aware of the experiential impact of their surroundings, finding the museum, for example, awe-inspiring, or calming, or "restorative" (Kaplan, Bardwell, & Slatker, 1993).

The art museum curriculum, though individualized by each visitor's choices in ways rarely experienced in school, is a deliberately shaped body of subject matter and teaching strategies. Both curators and educators, in their different ways and with sometimes different understandings of what the audience already knows, seek to provide aesthetically powerful experiences to a public that includes both first-time visitors and reliably informed "regulars." Though most students pick and choose among galleries and programs, we know what the major curricular options are for our students: We know that our museum includes XYZ cultures, artwork in specific media, extended labels or not, audio tours or not, frequent or rare docent tours, frequent or rare classes, lectures, and special programs. We can describe the curriculum we offer to students, even though we can rarely know for sure what curriculum any given student actually follows on any given visit. To an educator accustomed to the predictability of K-12 schools with their known students and curriculum, the museum is a wildly open educational milieu, but the commonplaces clearly pertain even in this setting.

Therefore, an educational criticism of an art museum's program can appropriately focus on the commonplaces of any of a number of mini-curricula pursued by students: Some students may attend only the scholarly symposia, where very finite topics are explored with fellow scholars in lecture halls and galleries; other students may make a point of attending every weekly Gallery Talk, thus cruising through a curriculum focusing on individual works of art in a variety of cultures over time; other "students" come as families with young children, whose chosen museum curriculum may be only the hands-on family programs offered on weekends. Area teachers may attend teacher workshops, use the teaching materials the museum has developed, and bring their students on docent-led tours. The possibilities of curricular experience are nearly endless.

In a sense, a complete educational criticism of a museum program might be analogous to a series of reviews of a symphony orchestra's season: The final judgment of the quality of the curriculum must be built up from studies of microcosms of what the curriculum offers, with a slightly different subject taught by the same players each time to a somewhat fluidly varying audience, no one performance being the definitive picture of the program just as no one visitor's trip through the galleries is a definitive picture of what a museum offers. But museum educators, like most teachers, already think in terms of aesthetic quality of both art objects and experiences. Though practical concerns require them also to track such data as attendance and Zip code distributions, they tend normally to accrue tacit records of evaluative judgments: They know when a program is "good" because its form was coherent and content-rich; they talk with visitors whose smiles, compliments, and suggestions seem to reflect their response to the experience as (in Dewey's terms) a memorable aesthetic experience; and they report these judgments in succinctly upbeat news items in the members' magazines (Vallance, 1996).

It is arguable, then, that aesthetic modes of knowing and at least a tacit process of educational criticism are built into assessing the art museum curriculum, since most parties are already thinking in these terms. Certainly, the development of connoisseurship and critical ability is the ultimate goal of most art museum programs themselves. The art museum experience is both a source of the ideas Eisner has been developing throughout his career and a natural place to apply them more systematically than has always been done. Art museum education offers a beautiful case study setting for educational criticism; we'll explore some research implications of this setting later.

TEACHING ART NOVICES TO BE CRITICS: ONE EXAMPLE

But can connoisseurship, a term developed with the fine arts (and wine) in mind, be applied to visual culture, and by people with little art background? I think so, and I think the connection between the two worlds may be one of the great contributions of Eisner's work. The pre-service course for elementary teachers explored here is the one I teach at Northern Illinois University. This may be the only art course some of these students ever take. They choose it over music education and physical education, and many enroll hoping for a collection of hands-on craft projects to do in classrooms, believing that they are "terrible at art," "have no art talent," and so forth. Many fear that they will be graded on their art ability. In this course, students are introduced to a variety of art media, styles, cultural traditions, accessible subject matters, and hands-on activities that can help children to explore and reinterpret works of art and other designed features of visual culture. The course combines slide lecture, discussion, informal gallery talk formats, museum/gallery visits, hands-on activities, critique of textbook activity ideas, regular writing about art and visual culture, lesson plan design, and micro-teaching.

The case of the elementary education majors suggests how art novices can develop skills in criticism. These students are not graded on their art ability, but they are graded on their ability to respond to and reinterpret art and artful objects for the purposes of teaching with them: Students are required to become critics with little or no background in art or criticism. Most are surprised to find writing requirements in an art course; they write eight Art Response Papers, hesitantly at first but their observations and writing improve over the semester. Four papers must respond to works of art defined rather restrictively to exclude sunsets and favorite baubles: one-of-a-kind objects, deliberately made and now on public view, accessible to many. One paper must address an art exhibition on campus or in area museums. One paper must respond to a live performance or film, assessed for its visual impact. One paper must respond to a storefront display in a non-chain establishment, reflecting the individual design decisions of an individual shopkeeper. And one must explore an "accidental arrangement" of objects that has an aesthetic appeal to the student. It is these last two categories that interest me most, as students learn to see the world in aesthetic terms. In all the ARPs, students are required to describe the object or arrangement in vivid enough terms that a reader could imagine it (this addresses Eisner's "description" step), to give two reasons why they noticed it (this is not exactly "interpretation," but it does require minimal analysis to identify sources of aesthetic impact), to suggest one way they could use the object in their teaching (this requires tacit interpretation), and to suggest two possible changes, including how a piece of colored yarn assigned to each student on the first day of class might be incorporated into the design, and what impact these changes would have on the total effect. This last point gets at "thematics," for it requires that students assess how simple changes can affect the unifying visual theme of a work. The papers are not pieces of criticism per se, but they do build the rudiments of a critical perspective that these future teachers should be able to use in a variety of settings.

Does this assignment "work," as an introduction to aesthetic modes of knowing? A full answer would require a rigorous analysis of student selections and writing, something I hope to do soon. But students report that the Art Response Paper requirement, though sometimes difficult, does force them to notice things in their environment that they would not normally notice. "The assignments, especially the ARPs, require me to notice and look for art that I would typically not pay attention to. I find myself having many aesthetic experiences. I was never aware of all of the art that surrounds me until I began this class," wrote one student in her class journal. Another said, "I am really enjoying this class more than I thought I would. Now I understand that you don't necessarily have to be artistically talented to enjoy art. You have to be creative and open to new experiences." A third wrote, "Doing the Art Response Papers has motivated me to find interesting works around the area and I enjoy critiquing them." One of the few male students, at first openly resistant to art and the class assignments, wrote this entry about a third of the way into the semester: "While I don't like writing the ARPs, that particular assignment has definitely increased my awareness of art," and cited a sculpture on campus that he had walked by hundreds of times and never noticed until selecting it for this assignment.

That many students are open to finding art in unexpected (or simply overlooked) places seems a good thing. But it's especially interesting to note what sorts of aesthetically compelling arrangements students are selecting from the wealth of visual information around them. They have found shop windows of artfully arranged puppets, lace curtains, toys, used clothes, antiques, bridal/groom accessories, pottery, garden furniture, yarn, and others. The accidentally aesthetic arrangements of objects appearing in Art Response Papers include library shelves with all brown book spines punctuated by one red one, multicolored plastic weights tossed like Pick-Up Sticks on the wood floor of a dance studio, four yellow cars arranged in a rectangle in an otherwise empty parking lot, Army rations suddenly seen as a still-life composition on a table, a rock collection arranged as a still-life on a coffee table, rolls of wire fencing stacked on a flatbed truck and seen from the rolled ends, old farm tools hanging on the exterior of a barn, the patterns of colored bricks in a campus bridge, blue exercise balls scattered randomly across the floor of a gym. Students use their yarn pieces—actually, when possible, or conceptually—to add order to these arrangements (for example, adding a red border framing the group of rocks, or wrapping the rolled wiring in red), to highlight and focus attention on unique items within them (for example, highlighting the zigzags in the brick pattern), or to change the focus of a coloristically unified composition (for example, adding a hot pink border around a white pillow in an all-white bedroom motif outlined by lace curtains). In Eisner's terms, they are analyzing the "thematics" of these elements of the visual environment and suggesting how additional color might change the focus or enhance the unity of them. Students' writing about these found objects is sometimes quite astute. The student with the colored weights first ran her white yarn through the pile of weights in a straight line, but found the straight line to be too harsh a juxtaposition to all the knobby curves; better was to work it into a spiral configuration: "The yarn served to move the viewer's eye through the pile without imposing on that gloriously random splash of color." The student adding hot pink to an array of white pillows in the lace store window observed that it "would be a harsh change to the display," contrasting with the "soft, natural colors," and would "attract and perplex someone passing by." About the antique tools on the side of a barn, the student wrote, "The tools are old, dark, rusted, and weathered and arranged haphazardly on the wall. The tools look like they were thrown at the wall and where and how they landed is where they stayed," and she would change the composition by making the color of the wall a lighter color, highlighting the contrast of the tools, and outlining the unfamiliar tools in red yarn.

These student accounts of aesthetic experiences, while scarcely examples of educational criticism, provide evidence of art novices—future teachers—being able to see aesthetically and assess these aesthetic experiences for their uniqueness, unity, and completeness. The general success of these assignments suggests that description, in aesthetic terms, is accessible to non-connoisseurs, and that these beginning critics are also quite capable of identifying the unifying thematics in interpreting and judging what works best about these found objects. It remains to be seen whether these students will continue to be so attuned to their visual environments,[1] or especially whether they can learn to apply educational criticism to their own teaching in the

---

[1] I am indebted to a tale told by a former colleague at the Saint Louis Art Museum, Linda Kulla, who once taught a college course on art appreciation for area police officers. The police officers, at first skeptical about how useful this course could be to them, later reported to her that the course had helped them to write better crime-scene reports: They paid better attention to details and to the patterns in which these details were accidentally or not arranged.

future—but the evidence of the practical usefulness of some of the steps in criticism is encouraging.

SOME EMERGING QUESTIONS

As venues for exploring the role of educational criticism, the two settings studied here raise different sorts of questions: One venue sets the stage as a perfect subject of criticism, and the other suggests some ways that art novices can be encouraged to become critics. The art museum case is one where aesthetic modes of knowing are built into much of the dialogue about the learning experience and certainly into the subject of most programs. This, an almost best-case scenario for applying educational criticism, brings together students seeking aesthetic experiences in milieus designed to enhance the very visual subject matter in loose, individualized curricula. Of all the nontraditional learning environments, art museums are probably the most equally balanced in terms of both the relative weight of each of Schwab's commonplaces and the applicability of each of Huebner's five rationales. Educational criticism happens regularly, if tacitly, in art museums. Some research questions about educational criticism arising from this setting, then, include these: Does the "aesthetic experience" so explicitly promoted by the museum seep into the language of those assessing museum programs for audiences, such as the Boards or potential funders, and do art museums differ from other museums in this respect? If art museum educators and curators tend to assess their work at least partially in aesthetic terms, could (and should) other staff (such as guards observing visitors in galleries, or frontline staff at entrances) be taught to report on visitor experiences as "critics"? What might educators learn from these frontline critical assessments of visitor experience that they can't learn by assessing actual programs? Do repeat visitors in fact become more adept at doing criticism of works of art, and perhaps of their own visits? If so, what is it about the museum experience that contributes most to this growth—does explicit teaching have a greater impact than repeat visits with good extended labels? If repeat visitors learn to make finer discriminations and/or more interesting connections among the art on view in the building, and to explore objects they might earlier have missed, does this ability extend to their responses to other objects in the broader visual culture? Do museum visitors become better-informed critics of their visual worlds?

The undergraduates struggling to explore the aesthetic forms in their everyday lives are a case study of teaching art novices to see and think in aesthetic terms: The Art Response Papers require students to identify and portray aesthetic moments within the visual chaos of their days. The larger question raised by this exercise is whether being forced to frame and report on such experiences translates later into a greater sensitivity to them, as I hope.

So I would pose these research questions: Do critiques of the everyday visual culture improve with more exposure to works of fine art? Do students who have spent a semester seeking and responding to visual design remain attuned to visual design after they leave this course? Do non-art students who study visual design through regular art criticism assignments become more attentive to using visually interesting patterns in their teaching? Does this practice with writing criticism in fact reeducate their perception of artful qualities in the visual culture? Do these students, more than those who have not been through this sequence, delight in existing forms and build lessons around them rather than focusing on Popsicle-stick log cabins and "sparkly bunnies" when inspired to do "art" with their students? If these students were asked to photograph interesting sights in their everyday lives before and after having written about the accidental arrangements, would they become more interesting and more idiosyncratic photographers? Would this matter to how they use art in their teaching? And can these students begin to apply principles of criticism in assessing their own teaching— about art or any other subject?

Elliot Eisner's work has encouraged us to approach the world as if every moment of our experience could be assessed as a work of art. He has encouraged educational researchers to go beyond the accepted technical, political, and traditionally scientific ways of understanding what happens in schools, and has developed over the decades a qualitative approach to research that has widened our access to things known. The chapters in this important book suggest some of the ways that Eisner's thinking, by reeducating our perceptions of the options open to us as we seek to understand the world of school, has shaped the direction of inquiry about education in recent decades. It now seems unimaginable that we would ever go back to using only the old ways: We learn too much by discussing the world in the aesthetic terms that reflect our most vital experiences. The worlds of understanding education and understanding the aesthetic experience were once two quite separate realms. Elliot Eisner, among the first of a long line of researchers working to bring them together, has been by far the most impassioned and articulate about the potential for doing so, and about the importance of doing so. His will be a lasting impact on how we think about how we see, learn, and teach.

REFERENCES

Dewey, J. (1958). *Art as experience*. New York: Capricorn Books. (Original work published 1934)

Eisner, E. W. (1985). Aesthetic modes of knowing. In E. W. Eisner (Ed.), *Learning and teaching the ways of knowing: Eighty-fourth yearbook of the National Society for the Study of Education* (pp. 23–36). Chicago: University of Chicago Press.

Eisner, E. W. (1991). *The enlightened eye: Qualitative inquiry and the enhancement of educational practice*. New York: Macmillan.

Falk, J. H., & Dierking, L. D. (1992). *The museum experience*. Washington, DC: Whalesback Books.

Hein, G. (1998). *Learning in the museum*. New York: Routledge.

Huebner, D. (1966). Curricular language and classroom meanings. In J. B. Macdonald & R. R. Leeper (Eds.), *Language and meaning* (pp. 8–26). Washington, DC: Association for Supervision and Curriculum Development.

Jackson, P. W. (1998). *John Dewey and the lessons of art*. New Haven and London: Yale University Press.

J. Paul Getty Trust. (1991). *Insights: Museums, visitors, attitudes, expectations: A focus group experiment*. Los Angeles: J. Paul Getty Trust.

Kaplan, S., Bardwell, L. V., & Slatker, D. B. (1993). The restorative experience as a museum benefit. *Journal of Museum Education, 18*(3), 15–17.

Lawrence-Lightfoot, S., & Davis, J. H. (1997). *The art and science of portraiture*. San Francisco: Jossey-Bass.

Pepper, S. C. (1945). *The basis of criticism on the arts*. Cambridge: Harvard University Press.

Schwab, J. (1969). The practical: A language for curriculum. *School Review, 78* (November), 1–23.

Schwab, J. (1971). The practical: Arts of the eclectic. *School Review, 79* (August), 493–542.

Schwab, J. (1973). The practical: Translation into curriculum. *School Review, 81* (August), 501–522.

Soren, B. (1992). The museum as curricular site. *Journal of Aesthetic Education, 26*(3), 91–101.

Vallance, E. (1979). Lessons from the non-ivory tower, or what curriculum theory can learn from adult post-secondary education. *Journal of Curriculum Studies, 11*(3), 221–231.

Vallance, E. (1995a). *The lively non-curriculum of the museum curriculum*. Keynote address at American Association of Museums' Seminar on Learning in Museums, Chicago, 16 November.

Vallance, E. (1995b). The public curriculum of orderly images. *Educational Researcher, 24*(2), 4–13.

Vallance, E. (1996). Issues in evaluating museum education programs. In D. Boughton, E. W. Eisner, & J. Ligtvoet (Eds.), *Evaluating and assessing the visual arts in education* (pp. 220–236). New York and London: Teachers College Press.

8

Eisner in the United Kingdom

John Steers
General Secretary of the National Society for Education in Art
and Design, United Kingdom

What can be said about Elliot Eisner's contribution to and influence on the development of art education beyond the shores of the United States? Very much more than can be related in this short chapter, which of necessity will concentrate on the impact of his ideas in the United Kingdom. Even then, it will be a partial and rather personal perspective—Eisner's presence in the art education scene over the past three decades is readily perceived, but "not everything that matters can be measured," or directly attributed.

Eisner's work in the fields of cognition and representation, school reform, and qualitative research methods are all well known and respected in the United Kingdom, as opportunities to address the Royal Society of Arts (RSA) and an honorary doctorate from De Montford University will testify. However, my brief is primarily to consider his work in arts education.

BRITISH ART EDUCATION

To appreciate something of Eisner's contribution to British art education, it is necessary to understand that there are important differences between the education systems in the United Kingdom and the USA. Most significantly, since 1988 there have been statutory national curricula in each of England, Wales, and Northern Ireland; in contrast, Scotland has nonstatutory curriculum "guidelines." Under this legislation, "Art and Design" is a compulsory subject in all state-maintained schools for all 5- to 14-year-olds, after which it becomes an optional subject. The term *art* in schools can be taken to mean "art, craft, and design" rather than simply visual or fine arts. Thus the expected range of the subject is broader than in many American schools.

It might be expected that the National Curriculum Statutory Order for Art in England, introduced in 1992 and subsequently twice modified, was the outcome of a rare opportunity to consider the philosophy, purpose, and content of the subject from first principles. What emerged was a far from radical conceptual framework—a rough and ready domain structure—that essentially codified an existing tradition. Political pressure distorted this to create an artificial divide between theory and practice with two attainment targets (domains): "Investigating and Making" and "Knowledge and Understanding."

The revised English art and design curriculum introduced in 2000 had a single attainment target—"knowledge, skills, and understanding," with four strands: (1) investigating and making art, craft, and design; (2) exploring and developing ideas; (3) evaluating and developing work; and the remaining strand, (4) knowledge and understanding, which is expected to inform all these processes.

In England, the curriculum, schools, and teachers are subject to rigorous accountability procedures principally achieved through regular inspections by a government department, the Office for Standards in Education (OFSTED). Testing is now rife in primary and secondary schools and national "league tables" of schools' relative performance are published annually. A long tradition of national examinations, taken by students at age 16+ and 18+, has a profound effect both on what is taught and how it is taught in secondary schools. Approximately 30% of 16-year-olds opt to take the art and design examinations.

Secondary teacher education is also different from the USA because the vast majority of art teachers have a university degree in an art and design discipline (e.g., fine art, fashion, textiles, graphic design, product design, etc.), rather than a degree specifically in art education. This is often preceded by a one-year foundation course in art and design to make four years of higher education after leaving secondary school. Those who choose to teach then complete an additional year of Postgraduate Certificate in Education courses (PGCE). (As in the majority of USA school districts, most primary school teachers are generalists with variable and often inadequate experience of art and design in their initial education leading to teacher licensure.)

There are advantages and disadvantages to educating secondary art teachers in this way. On the one hand, they have considerable experience in their specialist art and design discipline. On the other hand, their understanding of pedagogy is grafted onto this experience in the course of a very intensive nine-month-long course. As a consequence, newly qualified teachers very often have a pragmatic, studio-based understanding of art and design rather than a coherent grasp of the theory and philosophy of art education that perhaps is needed to sustain and enrich their practice.

It sometimes seems that the main aim of government over the past 15 years has been to try vainly to design a "teacher-proof" curriculum. In the current British education climate, Eisner's all too prophetic warning is particularly apposite:

> Infatuation with performance objectives, criterion referenced testing, competency based education, and the so-called basics lends itself to

standardization, operationalism, and behaviorism, as the virtually exclusive concern of schooling. Such a focus is, I believe, far too narrow and not in the best interests of students, teachers, or the society within which students live. Empathy, playfulness, surprise, ingenuity, curiosity, and individuality must count for something in schools that aim to contribute to a social democracy. (Eisner, 1985b, p. 367)

Today, as in the USA, there are calls in the UK (unheeded by government) to reconceptualise essentially modernist art and design practice. Arthur Hughes criticised the present curriculum as arbitrary, no more than tradition handed down over the years and through a process of accretion absorbed to form the canon of the subject:

The result is a set of procedures, processes and practices which are a kind of historical trace of past theories of art education, child development or art, craft and design practice, all existing simultaneously and each exemplified by activities which jockey for time and space. (1998, p. 45)

The extent of international influences on British art education may seem surprising. There has been substantial interchange of ideas and practices for more than a century, facilitated, partly, by international organizations such as the International Society for Education Through Art (InSEA). The keen observer can still discern traces of the French atelier system, the Weimar Bauhaus, Scandinavian craft activities, and the last vestiges of liberal, child-centred ideas of education with a lineage from Jean-Jacques Rousseau, through Johan Pestalozzi, Friedrich Froebel, and Franz Cizek, to Marion Richardson and Herbert Read. In the 1960s and 1970s, theories of child psychology had a strong influence on art education, in particular the work of Viktor Lowenfeld, Helga Eng, and Anton Ehrenzweig. At the same time, "Basic Design" courses, with their origins in the work of the Bauhaus, had an impact on schools and colleges through the work of Tom Hudson, Victor Pasmore, Harry Thubron, Kurt Rowland, and Richard Hamilton. The "Design Education" movement grew in the 1970s as a consequence of pioneering work by Bruce Archer, Ken Baynes, and Peter Green. In art teacher education, the work of Dick Field was particularly significant. Although now somewhat in decline, crafts had a strong place in art education activities from the 1920s to 1980s.

Of course, very little stemming from these distinctive and often contradictory philosophies will be encountered in a pure form in British classrooms; instead, half-grasped beliefs, with their origins in a variety of rationales, filter their way into the consciousness of art and design teachers. Until the 1970s, it seems that trade in art education ideas was mainly one way—east to west across the Atlantic. Stuart MacDonald's (1970) seminal history and philosophy of art education has few references to American influence in Britain, apart from the occasional mention of Arnheim, Dewey, and Lowenfeld. But in the 1970s, that changed and American thinking about art education began to enrich the British scene, not least through the work of Elliot Eisner.

CONNECTIONS

Eisner's connections with the United Kingdom began in 1970, when he lectured at the University of Leeds at the invitation of Brian Allison. In 1971–72, John Newick and Dick Field invited him as a visiting scholar to the prestigious University of London Institute of Education. The British art education cognoscente already knew *Readings in Art Education* (Eisner & Ecker, 1966), and Field (1970, p. 55) cites Eisner in his *Change in Art Education*, probably the first British publication to do so. During this period he spoke at other art education centres in England and Wales, thus introducing his ideas at first hand to a new generation of art teachers. This was followed by another stint at the Institute in 1979–80. The latter visit helped to make Eisner more widely known in the United Kingdom through talks at many of the major art education institutions and partly because, by that time, *Educating Artistic Vision* (1972) was a well-established text on the reading lists of art education courses.

In the late 1970s, Ralph Jeffery was the most senior of Her Majesty's Inspectors of Schools (HMI) responsible for art and design education—a very influential position. Jeffery remains a staunch admirer of Eisner, whom he introduced to senior civil servants and HMI because of his highly articulate advocacy of the arts in general education. I spoke recently to Jeffery, now retired for more than 20 years, and asked him whom he thought had most influenced British art education, politicians apart, in the second half of the 20th century. Herbert Read was mentioned, as was Dick Field, a less well-known name internationally, but he said, "Elliot was someone who really moved things forward; he was clear-thinking, articulate, and persuasive"—a description echoed time after time by those I interviewed in the course of writing this chapter.

Jeffery invited Eisner to contribute to a major HMI conference for art educators held in Bournemouth in 1977, when Eisner gave a seminal paper entitled "The Preparation of Art Teachers: A Pluralistic Perspective." He asked politely, but pointedly, why the British had no significant journal for art education or a professional association that could compare with that in the USA.

Eleven years later, Eisner was again invited to speak, coincidentally at Bournemouth, this time at the centenary conference of the National Society for Education in Art and Design (NSEAD), which, in the interim, had become much more active. Eisner was able to comment on this occasion about the relatively newly founded *Journal of Art & Design Education* (*JADE*):

> When I was here some 11 years ago I made a plea that British art educators should devote their efforts to creating a first rate journal. I said that

I thought that those of us in the United States should not be deprived of British insight. ... I applaud your initiative and the field values your journal. Let me tell you candidly that in many respects it's better than anything that we have in the United States. It's thoughtful ... it's well designed. It displays the best levels of current scholarship here without being stuffy. It's something that will create an important legacy for those who come into the field in the future. (Eisner, 1989, p. 154)

Whether Eisner was aware of the extent to which his earlier comments had struck a chord and stimulated renewed efforts by British academics to launch a British journal is a moot point. He served as an overseas consultant to the *JADE* editorial board from its inception in 1982 until 1988 and over the years has regularly contributed papers to the journal.

Eisner also commented on the increase in cross-continental contact between British art educators and those in the USA, noting that it appeared to be easier to fly from England to America than the other way around, judging by British involvement in NAEA conventions and other conferences in the USA. But, he concluded, "the fact that you have invited Howard Gardner and me to give major presentations here underscores the growing intercontinental character of our field. The traffic has become heavier" (Eisner, 1989, p. 154). This was true, although from the 1970s onward, Manuel Barkan, Arthur Efland, Kenneth Marantz, and Brent Wilson were all familiar figures on the British art education scene.

The editor of the *Journal of Art & Design Education*, David Thistlewood, noted that Eisner chose to adopt the role of detached observer and critical friend. He commented (a touch optimistically, as things panned out with the development of the national curriculum):

This was a substantially praising—though partly critical—survey of how the discipline in Britain had already reformed itself, of its own volition rather than in response to external pressures, into a more rigorous and properly-motivated body of theory and practice, in anticipation of the role it would be required to play in the new climate of accountability. (Thistlewood, 1989, p. 114)

The launch of *JADE* in 1982 also had the effect of making visible the current influences on United Kingdom art education, and a simple count establishes beyond any doubt that the most frequently cited author in the first 10 years of the journal was Elliot Eisner. One outcome of the journal's existence was that it prompted more British art educators to write. And having cut their teeth writing for *JADE*, many went on to write more substantial texts, with the result that there is now a wide-ranging and vibrant British art and design education literature that contrasts sharply with the sparse offerings of the 1970s.

There are other less obvious and subtler ways in which Eisner's work has influenced the development of art and design education in the United Kingdom. These include development of rationales for the place of art education in general education, elaboration of domain-based models of the art curriculum, and the place in the curriculum of what in Britain are called critical and contextual studies. These are discussed in the sections that follow.

RATIONALES

A constant theme in Eisner's work has been the development of rigorous, persuasive, and robust rationales for the arts in education. Already in 1972, he rejected extrinsic rationales—for example, the arts as a leisure activity or to provide emotionally cathartic experiences—as inadequate justification for the field of art education, principally on the grounds that such claims could be made also by a host of other school subjects. He affirmed that the prime value of the arts in education lies in the unique contributions they make to the individual's experience and understanding of the world.

The visual arts deal with an aspect of human consciousness that no other field touches on: the aesthetic contemplation of visual form. The other arts deal with other sensory modalities, whereas the sciences and the practical arts have still other ends. Scientific inquiry aims at producing knowledge couched in propositions about the world. The claims of science are generalizations and subject to the limits of language. The practical arts aim at the completion of a significant task; their end is to efficiently complete an action. The visual arts provide for our perception of form that vivifies life and that often makes an appraisal of it. In short, we can learn of the justification of art in education by examining the functions of art in human experience. We can ask: What does art do? To answer this question we need to turn directly to works of art themselves (Eisner, 1972, p. 9).

Since that time, Eisner has argued persistently and consistently that the arts make a vital contribution to education and, moreover, he has taken pains to ensure that a wide audience hears his arguments. Undoubtedly, his rationale for what the arts teach best has become more compelling as it has become more refined over the years. He reminds us of key features of arts education, including the importance of attention to relationships, flexible purposing, using materials as a medium, shaping form to create expressive content, exercise of the imagination, learning to frame the world from an aesthetic perspective, as well as the ways in which visual experiences can be transformed into speech and text:

> Work in the arts, when it provides students with the challenge of talking about what they have seen, gives them opportunities, permission, and encouragement to use language in a way free from the strictures of literal description. This freedom is a way to liberate their emotions and imagination. (Eisner, 2002, p. 89)

CURRICULUM DOMAIN MODELS

Eisner (2002, p. 27) acknowledges that the theoretical, domain-orientated curriculum model of Discipline-Based Art Education (DBAE) has its origins in the ideas of Jerome Bruner and a seminar held at the Pennsylvania State University in 1963.

Stanford University's late-1960s Kettering Project identified three domains: the productive, the critical, and the historical (Eisner, 1969). The NAEP objectives (U.S. Department of Education, 1970) included an additional aesthetic education dimension, and it was not long before similar models emerged in the United Kingdom. Initially, these ideas were promoted forcefully by Brian Allison, who encountered them on a visit to California. In 1977, Allison played a key part in formulating proposals for a new examination structured around a four-domain model: Expressive/Productive, Perceptual, Analytical/Critical, and Historical/Cultural (Schools Council, 1977, p. 9). By 1982 this domain structure had been appropriated by Allison and, extraordinarily, was published (Allison, 1982, p. 62) without reference to its origins in what is still regarded as a seminal paper identifying "Allison's domains"!

Although the origins are murky and often non-attributed (national curriculum documents and examination syllabuses do not cite references), a domain model has been at the core of the development of criteria for British public examinations in art and design from the 1980s onward and in the subsequent development of attainment targets for the national curricula.

Perhaps because an apparently "homegrown" domain structure is embedded in the statutory requirements for art and design in schools, Discipline-Based Art Education has been the subject of passing academic rather than practical interest in the United Kingdom. Nevertheless, to complete the record, I invited Eisner to contribute a paper to *JADE*, placing DBAE in perspective, identifying its roots and reflecting on the robust debate then taking place in the USA. "Structure and Magic in Discipline-Based Art Education" appeared in 1988 and, curiously, the paper attracted little comment from the British audience. It did however prompt a scathing, almost vitriolic attack from an American colleague who accused Eisner of no more than mastering the art of seductive prose:

"He makes his notions appealing and accessible, uses attractive examples, and creates a writing rhythm which lulls us into nodding acceptance of his propositions" (Marantz, 1990, p. 197).

At the root of Marantz's criticism is his view that DBAE is a "conservative political movement," elevating a canon of "fine arts" above the "popular" arts: "But for the vast majority of our citizens, their art world is filled with more mundane matter, much of it related to utilitarian objects like coffee pots, posters, automobiles, calendars, book illustrations, lawn sculptures, public monuments, and bank murals" (Marantz, 1990, p. 198). Given that British art education has a tradition of encompassing art, craft, and design, perhaps it was simply taken for granted in the United Kingdom that the DBAE model could be adapted for a wide range of content.

CRITICAL AND CONTEXTUAL STUDIES

The fact that the *JADE* audience was willing to find a typical British compromise between the apparently diametrically opposed views of Eisner and Marantz can be explained by the development of "critical and contextual studies," which are now firmly embedded in the examination system and national curricula.

The idea that art education should not be confined to studio practice appears to have been "in the air" in the late 1960s, perhaps as much in the United Kingdom as in the USA. For example, Dick Field—who certainly was aware of Eisner's work by this time—argues for an enhancement of practical studio work, partly as an escape for students from having to "make art to order," and "in the sense that other studies must relate to practical work and must elucidate it" (Field, 1970, p. 122). He recognises that this will make additional demands on art teachers who will need to "move with some freedom through the realms of philosophy, criticism, and history." Field also points to a key tenet of British art education: the complementary and interrelated nature of theory and practice. Nevertheless, Arthur Hughes maintains:

> The foundations for the introduction of what is (somewhat optimistically) called critical studies were laid during the late 60s and early 70s with the introduction to England of North American texts by now familiar names such as Eisner, Ecker, Smith, Efland, Hurwitz, Wilson, and Broudy. There followed a gestation period of more than a decade during which United Kingdom art educators began to formulate curriculum philosophies reflecting the perceived importance of a firm basis of contextual knowledge and understanding as a necessary outcome of a good art syllabus. It is to a large extent due to the visionary and pioneering work of Rod Taylor (1986) that we owe both its assimilation into the public examination system ... and its later introduction ... into the overwhelmingly performative-based National Curriculum. (Hughes, 1999, p. 369)

Not for the first time in this narrative, the American and British strands in this development seem to be inextricably intertwined but, once again, Eisner is identified as a significant influence.

CRITIQUES

Generally speaking, British critiques of Eisner have been few and far between. There seems to have been a remarkable congruence between Eisner's views and the readiness of British art educators to accept them—see, for example,

99

Thistlewood's (1985) warm review of *The Art of Educational Evaluation* (Eisner, 1985a). Perhaps one of Eisner's strengths has been to take ideas that seemed to be vaguely "in the air," at least in the United Kingdom, and through his lucid and accessible writing, present coherent accounts of a range of complex issues. With the advent of postmodernist perspectives in art education, which are as evident in the United Kingdom as the USA, there are suggestions—usually without naming Eisner directly—that art education philosophies from the 1970s and 1980s are too elitist, too focused on high art, too Western and Eurocentric, and too conservative.

While it is an irony that the strongest criticism in the British literature comes from a fellow American, Eisner has prompted debate. The philosopher David Best has discussed at some length the confusion that he believes exists about subjectivity and objectivity in the arts (Best, 1982). He includes Eisner in a list of those who implicitly or explicitly have adopted a subjective view of artistic practice. He criticises in particular Eisner's belief that privately held conceptions could be externalised and transferred into public images. This, argues Best, is an untenable conception of mind:

> It is assumed that, because of his [*sic*] social nature, man invents, or decides to create, forms of representation and communication, in order to share with others his inaccessibly private thoughts. How on earth could he achieve this? Hold a committee meeting in order to create a language of communication? (Best, 1982, p. 377)

Best concludes that the public, shareable practices and concepts of language and the arts are the preconditions of the individual and private, not constructs out of them. However, Best did not go unchallenged, and an inconclusive and sometimes vitriolic debate rumbled on in *JADE* for another year or so (Best, 1983; Winterbourne, 1983).

Diarmuid McAuliffe offered a thoughtful review of *The Kind of Schools We Need*, in which he notes that the American pragmatist, John Dewey, and the influential educationist, Jerome Bruner, are Eisner's most formidable influences, and "undoubtedly *Art as Experience*, and *The Process of Education*, respectively, his most seminal texts" (McAuliffe, 1999, p. 368). He acknowledges the significance of Eisner's contribution to educational research, particularly because of the way in which he elucidates how the arts can be used to study, understand, and improve educational practice. However he questions the validity of Eisner's arguments for the arts as a neglected resource in schools:

> Here we see Eisner's plea for the arts at its weakest, repeatedly drawn into contention with the sciences in order to illustrate that the arts do indeed contribute something unique to education. A contention that invariably weakens, rather than strengthens, the case for the arts in education. ... [Eisner] asks, what's the point of it all? He does so with the tacit acceptance that "we do the arts no service when we try to make their case by touting their contributions to other fields"—a conclusion

that emphatically questions the very point of Eisner's argument in the first instance. (McAuliffe, 1999, p. 368)

The debate about the transferable effects of arts education was boosted in the late 1990s by press reports of the so-called "Mozart effect." Eisner addressed this issue on two occasions in the United Kingdom: first at the InSEA European Congress held in Glasgow in 1997 (Eisner, 1998a) when he questioned whether the arts boost academic achievement and reached the conclusion that such claims by researchers could be often ascribed to the "Hawthorne effect." He called for further research studies that were more methodologically sound and proposed some parameters for a convincing study.

The second occasion was when he spoke as part of the "Minding the Arts" series of lectures at the RSA in London in January 1998 (Eisner, 1998b). At this time the Royal Society had commissioned the National Foundation for Education Research (NFER) to undertake just such a major study into the effects and effectiveness of secondary school arts education in England and Wales (Harland et al., 2000). Included among the key aims of the study was an examination of the extent to which high levels of institutional involvement in the arts correlated with qualities known to be associated with successful school improvement and school effectiveness. The findings were broadly in line with Eisner's 1998 review of the literature— that is, there is no clear correlation.

In conclusion, I am conscious of the limitations of this brief account. For example a further lengthy chapter could be written about Eisner's long-standing association with InSEA. This included a term as president in 1988–91 and culminated in the presentation of the organization's Sir Herbert Read Award in 1997. For three decades Eisner has regularly contributed to InSEA events worldwide and has generously given time to innumerable conferences and seminars at the invitation of InSEA members.

It will be evident that Elliot Eisner's associations and relationships in the United Kingdom have stood the test of time and that he is held in as high regard in these islands as in the USA. Undoubtedly, his ideas are woven into the anonymous tapestry of the national curriculum and examinations system, although discerning the individual threads is difficult. As I drafted this chapter, *The Arts and the Creation of Mind* landed on my desk. It was at once clear from even the most cursory reading that his thinking is set to influence new generations of art teachers at the beginning of the 21st century with much the same impact that *Educating Artistic Vision* had on me as a young teacher in the early seventies.

REFERENCES

Allison, B. (1982). Identifying the core in art and design. *Journal of Art & Design Education, 1*(1), 59–66.

Best, D. (1982). Objectivity and feeling in the arts. *Journal of Art & Design Education, 1*(3), 373–390.

Best, D. (1983). Objectivity and feeling in the arts. *Journal of Art & Design Education, 2*(2), 234–238.

Eisner, E. W. (1969). *Teaching art to the young: A curriculum development project in art education*. Stanford, CA: Stanford University, School of Education.

Eisner, E. W. (1972). *Educating artistic vision*. New York & London: Macmillan.

Eisner, E. W. (1985a). *The art of educational evaluation: A personal view*. London: Falmer Press.

Eisner, E. W. (1985b/1994). *The educational imagination*. New York: Macmillan.

Eisner, E. W. (1988). Structure and magic in discipline-based art education. *Journal of Art & Design Education, 7*(2), 185–196.

Eisner, E. W. (1989). Current issues in art and design education: Art education today: A look at its past and an agenda for the future. *Journal of Art & Design Education, 8*(2), 153–166.

Eisner, E. W. (1998a). Does experience in the arts boost academic achievement? *Journal of Art & Design Education, 17*(1), 51–60.

Eisner, E. W. (1998b). What do the arts teach? *Royal Society of the Arts Journal, CXLVI 2/4*. London: Royal Society of Arts.

Eisner, E. W. (2002). *The arts and the creation of mind*. New Haven & London: Yale University Press.

Eisner, E. W., & Ecker, D. (Eds.), (1966). *Readings in art education*. New York: Blaisdell.

Field, D. (1970). *Change in art education*. London: Routledge & Kegan Paul.

Harland, J., Kinder, K., Lord, P., Stott, A., Schagen, I., & Haynes, J. (2000). *Arts education in secondary schools: Effects and effectiveness*. Slough, England: National Foundation for Education Research.

Hughes, A. (1998). Reconceptualising the art curriculum. *Journal of Art & Design Education, 17*(1), 41–50.

Hughes, A. (1999). Book review: Institute of International Visual Arts: Education Packs. *Journal of Art & Design Education, 18*(3), 369–370.

Macdonald, S. (1970). *The history and philosophy of art education*. London: University of London Press.

Marantz, K. (1990). Correspondence: On deconstructing Eisner's sermon from Mount Getty. *Journal of Art & Design Education, 9*(2), 197–199.

McAuliffe, D. (1999). Book review: The Kind of Schools We Need. *Journal of Art & Design Education, 18*(3), 368–369.

Schools Council. (1977). *Report of the 18+ Art Syllabus Steering Group*. London: Schools Council.

Taylor, R. (1986). *Educating for art*. London: Longman.

Thistlewood, D. (1985). Editorial: The added value of art education. *Journal of Art & Design Education, 4*(3), 293–294.

Thistlewood, D. (1989). Editorial: Past practices, future trends. *Journal of Art & Design Education, 8*(2), 113–119.

U.S. Department of Education. (1970). *National Assessment of Educational Progress—Art Objectives*. Washington, DC: U.S. Department of Education.

Winterbourne, A. (1983). Objectivity and feeling in the arts. *Journal of Art & Design Education, 2*(1), 120–124.

9

Eisner's Thinking from a Music Educator's Perspective

Bennett Reimer
Northwestern University

Throughout their histories in the United States, the art education fields—music, visual arts, dance, and theatre—have functioned almost entirely autonomously. Rarely has there been a serious attempt to cooperate or coordinate in any substantive way. Even the development of national standards for the arts in the early 1990s was undertaken by separate task forces in each field, coordination existing only at the administrative level (Music Educators National Conference, 1994). No attempt was made by the task force members, who were well-recognized leaders in each field, to meet together to forge a unified stance based on shared principles and goals. The commonalities that emerged among the four standards documents were a function of natural similarities among the arts and a generally shared philosophical orientation to education that pervaded the thinking of leaders across the arts fields at that time (and to the present).

Those similarities suggest that substantive coordination among arts educators—inclusive of dimensions of philosophy, advocacy, policy, research, and program implementation—is indeed possible, at least theoretically. Its absence cannot be attributed to inherent incompatibilities among the arts (although there are certainly important characteristics that mark each of them as distinctive), but to historical patterns of subject matter self-containment in all of American education, reflected as well in the arts, where each field tends to act within and be protective of its own borders. Each has its own school program, its own literature of journals and books, its own teacher education and research endeavors, and its own conferences and activities peopled almost exclusively by its members.

The most thorough attempt to bring people from all four arts fields together to forge a common philosophy and curriculum was the Aesthetic Education Program administered by the Central Midwestern Regional Educational Laboratory in the 1960s, in many ways the most important cross-arts endeavor in American educational history. The books published under its auspices remain a unique achievement of arts education inter-disciplinary cooperation.[1] They are seldom referenced any more, the separatism endemic to subject matter fields, the arts included, having reestablished itself securely. At present there are two instrumentalities for sharing ideas across the arts in education. In the journal *Arts Education Policy Review*, a variety of matters impinging on all the arts are discussed, primarily focused on policy issues broadly conceived, single-art articles also appearing regularly. And, of course, the seminal *Journal of Aesthetic Education*, published since 1966, remains a bulwark of thoughtful scholarship relating to the arts and education. The book *The Arts, Education, and Aesthetic Knowing*, one of the yearbooks of the National Society for the Study of Education, also focused on issues relating to all the arts in education (Reimer & Smith, 1992).

Despite these and occasional other attempts to view the arts in education as a coherent domain, expertise resides almost entirely within the boundaries of each field. Few individuals have had the interest or the breadth of vision to communicate with professionals outside their own art or have been perceived as being capable of doing so. One such person has been Elliot Eisner. While well established as a leading thinker and activist in his home base of the visual arts, his reputation and influence have spread to a variety of additional fields, as this book amply demonstrates. One of those fields has been music education, where he has addressed prestigious conferences and where his writings have received unusual visibility for a field, like the other arts, fixated on its own issues and accustomed to listening only to its own voices.

In this chapter I will attempt to explain why Eisner's thinking has been conceived as being supportive of central constructs existing in music education for much of the 20th century and to the present. His approach to those constructs, while compatible with their articulation within music education, casts a refreshing perspective that deepens and expands them. He also adds corroboration as a distinguished scholar who is at once inside, as part of the arts in education establishment, and outside, as not based within the tight confines of music education. This is comforting to music educators, their beliefs being supported by a well-known figure perceived as being a member of the extended family, and also enlivening, in the different ways Eisner approaches the beliefs given his not being a member of the immediate family.

I will organize my examination of Eisner's ideas, as they are both parallel to and expansive of those in music education, into three categories,

---

[1]Four books were published under the general heading Yearbook Series on Research in Arts and Aesthetic Education: *Arts and Aesthetics: An Agenda for the Future* (1977); *The Arts, Cognition, and Basic Skills* (1978); *The Teaching Process and Arts and Aesthetics* (1979); and *Curriculum and Instruction in Arts and Aesthetics Education* (1981). St. Louis: Central Midwestern Regional Educational Laboratory, Inc.

each of them dealt with by Eisner in contexts inclusive of all the arts in education. They are: (1) the role of the arts in human consciousness and cognition, (2) transfer from arts learnings to non-arts learnings, and (3) policy for arts education. I will deal with the first category more fully than the other two.

THE ROLE OF THE ARTS AND EDUCATION IN THE MAKING OF MIND

> My thesis is straightforward but not widely accepted. I will argue that the arts are cognitive activities guided by human intelligence that make unique forms of meaning possible. (Eisner, 1981, p. 48)

These initial sentences in Eisner's "The Role of the Arts in Cognition and Curriculum" summarize his rich, extensive contributions to the philosophy and psychology of art and of education. They portray his long-standing, ongoing focus on constructs that form the basis of his philosophy and of their psychological/educational implications. For him, all else flows from these convictions that the arts are constructions of the human mind; that human minds are fashioned from the influence of cultural institutions, the most important of which is education; that the operations of mind that the arts call upon are instances of intelligence, and that the education-enabled, mindful, intelligent products and processes we call "the arts" offer meanings available in no other way. Much of Eisner's prolific output, written and oral, can be understood as a gloss on these central, powerful ideas as they impact on what a humane education should entail.

Several recurring themes stem from Eisner's foundational beliefs, presented by him in a variety of guises and contexts. He points out that in long-standing models of human cognitive functioning in American philosophy and psychology of education there is a separation between mind, body, and feelings, traceable all the way back to Plato. Because the arts are not conceived to be dependent on rationality and are not grounded in logic, they are traditionally regarded as arational and therefore not productive of meaning. Meaning, in this more traditional view, requires propositional logic, characteristically lacking in arts involvements, which are dependent, instead, on a kind of emotive intuition. In his typically felicitous and clever way of illustrating his points, which accounts, I believe, for much of the persuasive power of his arguments, Eisner reminds us of the perennial dismissal of subjects regarded to be unintellectual as tantamount to basket weaving—that is, working with the hands instead of the mind and therefore regarded to be at the bottom of the status hierarchy in education. "I reject mindless forms of basket weaving in school," Eisner asserts. "But let me add quickly that I also reject mindless forms of algebra and that I find nothing inherently more intellectually complex in algebra than in basket weaving"

(Eisner, 1981, p. 48). Here the gauntlet is thrown decisively. The arts are as intellectually challenging, as much the operation of intelligence, and as much the creation and sharing of meanings central to the human condition and to human welfare as anything else people do. And their importance in education must be no less.

The essential difference between the arts and other subjects is the same as the difference between each other subject, Eisner explains. Each subject produces meanings by the way the subject allows us to represent meanings. Each form of representation allows us to create meanings not available from the others. "Some forms of representation can illuminate some aspects of the world that others can not. What one can learn about the world through visual form is not likely to be provided through auditory form. What one knows takes shape in the empirical world through a vehicle that makes such knowing public. The vehicles employed are the forms of representation" (Eisner, 1981, p. 50). Basket weaving, then, and all other manifestations of artistic representation, make meanings available for public sharing, just like the forms of representation in algebra, science, history, and so forth.

But the meanings the arts create are distinctive in that they come into being through a process of imaginative exploration and discovery requiring the manipulation of the forms each art makes available through its media. Artists manipulate the media of their art—creatively form them—and in so doing create meanings never before existent. Unlike the rule-following operations of standard school subjects, Eisner points out that the arts are created through acts of imagination in pursuit of expressiveness. Each such pursuit requires a unique solution to the task at hand, which is to make meanings through judgments about how to form materials (visual, aural, kinetic, etc.) into aesthetically compelling objects and events. That process, including the creation of artistic meanings and the sharing of them by those who attend to them, are acts of mind, of intelligence, of cognitive mental ability.

The educational implications of this stance, Eisner points out again and again, are clear. We must expand our conception of subjects worthy of education beyond the traditional "basics," to include the arts as essentials of any complete and valid curriculum. We must provide educational equity by counting excellence in the arts to be as being as valuable as any other achievements of excellence; by calculating high school GPAs to include the arts; by expecting colleges and universities to accept those GPAs as being valid for admission; by regarding giftedness in the arts as equal to any other form of giftedness, and by providing rich opportunities for its development. Until educators around the world recognize that human cognition goes far beyond language literacy and numeracy, and includes artistic/aesthetic cognitions only the arts afford, the arts will continue to be neglected unconscionably in schooling. "Indeed," says Eisner, "there is no country I have visited where the arts are regarded as having parity with algebra or geometry, chemistry or physics, foreign languages or history" (Eisner, 1980, p. 2). The consequences of this disparity are severe, for what is not attended to in schooling can not be developed. "The kinds of opportunities the environment provides shape the forms of consciousness and the kinds of intelligence that humans can employ in dealing with the world. ... The inability to think in any particular form is an inability to access the meanings that are projected in that form" (Eisner, 1980, p. 4).

These themes, expanded, developed, applied in a variety of contexts, remain constant throughout Eisner's work on the arts in education. In musical terms they are his *ostinati*, persistently repeated phrases occurring throughout a composition or section. Such *ostinati* are found as well in their musical setting—that is, in music education.

Serious philosophical and psychological work in music education, as we now construe what that consists of, has been produced only fairly recently. Of course, speculation about the nature and importance of music stretches back to ancient Greece and has occupied the energies of major thinkers in Western history ever since. But such work by music educators, focused specifically on the values of music in education and the most opportune ways of realizing those values, can be traced back only to the 1930s and 1940s. The leading voice in those times was that of James L. Mursell, whose many influential books and articles proposed that there is an "essence" of music that defines both its value to humans and the ways an education in music should be conducted. "Of all the sensory media," he claimed, "tone is most closely connected to emotion. ... Thus music is the most purely and typically emotional of all the arts. Here we find its essence. This must be our chief clue to its proper educational treatment, for it is the central secret of its human appeal and its power in the lives of men" (Mursell, 1934, p. 35). The "meaning" of music, for Mursell, is its mediation, or representation, of ineffable feelings as organized by human intelligence and creativity. The capacity to create occasions for feeling as musicians do, and to respond to them as audiences do, is inborn. All humans have some degree of "musicality"—the ability to create and respond to the meanings music distinctively makes available.

Such ideas, elaborated by Mursell both philosophically and psychologically, have permeated music education scholarship and research to this day. The major challenges of this work, and its major controversies, center on issues of the nature of musical feeling; how, why, and when it is created; and how to best enhance musicality through a balanced, sequential, and comprehensive music curriculum. Impetus for this work was provided by the rise of the aesthetic education movement in music education in the middle of the 20th century, which emphasized musical feeling as the central construct in musical cognition and meaning. That movement continues in influence to the present, in ways both congruent with and divergent from its early articulations, some of those articulations having withstood the test of time quite well, others having been abandoned or reconstituted as new and competing understandings have arisen.[2]

It would be impossible within this chapter to trace the many debates about foundational constructs of musical experience, creativity, affect, meaning, thinking, intelligence, cultural influences, social issues, and on and on, with the plethora of matters vigorously debated in contemporary music education scholarship. Suffice it to say that Eisner's key constructs—that the body and feelings are essential components of the human mind, that the arts provide instances of human mindful functioning at its highest levels, that the meanings the arts add to human experience are culturally grounded, that imagination and creativity are at the core of artistic/aesthetic functioning—all resonate strongly within contemporary music education thinking. While divergent positions are taken about details of each of these constructs, all are influential in present scholarly work and are widely accepted as persuasive by informed music teachers in school settings.

What Eisner adds to those constructs is his breadth of conception, in which the many specifics of music are cast in the larger terms of a shared commitment to the contribution all the arts make to the quality of human life. That breadth is notoriously lacking in music education and in the other arts education fields, as previously mentioned.[3] I observe little interest within music education in becoming actively involved in the larger sphere of cooperative, coordinated arts issues, either philosophically or practically, and in fact, observe a good deal of suspicion about the efficacy and validity of doing so. Nevertheless, Eisner's representation of those issues to music educators, in tones so harmonious with their own interests, tends to solidify the validity of their interests. In a sense, this relieves music education scholars and researchers from feeling there is any need to pursue them with their counterparts in the other arts, practically all of whom are complete strangers to them. Eisner serves as a kind of friendly envoy from a not-so-distant land, treated with respect and admiration and then sent home to wherever it is he dwells.

---

[2]The inception and progression of the aesthetic education movement in music education can be traced through writings such as the following: M. L. Mark, *Contemporary Music Education,* 3rd ed. (New York: Schirmer Books, 1996); C. Leonhard & R. W. House, *Foundations and Principles of Music Education* (New York: McGraw-Hill, 1959); N. B. Henry (Ed.), *Basic Concepts in Music Education* (Chicago: University of Chicago Press, 1958); R. J. Colwell (Ed.), *Basic Concepts in Music Education II* (Niwot: University Press of Colorado, 1991); B. Reimer, *A Philosophy of Music Education* (Englewood Cliffs, NJ: Prentice Hall, 1970; 2nd ed., 1989); B. Reimer, *A Philosophy of Music Education, Advancing the Vision,* 3rd ed. (Upper Saddle River, NJ: Prentice Hall, 2003); D. J. Elliott, *Music Matters: A New Philosophy of Music Education* (New York: Oxford University Press, 1995); and the issues of the *Philosophy of Music Education Review,* which began publication in Spring 1993.
[3]A penetrating discussion of the isolation of the arts fields from each other in American education is C. Detels, *Soft Boundaries: Revisioning the Arts and Aesthetics in American Education* (Westport, CT: Bergin & Garvey, 1999).

But we should not underestimate the salutary effects of his occasional, if ceremonial, presence in music education, in reminding its denizens that, after all, they are not entirely alone in the world, they do not have all the answers, there are impressive thinkers out there beyond their own, and they had better stay honest because other eyes are sometimes cast on their thinkings and doings. Eisner, I believe, connects music educators to a reality beyond their own, in most impressive terms, and thereby provides breaths of fresh air when he is given the opportunity to do so in person and when his writings are cited to shore up various arguments. Would that we had a greater number of such consciousness raisers!

Conversely, however, many contemporary debates and ideas within music education can add to Eisner's repertoire of arguments in ways that would deepen and expand them. Influences on musical experience of gender, race, and other societally grounded identifications, and the issue of the relation of music to ethics and morality, have occupied the attention of many thoughtful commentators in music education, as has occurred in the other arts as well. Some who discuss social issues as reflected in music education call into question the validity of previous interests in artistic forming as the basis for musical meaning and significance ("inherence"), stressing instead the societally relevant aspects of musical experience ("delineation"). Others continue to give credence to the essentiality of inherent dimensions. Still others argue that the two—delineation and inherence—are in fact reconcilable, that the meanings created by inherent form are not in conflict with the delineated social issues music also addresses meaningfully.[4]

Details of cognition, perception, feeling, and intelligence have been explored in some depth by scholars in music education, as influenced by recent advances in understandings from philosophy and the cognitive sciences. For example, the notion of intelligence, as applied to the arts, is recognized by Eisner as applying to what artists do as they work with their materials. He often mentions Howard Gardner's theory of multiple intelligences in this regard but does not probe the insufficiencies of that theory, accounting for its limited utility in arts education beyond its use as an advocacy tool. Is there a general "arts intelligence"? Or, as Gardner tends to argue, a general intelligence for each of the arts fields but with music the only one with its own "frame of mind," as his conceptualization implies? An argument has been made that we need to take Gardner's theory of multiple intelligences further, recognizing that each role in each art calls upon a distinctive way to be intelligent, accounting for the very strong identification with and achievement in a particular role by most artists within each art. That argument also implies the need for education in the arts to be specifically role-focused rather than generally art-focused if it is to achieve the

---

[4]See my discussions of the inherent/delineated debate in *A Philosophy of Music Education*, 3rd ed., note 2, chapter 2, and p. 89.

cultivation of the many and diverse intelligences the arts encompass. (The argument has significant implications not only for the arts in education, but for education as a whole [Reimer, 2003, chapter 7].)

Issues of whether music-creating is the primary or exclusive route to success in all musical involvements, as some in music education would argue (Elliott, 1995); whether those who engage with music as respondents are lesser in accomplishment and in need for education than those who create; whether, in fact, musical respondents can also be conceived as being creative; whether conceptual learnings play a function in music—and many other such matters—are front and center in current music education work. It must also be mentioned that the impact of electronic technologies on the art of music, hence on music education, has been profound in recent decades. Technology has opened up unprecedented opportunities, such as in musical composition, and also serious dilemmas, such as whether performance on traditional instruments will remain viable when they have increasingly become optional. Such challenges are likely to change the face of music education fundamentally. Also, of course, the applications of technology to teaching, while being explored with great energy, have only begun to fulfill their potentials.

These and other ongoing developments in music education call for serious reflection as to their implications for the other arts in education, such reflection possibly leading to more inter-arts collaboration than has existed before, raising provocative issues as to the benefits and hazards such collaborative work might entail. Further exchanges with leaders like Eisner would be extremely efficacious.

TRANSFER OF LEARNINGS

Eisner's writings on transfer focus on the ways that arts learnings have been justified because of their utility for learning other subjects. He makes an important distinction relating to the notion of transfer. Proximal (or specific or in-domain) transfer applies what one has learned to situations highly related to the initial learning. Distal (or general or out-of-domain) transfer relates learnings to others quite different from them. Research on the transfer of arts learnings has focused on distal transfer, as from music to mathematics, or visual art to science. Eisner's interest is not so much in the research itself, hence the perfunctory nature of his review of it (Eisner, 1998), as compared with the exhaustive work done by, for example, Ellen Winner and Lois Hetland (Winner & Hetland, 2000). His concern is about the propriety of the assumptions the research embodies, that the arts are valuable to the extent they affect learnings in the subjects that "matter." That kind of distal transfer is, for Eisner, as for many other educators in the arts, entirely ancillary to the genuine values the arts afford.

This is not to suggest that it is improper to situate the arts within the cultures in which they inevitably exist, according to Eisner, by studying the beliefs, attitudes, and perceptual styles each culture provides for all the human transactions within it. Art needs to be understood within the cultural milieu in which it operates. In that sense there is a natural affinity between art learnings and historical/social studies learnings, the latter contextualizing and thereby enriching the former. There is also the reverse effect, in that studying the arts as an integral part of social studies and history enlarges the array of meanings those subjects afford, vivifying them beyond their typical language-based treatment (Eisner, 1991). Nevertheless, Eisner argues, whatever fruitful coordination of learnings might exist between the arts and non-arts subjects, "we do the arts no service when we try to make their case by touting their contributions to other fields. When such contributions become priorities the arts become hand-maidens to ends that are not distinctively artistic and in the process undermine the values of art's unique contributions to the education of the young" (Eisner, 1998, p. 59).

Eisner's concerns with justifying the arts as an integral component of education are echoed strongly within music education, where the issue of justification has been ongoing throughout its history. From its inception as a sanctioned school subject in the United States in the late 1830s, music educators have struggled mightily to persuade others of its value, sometimes being willing to do whatever it might take, veracity be damned. Whatever the public has focused on as being essential for education to provide, reflecting various values as societal needs and interests have identified them over time, some music educators have been quick to leap on the bandwagon by claiming that music education will, at the least, contribute significantly to them, and at most, be the royal road to their attainment. Continuing to this day, results ancillary to music are often claimed to be what music study exists to provide, whether higher test scores, brain development unrelated to music, or the "Mozart Effect."[5]

Some in music education decry any and all such claims, seeing them as perversions of the genuine nature of music. Others take a midpoint view, stressing that musical learnings must be central in any delineation of the basis of a comprehensive music education—such as in the national standards for music education, discussed in the following section—while any other (distal) learnings, if actually produced or enhanced, can be taken as supplementary without endangering what music uniquely offers. If history is any guide, it would seem safe to say that all these positions are likely to coexist in music education, and in the other arts as well, in the foreseeable future. Eisner's reflections on this matter provide a sound basis for avoiding the trap of unwarranted, self-serving advocacy while not being dismissive of

---

[5]For my discussion of the possible negative effects of justifying music education on the basis of the "Mozart Effect," see "Facing the Risks of the 'Mozart Effect,'" Grandmaster Series, *Music Educators Journal, 86*(1), July 1999. Reprinted in *Arts Education Policy Review, 101*(2), November/December 1999; and in *Phi Delta Kappan, 81*(4), December 1999.

potential enhancements the arts can offer to valuable learnings and dispositions for which education should reasonably be responsible.

POLICY FOR ARTS EDUCATION

Eisner's contributions to policy issues in arts education relate primarily to his concerns about advocacy based on faulty values, as discussed in the previous section, and to the possibly deleterious effects of the standards movement in both arts education and education generally. His reservations about the arts standards are an echo of those expressed by many commentators in education as a whole, that they are "predicated upon assumptions of uniformity and predictability that are not always congenial to the deeper aims of the field" (Eisner, 2000, p. 4). Arts education is about individuality, risk taking, and exploiting the unpredictable, Eisner points out. The standards movement is much more closely aligned with the kind of technical rationality associated with efficiency and behavioral objectives. "In fact, the so-called standards are not standards at all in the sense of constituting a unit through which something can be measured; at best they are standards in the way a flag is a standard; as symbols of what a field values. Nevertheless, the term implies a means through which teachers and students can be held accountable for the realization of specified outcomes" (Eisner, 2000, p. 5).

I believe Eisner falls into the trap, here, of confusing the original intent of the term *standards* (to designate the desired content of a curriculum) with its more common meaning of a level of expected achievement of detailed, stipulated objectives. The arts standards "are intended to create a vision for learning, not a standardized instructional system," according to the official document presenting them. In that document the standards are divided into Content Standards and Achievement Standards. As to content—what students should know and be able to do in the arts by the time they have completed secondary school—five general aims are listed:

1. They should be able to communicate at a basic level in the four arts disciplines, including knowledge and skills in basic vocabularies, materials, tools, techniques, and intellectual methods of each.
2. They should be able to communicate proficiently in at least one art, including the ability to define and solve artistic problems with insight, reason, and technical proficiency.
3. They should be able to develop and present basic analyses of works of art from structural, historical, and cultural perspectives.
4. They should have an informed acquaintance with exemplary works from a variety of cultures and historical periods.
5. They should be able to relate various types of arts knowledge and skills within and across the arts disciplines, including understandings and competencies in art-making, history and culture, and analysis.

The knowledge and skills called for in these five aims require study in a wide array of areas and the development of several skills, including "creation, performance, production, history, culture, perception, analysis, criticism, aesthetics, technology, and appreciation. ... As a result of developing these capacities, students can arrive at their own knowledge, beliefs, and values for making personal and artistic decisions. In other terms they can arrive at a broad-based, well-grounded understanding of the nature, value, and meaning of the arts as a part of their own humanity" (Music Educators National Conference, 1994, pp. 18–19).

Eisner would probably state these aims in terms compatible with his particular ways of understanding them, but it is difficult to believe that he would take exception to their thrust. Certainly they are more ambitious—perhaps unreasonably so given the historical separatism of the arts in education—than anything heretofore claimed. But, to use Eisner's own terms, they just as certainly herald, as a flag does, a symbol of what a field values. In this I, and I think Eisner as well, can only gasp at the grandness, even audacity, of the conception they embody, and embrace that conception as worthy of our best hopes. In the implementation of these values the various arts fields are likely to desire—even demand—more specificity than the content standards are intended to offer. In that case we can share our anxiety about the dangers of specificationism as it was most pathologically demonstrated in the behavioral objectives movement (long since laid to rest). But understood as a goal for content, the standards represent, I would argue, an historical movement toward comprehensiveness of arts learnings beyond the detailed objectives on which arts educators have traditionally focused.

Certainly in music education these learnings—embodied in the nine music content standards as embracing singing; playing; improvising; composing; reading and notating; listening, analyzing, and describing; evaluating; understanding relationships of music to the other arts and other subjects; and understanding music in its historical and cultural dimensions—take the field light-years beyond its historically narrow focus on singing and playing alone, with radical consequences for its conception of what a comprehensive curriculum must offer. (The nine music content standards are not listed in priority or hierarchical order, but by level of familiarity, so as to forestall undue anxiety about the comprehensiveness of what the nine require.)[6] Music educators all over the world have acknowledged the validity and desirability of the music content standards as a model for what a comprehensive curriculum should include. While there is no place in the world, including the United States, that has achieved its vision, the standards have effectively established a new conception of inclusivity in regard to the aims of the field of music education.

---

[6]My challenge to the music education profession to both reconceptualize the nine standards as reflecting distinctive musical intelligences, and to reconceive the general music and elective music programs accordingly, is presented in *A Philosophy of Music Education*, 3rd ed., note 2, chapters 8 and 9.

In this chapter I have discussed Eisner's views on the arts as cognitive domains worthy of full membership among the subjects basic to a valid education, his objections to justifying the arts as valuable for reasons ancillary to their nature, and his concerns about the possible negative effects of the standards movement on the individuality and creativity on which the arts depend. Each of his positions has counterparts in and implications for music education. Other chapters in this book will apprise readers of many further issues Eisner has addressed, practically all pertinent to his sister art field. Few if any thinkers, other than Elliot Eisner, have accomplished this breadth of relevancy. He has bequeathed a singular legacy, one we can hope will be enhanced even further by his continuing professional creativity.

REFERENCES

Eisner, E. W. (1980). The role of the arts in the invention of man. *New York University Quarterly, 11*(3).

Eisner, E. W. (1981). The role of the arts in cognition and curriculum. *Phi Delta Kappan, 63*(1), 48–52.

Eisner, E. W. (1991). Art, music, and literature within the social studies. In James P. Shaver (Ed.), *Handbook of research on social studies teaching and learning* (pp. 551–558). New York: Macmillan.

Eisner, E. W. (1998). Does experience in the arts boost academic achievement? *Journal of Art & Design Education, 17*(1), 51–60.

Eisner, E. W. (2000). Arts education policy? *Arts Education Policy Review, 101*(3), 4–6.

Elliott, D. J. (1995). *Music matters: A new philosophy of music education.* New York: Oxford University Press.

Mursell, J. L. (1934). *Human values in education.* New York: Silver Burdett.

Music Educators National Conference. (1994). *National standards for arts education: What every young American should know and be able to do in the arts.* Reston, VA: Music Educators National Conference.

Reimer, B. (2003). *A philosophy of music education, advancing the vision* (3rd ed.). Upper Saddle River, NJ: Prentice Hall.

Reimer, B., & Smith, R. A. (Eds.). (1992). *The arts, education, and aesthetic knowing.* Chicago: University of Chicago Press.

Winner, E., & Hetland, E. (2000). Special Issue: The arts and academic achievement: What the evidence shows. *Journal of Aesthetic Education, 34*(3), 3–4.

PART 3

Research and Evaluation

10

Arts-Based Educational Research and the Professional Heroism of Elliot Eisner

Tom Barone
Arizona State University

*T*hose of us familiar with the professional career of Elliot Eisner know that it is a study in intellectual courage. Over the years, Eisner has demonstrated a penchant for taking bold positions that place him outside of the prevailing currents of educational thought. To a great degree, Eisner's contrariness has been fueled by a passion for the arts, and marked by an unswerving dedication to securing their rightful place in the field of education. But the greatest professional risks taken by Eisner in his career are not, I suggest, found in his championing of arts education. One might expect an aficionado of the arts and former art teacher to be intensely committed to the cause of arts education in the public schools. I believe that the most controversial and courageous aspects of Eisner's work—its most boldly imaginative elements—can be found in his advocacy of a view of educational artistry that extends far beyond the realm of education in the arts.

Early on and often, Eisner has appreciated and conveyed the relevance of aesthetics to the many dimensions of the educational enterprise. They include those highlighted in this book—teaching, teacher education, school curricula, program evaluation, as well as the dimension that is the focus of this essay: educational research. In this regard, Eisner has been deeply influenced by the works of John Dewey, especially his *Art as Experience* (1934/1958), a book that Eisner has referenced repeatedly throughout the decades. Dewey reveals the connections of art to the mundane affairs of everyday commerce. Extrapolating from Dewey's writings, Eisner has imagined education not solely as an undertaking of social science but one with profoundly artistic features. Operating against a highly technicized field of study, Eisner has insisted upon a consideration of the arts with a persuasive eloquence that has been difficult to ignore.

EARLY HISTORY

The most courageous interventions by Eisner into the professional dialogue have indeed been, I believe, in behalf of educational research. The precise date of Eisner's initial disturbance of the prevailing consensus about the exclusively scientific nature of educational research is impossible to discern from his publication record. But before introducing the term *arts-based educational research (ABER)* to the field, Eisner first explored the place of artistry in the evaluation of educational programs.

In 1976, Eisner published an article in the *Journal of Aesthetic Education* linking the notions of "connoisseurship" and "criticism" in the arts with the practice of educational evaluation. For Eisner, "educational connoisseurship" implied an appreciation of subtle qualities within educational programs and settings. "Educational criticism" was a disclosure, a vivid rendering of those qualities appreciated by the connoisseur. The introduction of these concepts into a field that for so long had privileged the premises and practices of scientific forms of evaluation research represented a brave interruption of an ongoing professional conversation. Especially through his groundbreaking book *The Educational Imagination* (Eisner, 1979), he succeeded in popularizing the concepts.

By the 1980s Eisner was addressing educational research outside of the realm of program evaluation. In the preceding decade qualitative research had achieved a significant amount of recognition and respectability. Lagemann notes that after the founding of the Council on Anthropology and Education in 1970,

> [educational] researchers increasingly turned to anthropology, more specifically to the ethnographic methods anthropologists had discovered. ... According to some proponents, the shift toward qualitative methods was generally inspired by the recognition that there were severe limitations in the assumption "that 'what cannot be measured cannot be important' [Rist, 1982, p. 439]." (Lagemann, 2000, p. 222)

Indeed, Eisner's early awareness of such limitations had first inspired his arts-based notion of connoisseurship in educational evaluation before he addressed its relevance for educational research. But while the pioneers of educational ethnography, heroes themselves, could display the cachet of the social sciences in their quest for methodological acceptance and legitimacy, Eisner was intellectually bound to refuse the label of social scientist.

In an article published in *Educational Researcher*, Eisner (1981) first clearly distinguished between qualitative educational research with roots in the arts and qualitative educational research within the social sciences. The design elements employed within arts-based educational research texts, while similar to those found in, for example, ethnographic texts of the ethnographic storyteller Clifford Geertz, were revealed as generally unsuited to the traditional principles and premises of the social sciences.

At least in the dry stretch of time before the onset of the "stage of qualitative research ... [during which] ... boundaries between the social sciences and the humanities had become blurred" (Denzin & Lincoln, 1998, p. 18), the arts and the sciences still lived apart within Snow's (1993) famous "two cultures." Segregation of these two cultures within academia was strictly enforced and the living conditions were separate but not equal. A status hierarchy was (and still is) clearly in evidence. Indeed, one might suggest that the popular culture's valorizations of the technologies produced by scientists over the aesthetically pleasing but ephemeral works of artists have been replicated within academia-at-large and in the microcosmic field of education.

Postmodernists would come to recognize the idea of an invaluable modernist science as central to an unfortunate but nearly ubiquitous master narrative (Lyotard, 1984; Rosenau, 1992). This totalizing meta-story, itself taken for granted as true, nevertheless portrays science as the sole source of valid, reliable, trustworthy knowledge. The meta-narrative exists within a regime of truth that confers exclusive rights and privileges onto members of a professional class who have acquired the intellectual capital needed to generate new knowledge within their respective fields of the social sciences. Individuals without the requisite scientific credentials who nevertheless issue knowledge claims may be revealed as charlatans, equated with the likes of astrologists, numerologists, and phrenologists (Mayer, 2000).

So for an artist-outsider in the 1970s to knock at the door of the citadel of educational research and ask for the same rights and privileges accorded the scientists within was a gutsy move indeed. Of course, it was not unimportant that the apparent trespasser was himself professionally privileged in other ways, an increasingly distinguished member of the educational professoriate, tenured at the Stanford University School of Education, renowned in his own field of arts education, someone difficult to lump together with the phrenologists. Perhaps some of his colleagues incorrectly surmised that Eisner had simply misread the authorized maps of the professional terrain, and taken an unfortunate turn to find himself at the wrong gateway. Indeed, the first thumps were no doubt startling to some, puzzling to others, and largely ignored by most. There was surely some optimism that Eisner would soon reconsider and depart. But the tap-tap-tap persisted for years.

Now, postmodernists tend to dismiss the importance of heroes as singular individuals with the capacity to influence important historical trends and events (Rosenau, 1992, p. xii). I agree that courageous acts within the academy, whether scientific or artistic, and no matter how robustly imaginative, tend to arise from within a cultural milieu that extends beyond the local landscape of the protagonist's field of study. Developments within the field of education, for example, are often presaged by broader transformations of the human studies. And indeed, Eisner's aspirations for artistic forms of educational inquiry to complement traditional scientific research were sustained within an academic atmosphere recently altered in several ways. I will merely mention the successful incursions of literary criticism into the field of philosophy, the advancements of postmodernist theory, and the linguistic, literary, and narrative "turns" in the humanities that surely played a role in the prior legitimation of qualitative social science research. And Eisner was aware of, and perhaps emboldened by, the full status that was slowly being accorded to other sorts of qualitative social scientists within the educational research community. Indeed, Eisner's nearly exclusive early emphasis on literary forms of art may be at least partly explained by these prior shifts in the academic zeitgeist. Despite his awareness of the potential of nonlinguistic forms of art for expressing research findings, references to word-based texts dominated his arguments for arts-based research.

Moreover, Eisner could often be heard recommending an analytical component to complement the purely literary, "thickly" descriptive character of arts-based research texts. Especially in relation to educational criticism, Eisner argued that "description is almost never adequate without interpretation" (1991, p. 97). Educational critics must explain the educational significance of what they have described, "illuminating the potential consequences of practices observed and providing reasons that account for what has been seen" (p. 95). They must augment the descriptive element with explicit interpretation and evaluation, even employing various kinds of academic theory for the sake of "satisfying rationality, raising fresh questions, and deepening the conversation" (p. 95). Eisner preferred the same sort of theoretical envelope for the educational-novel-as-dissertation, a research genre that he forcefully championed in a series of high-profile debates with Howard Gardner at three annual meetings of the American Educational Research Association.

This recognition of a place for theory and explicit interpretation within ABER may suggest an allegiance to the traditional role of the academy as legitimator of research. Lest educational research become the province of dilettantes (including journalists and non-educationist members of the literati), educational connoisseurship was seen as achieved not only through reflections upon life experiences within classrooms but also through the broad range of coursework taken in pursuit of advanced degrees in the field of education. In my view, while Eisner's insistence on a presence for academic theory within arts-based research texts may have made his notions more palatable to some research traditionalists, it dulled slightly the sharp edge of his revolutionary vision of what educational research might become.

Most important in the promulgation of that vision was Eisner's sincere appreciation of the importance of the tools of science (including the social sciences) as means for exploring facets of the educational enterprise. Eisner has never advocated a new research orthodoxy in which the arts assumed the top spot on the research totem pole. Evidencing a generous and expansive outlook, he has never advanced the cause of arts-based research through a repudiation of the work of his scientist colleagues. Instead, he has consistently endorsed, although not as a calculated compromise, a kind of binocular vision that maintains the importance of both the arts and the sciences for generating full and deep understandings of empirical phenomena.

So, did Eisner's actions really represent a kind of heroism? It is undeniable that Eisner, like all of us, is a child of his culture. But in writing the history of arts-based educational research I find it is impossible to explain away the subject who was and is Elliot Eisner. Operating within a particular historical moment, the presence of a special combination of personal attributes—his enormous rhetorical talents, his passion for the arts and for education, his personal quest for melding those two hemispheres of his professional life, and especially his willingness to take professional risks—meant that he was exactly the right person at exactly the right time to profoundly influence the course of educational research.

PROGRESS

In the nearly three decades following his 1976 article on the potentials of the arts for educational evaluation and research, enormous progress has been made. Since that time Eisner has continued to advance his ideas in speeches and in print to untold numbers of audiences worldwide. Moreover, Eisner has mentored a number of graduate students (among them the authors of some of the chapters in this book) who have themselves continued to advocate forcefully for the legitimation and acceptance of arts-based educational research, to teach ABER-related university courses, and to infuse readings and discussions about ABER in qualitative research methods courses. These former students of Eisner's have, in turn, mentored like-minded graduate students of their own.

Many professional journals have become more willing to accept articles that advocate ABER, to discuss issues surrounding it, or to provide examples of studies employing this research approach. These journals include (among others) *Qualitative Inquiry, International Journal for Qualitative Studies in Education, Curriculum Inquiry*, the online *International Journal of Education and the Arts*, and the *Journal of Critical Inquiry into Curriculum and Instruction*. Some journals—most recently *Teacher Education Quarterly*—have devoted entire issues to examples of studies employing this approach. Additionally, chapters about ABER have appeared in handbooks and in anthologies of articles about research approaches, such as the second, and (upcoming) third editions of *Complementary Methods for Research in Education* published under the auspices of the American Educational Research Association (Barone & Eisner, 1997). As of this writing six Arts-Based Educational Research Winter Institutes sponsored by AERA have been conducted in

Palo Alto, California, and Tempe, Arizona. Twenty to thirty participants attended each of these two- to three-day "training seminars." Following one of these institutes, an electronic listserve was created for continuing communication and conversation between attendees and others about ABER-related matters.

Numerous sessions at the annual meetings of the American Educational Research Association and other professional educational organizations have been devoted to ABER. In 1996 an AERA Special Interest Group on Arts-Based Educational Inquiry was formed, and flourishes to this date. Two conferences devoted entirely to the research approach were held in 2000 and 2001. Additionally, a significant strand of the annual Curriculum and Pedagogy Conference has been reserved for ABER.

Other important developments included the birth and growth of educational research approaches closely related to ABER. Among them were Sara Lawrence-Lightfoot's *Art and Science of Portraiture* (Lawrence-Lightfoot & Davis, 1997), and *Narrative Educational Research*, the brainchild of D. Jean Clandinin and F. Michael Connelly (Connelly & Clandidin, 1990). The originators of these research approaches have each noted the prominent role of Elliot Eisner in their thinking.

Narrative research, in particular, has achieved a level of recognition equivalent to that of arts-based research, with AERA Institutes and an AERA Special Interest Group of its own. A type of narrative research called *narrative analysis* (Polkinghorne, 1995) or *narrative construction* (Barone, 2001a) may, in fact be seen as a species of ABER. In narrative construction, "researchers collect descriptions of events and happenings and synthesize or configure them by means of a plot into a story or stories" (Polkinghorne, 1995, p. 12).

In recent years, narrative-based educational researchers have experimented with a variety of literary genres for emplotting their data. These include (among others) poetry (Sullivan, 2000), the novel (Dunlop, 1999) and novella (Kilbourne, 1998), the life story (Barone, 2000, 2001b), the short story (Ceglowski, 1997), the ethnodrama (Saldana & Wolcott, 2001), autobiography and "self-narrative" (Buttignol, 1999), readers theater (Donmoyer & Donmoyer, 1995), and even the "sonata form case study" (Sconiers & Rosiek, 2000).

Arts-based educational researchers have also, somewhat belatedly and with mixed success, begun experimenting with nonlinguistic forms of the arts for alternative modes of representing research data. Various species of the plastic and performing arts have served as modalities for the representation of research findings at AERA meetings, in journals, dissertations and theses (Springgay, 2001), and books (Bagley & Cancienne, 2002; Diamond & Mullen, 1999; Mirochnik & Sherman, 2002). Throughout this period of enhanced prominence of ABER, Eisner has continued his own promotional efforts on its behalf through his speaking, mentoring, and writing. Especially significant was the publication of *The Enlightened Eye* (Eisner, 1991), a widely praised book that detailed his vision for the role of the arts in educational inquiry. But perhaps the apogee of Eisner's entire career was his election to the presidency of the American Educational Research Association in 1993. And the high point in his championing of the arts as a basis for educational research may have been his AERA presidential address, entitled *Forms of Understanding and the Future of Educational Research* (Eisner, 1993).

Watching Eisner at the podium as he delivered this history-making speech arguing for methodological pluralism in educational research—replete, for the first time in presidential addresses, with visual images on videotape—it seemed that a hero had gained access to a citadel. As a student of Eisner's who had, since my dissertation work on the uses of literary non-fiction in educational evaluation (Barone, 1978), played a supporting role in a campaign for professional acceptance of a research approach in which I believed deeply, I sat excitedly in the audience sensing sweet victory, believing that a new age of educational inquiry had arrived. The coming era would be one in which we arts-based researchers could divert our energies from the arduous tasks of convincing our scientist brothers and sisters of the potentials of our research approach, toward achieving our common goal—the improvement of educational policy and practice.

FUTURE PROSPECTS

At this writing, having descended from my euphoric state, I see that sustained, universal acceptance of the arts as a basis for some forms of educational research remains a goal yet to be achieved. Certainly critics of the approach have not desisted since the 1990s. Indeed, one of the most vocal, Denis Phillips, wasted little time in critiquing Eisner's presidential address (Phillips, 1995). Today, despite substantial progress due to the efforts of Eisner and many others, ABER remains on the margins of the field, still not mentioned, for example, in any major introductory educational research texts. Much misunderstanding about the nature and purposes of ABER lingers. A belief that proponents of ABER are antiscience can still be heard in some quarters.

We arts-based researchers are, after all, proposing a substantial deviation from the history of a field, one that will require a new set of understandings and talents for the conduct of educational research and for conveying research findings. As of this moment, schools and colleges of education have not implemented the curriculum changes needed to develop those capacities. Those of us who valorize these talents needed for ABER will likely continue to be perceived as threatening by many research traditionalists who have been professionally socialized into a predominantly science-based field. Of that fact, Eisner (1986) is aware, and explains its endurance in terms of a pervasive and persistent politics of methodology:

> Our methods and our power are intimately related to the games we are adept at playing. When the prospect for a new game arises, we quite naturally assess how good we are at playing it. The prospect of losing

competence or sharing turf is not, for most of us, attractive; the familiar is much more comfortable. So we have a tendency to keep the game as it is, particularly if we have been winning. Power, control, and admiration are not easy to share. (p. 13)

In addition, there are recent moves outside of academia to reinforce a research orthodoxy that many of us thought long relegated to the ash heaps of history. These moves toward a narrowing of the officially sanctioned methodological spectrum are found especially at the level of the federal government, and the passage of the No Child Left Behind Act of 2001 is the most prominent among them. The law calls explicitly and exclusively for the use of scientifically based research as the foundation for many education programs and for classroom instruction. Most retrogressively, this law does not sanction all forms of scientific educational research, but only the use of the kind of randomized clinical trials employed in medical research. Whether or not this methodological retrenchment at the level of national politics will jeopardize the future of ABER remains to be seen. An optimist might suggest that the installment of a regime that marginalizes even correlational and survey studies could actually encourage alliances between educational methodologists of many stripes. As just such an optimist, I propose that we arts-based researchers who are hardly unaccustomed to adversity continue with our program as best we can under the new set of conditions.

What, then, is one possible future agenda for arts-based researchers? Without presuming to speak for Elliot Eisner, it strikes me that two kinds of efforts are in line with his thinking about ABER. One type of activity would involve further reflections on the promises and potential pitfalls of arts-based educational research. A second would find us crafting and publicizing new examples of this research genre. Concerning the former, several facets of arts-based research need further exploration and discussion. Among them, I suggest, are the following:

1. Issues of fact versus fiction in ABER texts
2. The possibilities of new sorts of audiences for educational research texts, including educational practitioners, policymakers, and the general public
3. Issues regarding the place of the political in educational research
4. The limits and potentials of various kinds of representational modalities
5. Further elaboration of the purposes served by ABER and the epistemology that undergirds those purposes
6. The tension between the need for quality controls and the democratic impulse to share artistic expressions

In private conversations, Eisner has expressed concern related to item number six. The issue of quality within ABER is difficult and complex, but enormously important. Elsewhere (Barone, 2001a), I have framed the issue in terms of several questions: How do we judge whether a particular product of ABER is useful? How do we know whether it is worthy of dissemination? What degree of artistic achievement must it evidence? How compellingly and artfully composed must it be to deserve publication? Should we as a research community strive toward consensus about goodness criteria for ABER? And if so, what are the practical concerns related to the application of those criteria in specific venues such as conferences, dissertation committees, and journal publications?

It may be that the enduring consequences of Elliot Eisner's heroic efforts on behalf of the role of the arts in educational research will depend, at least in part, on the quality of the work of those of us who follow in his footsteps.

REFERENCES

Bagley, C., & Cancienne, M. B. (2002). *Dancing the data*. New York: Peter Lang.

Barone, T. (1978). *Inquiry into classroom experiences: A qualitative, holistic approach.* Unpublished doctoral dissertation, Stanford University.

Barone, T. (2000). *Aesthetics, politics, and educational inquiry: Essays and examples.* New York: Peter Lang.

Barone, T. (2001a). *Narrative as research: What's next?* Paper delivered at the American Educational Research Association annual meeting, Seattle.

Barone, T. (2001b). *Touching eternity: The enduring outcomes of teaching*. New York: Teachers College Press.

Barone, T., & Eisner, E. (1997). Arts-based educational research. In R. M. Jaeger (Ed.), *Complementary methods for research in education* (pp. 75–116). Washington, DC: American Educational Research Association.

Buttignol, M. (1997). Encountering little Margie, my child as self-artist: Pieces from an arts-based dissertation. In C. T. P. Diamond, & C. A. Mullen, (Eds.), *The postmodern educator: Arts-based inquiries and teacher development*. New York: Peter Lang.

Ceglowski, D. (1997). That's a good story, but is it really research? *Qualitative Inquiry, 3*(2), 188–201.

Connelly, F. M., & Clandinin, D. J. (1990). Stories of experience and narrative inquiry. *Educational Researcher, 19*, 2–14.

Denzin, N., & Lincoln, Y. (1998). Introduction. In N. Denzin & Y. Lincoln (Eds.), *The landscape of qualitative research: Theories and issues* (pp. 1–34). Thousand Oaks, CA: Sage.

Dewey, J. (1958). *Art as experience*. New York: Capricorn Books. (Original work published 1934)

Diamond, C. T. P., & Mullen, C. (Eds.). (1999). *The postmodern educator: Arts-based inquiries and teacher development*. New York: Peter Lang.

Donmoyer, R., & Yennie-Donmoyer, J. (1995). Data as drama: Reflections on the use of readers theatre as an artistic mode of data display. *Qualitative Inquiry, 1*(4), 402–428.

Dunlop, R. (1999). *Boundary Bay: A novel*. Unpublished doctoral dissertation, University of British Columbia, Vancouver.

Eisner, E. (1976). Educational connoisseurship and educational criticism: Their forms and functions on educational evaluation. *Journal of Aesthetic Education, 10*(3–4), Bicentennial Issue, 135–150.

Eisner, E. (1979). *The educational imagination: On the design and evaluation of educational programs*. New York: Macmillan.

Eisner, E. (1981). On the differences between artistic and scientific approaches to qualitative research. *Educational Researcher, 10*(4), 5–9.

Eisner, E. (1986, September). *The primacy of experience and the politics of method*. Lecture presented at the University of Oslo, Norway.

Eisner, E. (1991). *The enlightened eye: Qualitative inquiry and the enhancement of educational practice*. New York: Macmillan.

Eisner, E. (1993). *Forms of understanding and the future of educational research*. Presidential address, American Educational Research Association annual meeting, Atlanta.

Kilbourne, B. (1998). *For the love of teaching*. London, Ontario: Althouse Press.

Lagemann, E. C. (2000). *An elusive science: The troubling history of education research*. Chicago: The University of Chicago Press.

Lawrence-Lightfoot, S., & Davis, J. D. (1997). *The art and science of portraiture*. San Francisco: Jossey-Bass.

Lyotard, J-F. (1984). *The postmodern condition: A report on knowledge* (G. Bennington, Trans.). Minneapolis: University of Minnesota Press.

Mayer, R. E. (2000). What is the place of science in educational research? *Educational Researcher, 29*(6), 38–39.

Mirochnik, E., & Sherman, D. (Eds.). (2002). *Passion and pedagogy: Relation, creation, and transformation in teaching*. New York: Peter Lang.

Phillips, D. C. (1995). Art as research, research as art. *Educational Theory, 45*(1), 71–84.

Polkinghorne, D. (1995). Narrative configuration in qualitative analysis. In J. Hatch & R. Wisniewski (Eds.), *Life history and narrative* (pp. 5–24). London: Falmer Press.

Rist, R. C. (1982). On the application of ethnographic inquiry to education: Procedures and possibilities. *Journal of Research in Science Teaching, 19*, 349.

Rosenau, P. (1992). *Post-modernism and the social sciences: Insights, inroads, and intrusions*. Princeton: Princeton University Press.

Saldana, J., & Wolcott, H. (2001). *Finding my place: The Brad trilogy*. A play adapted by Johnny Saldana from the works of, and in collaboration with, Harry F. Wolcott. Performance Draft. Tempe: Arizona State University, Department of Theatre.

Sconiers, Z., & Rosiek, J. (2000). Historical perspective as an important element of teachers' knowledge: A sonata-form case study of equity issues in a chemistry classroom. *Harvard Educational Review 70*, 370–404.

Snow, C. P. (1993). *The two cultures*. Cambridge: Cambridge University Press.

Springgay, S. (2001). *The body knowing: A visual art installation as educational research*. Unpublished master's thesis, University of British Columbia, Vancouver.

Sullivan, A. M. (2000). Notes from a marine biologist's daughter: On the art and science of attention. *Harvard Educational Review, 70*(2), 211–227.

11

❦

Multiple Worlds, Multiple Ways of Knowing

Elliot Eisner's Contributions to Educational Research

David Flinders
Indiana University

*C*ollectively, the chapters in this book illustrate Elliot Eisner's ability to lead rather than follow contemporary trends, and to do so, it seems, in whatever fields of educational scholarship he chooses. This chapter focuses on research, yet another arena in which Eisner's work is found at the forefront of change. Foremost among recent changes in research has been the rise of qualitative methods and approaches. Not only has this trend reconfigured the field, but Eisner himself has played a major role in fostering its growth. As a result, Eisner's contributions surface time and again in the key debates and leading developments of the field.

My intention, however, is not to provide a chronology of Eisner's work. The problem with chronologies is that they tend to look to the past rather than to the future. In contrast, I believe that most of Eisner's ideas are forward-looking; that is, they serve better as launching pads than they do as landing strips. For this reason, I have tried to approach the chapter by looking ahead. In particular, which of Eisner's contributions are most important in light of emerging trends? Which of his ideas are likely to serve as beacons in the times ahead? What on Eisner's palette promises to guide future generations of educational research?

I will address three contributions that are brought forward by these questions. The first is Eisner's conception of *transactive knowledge*, a theoretical basis for redefining notions of truth, validity, objectivity, subjectivity, and other concepts central to our work. My argument is that while Eisner develops this theory to support qualitative forms of inquiry in particular, transactive knowledge is more broadly important today as a means of responding to the increasingly negative critiques of postmodern scholarship. Notions of truth in the present context are especially needed as a corrective to extreme positions on both sides of the postmodernism debate (Noddings, 1995, pp. 72–76). The second contribution is *educational criticism*, a specific genre of qualitative inquiry. This approach is more closely associated with Eisner than with anyone else in the field. As a form of research that draws on the arts and humanities, criticism continues to offer a genuine alternative to those who are not attracted to the broadening reach of educational science. Eisner's third contribution is *epistemic seeing*. This is the important notion that knowledge structures perception, and as such, the mind can be used to further as well as restrict what we come to know in the future.

Although this chapter is organized more around Eisner's topics of scholarship than it is around their history, one ongoing debate is important to note up front because it helps provide an underlying context for situating specific contributions within the intellectual landscape of Eisner's work as a whole. This long-standing argument stems from what Thomas Kuhn (1962, p. 102) referred to as *paradigm clash*, and which in education is commonly associated with the commensurability-incommensurability debate. Those on the commensurable side of the debate argue that quantitative and qualitative research are fundamentally the same. Both are forms of empirical inquiry, both are systematic, and both strive toward the same ends (e.g., a better understanding of educational phenomena). In contrast, the incommensurable standpoint views quantitative and qualitative research as fundamentally different. Each category of research represents a separate species of inquiry with its own genetic history, epistemology, functions, languages, evaluation criteria, and units of meaning. I will not argue that Eisner takes a stand on one side of this debate or the other. Instead, what seems important are the tensions of the dichotomy itself, the striving to transcend forced compromises and thereby move beyond either-or positions. My thesis is that discomfort with such dichotomous thinking stands behind many of the ideas discussed in this chapter. To put this thesis specifically in terms of research, yes, Eisner does want qualitative research to have a seat at the table, but he also wants it to be welcomed there on its own terms rather than for its ability to mimic those already seated.

TRANSACTIVE KNOWLEDGE: SAYING YES TO THE WORLD

> I hope that by reconceptualizing the way in which we create and relate to the worlds in which we participate, we will be able to secure a more reasonable and useful way of thinking about the status of our empirical beliefs. (Eisner, 1991, p. 43)`

Today the field of educational research is once again defined in terms of a rather broad dichotomy. The contemporary split is between believers, whom we still label "modernists," and the unbelievers, labeled the "postmodernists." Most scholars would be quick to point out that the labels themselves are elusive. Nevertheless, more than a few careers have been made by one side in this intellectual debate building arguments against the other side.[1] In a nutshell, the unbelievers are those who reject truth as anything absolute or independent of our beliefs. From this perspective, beliefs are just another form of text, and any text, be it an Elizabethan sonnet or a scientific report, refers only to other texts. Human thought is right or wrong only with respect to its intertextual references.

The believers argue that if there is no truth, only the language games of intertextual analyses, we lose any basis for drawing conclusions, supporting a judgment, exercising authority, or acting intelligently. All of these possibilities—judgment, authority, intelligence—require that truth exceed beliefs. Truth does so, according to the believers, because it references an independent, objective world.

At one of Eisner's lectures in 1996, a philosopher in the audience hoped to pin Eisner down on just this issue. Was he a believer or an unbeliever? In Eisner's talk, he had mentioned the importance of attending to the qualities of an educational experience, and the philosopher asked, "By qualities, do you mean something in the world, or something that we create in our heads?" Eisner hardly paused before answering, "Yes." His affirmative reply to an either-or question sought to confirm the world—or *worlds*, for that matter—and the possibility that these worlds can be known in multiple ways. This inclusive stance is at the heart of transactive knowledge.

Before exploring the logic of that approach, however, others reasonably might ask whether researchers should be expected to justify their work on such grounds to begin with. Don't we have enough to worry about without puzzling over philosophical questions? Eisner argues that philosophical questions are unavoidable because theories of knowledge shape our conceptions of truth, evidence, validity, objectivity, and other concepts that are at the very heart of what we do. Rather than shy away from such concepts, Eisner has integrated knowledge as a central theme in the corpus of his writings,[2] thereby asserting that "how we think about the status of our empirical beliefs" (Eisner, 1991, p. 43) should be viewed as a bread-and-butter issue. In short, doing research urges that we know something about its object of desire—that is, knowledge.

As a reformer, Eisner may also have other reasons for his close attention to the conceptual underpinnings of research. Conventional work can take for granted its positivist and neopositivist bases. Qualitative research cannot. To his credit, however, Eisner has not developed his alternative

---

[1]For a recent example of this debate, see the articles in the November 2002 issue of *Educational Researcher*, particularly Feuer, Towne, & Shavelson (2002), and St. Pierre (2002).
[2]See in particular *The Enlightened Eye* (1998), and chapters 8–12 of *The Educational Imagination*, 3rd ed., (1994).

approach on a negative basis; that is, transactive knowledge is not conceived as simply a rejection of conventional theories such as positivism. Instead, his approach builds on scholarship in two well-established fields—aesthetics and pragmatism—both of which have a long-standing concern for what it means to better understand the particular worlds that interest us.

From aesthetics, Eisner takes up the notion that perception and cognition are inseparable. To emphasize this point, Eisner often cites Gombrich (1969) who argued that artists not only paint what they see, but they see what they are able to paint. Drawing more broadly on scholars such as Ernst Cassirer (1960), Susanne Langer (1976), Michael Polanyi (1958), Rudolf Arnheim (1969), and Nelson Goodman (1978), Eisner argues that art provides a quintessential model in which knowledge is both empirical and reconstituted anew with each perception.

Eisner draws on an even broader range of ideas and scholarship from the American traditions of pragmatism. Following John Dewey's lead, he pursues the notion that because knowledge is the product of a transaction, it is, in a sense, larger than truth (Noddings, 1995, p. 31). In particular, Eisner argues that the transactions that result in knowledge take place between a postulated world and the subjective mind through which that world is experienced. Dewey (1938) described this process as a joining of forces between the external and internal conditions of life. By whatever terms, however, both Dewey and Eisner assert that knowledge is always bound up in commerce with the world. We live in particular times and places that make a difference in who we are and the types of knowledge we seek. As Eisner (1991/1998) puts it, "whatever we come to know about the world will be known through our experience. Our experience, in turn, is mediated by prior experience. Our prior experience is shaped by culture, by language, by our needs, and by all of the ideas, practices, and events that make us human" (p. 47).

This is the world that transactive knowledge affirms—the world of culture, language, ideas, and practices. As such, its affirmation does not necessitate that researchers embrace a single, unchanging reality. On the contrary, Eisner rejects the Newtonian belief that universal laws can be discovered on the basis of dispassionate objectivity. If objectivity is defined as knowing reality in its pristine form, then such knowledge is logically unobtainable. Again, we can only know the world through our perceptions and, as Eisner (1998) writes, "perception itself is a cognitive event" (p. 46). The danger of placing too much faith in an objective, certain reality is that doing so subordinates subjectivity, thus eliminating any possibility of transactions because the world has nothing with which to interact. On this point, Eisner cites Alan Peshkin (1985) who writes: "By virtue of subjectivity, I tell the story I am moved to tell. Reserve my subjectivity and I do not become a value-free participant observer, merely an empty-headed one" (p. 280).

This is about the point at which believers (modernists) step in to argue that rejecting objectivity forces us to abandon all criteria for judgment and authority. But is this necessarily the case? What prevents multiple worlds and multiple ways of knowing from producing authentic experience? Multiple worlds can be both multiple and coherent. They can also be useful, and they can even serve as the basis for agreement. These particular characteristics—coherence, agreement, and utility—are the criteria that Eisner (1998, pp. 107–114) views as appropriate to transactive knowledge. He develops these criteria using the terms *structural corroboration, consensual validation*, and *referential adequacy*.

Structural corroboration refers to the coherence of a work, or the relationship of its parts to the whole. This criterion may sound a bit esoteric; however, it is illustrated in everyday experience, as when we judge what is going on in a given situation, based not on certainty, but on the preponderance of the information at hand. Consensual validation refers to how robust our information is with respect to agreement *on points where we would expect such agreement*. We know from experience that although misunderstandings are common as we go about interacting with others, these misunderstandings can sometimes be resolved through reaching agreements. Moreover, these agreements can be reached without requiring that everyone believe in the same God or belong to the same political party. Referential adequacy, the third criterion, refers to how powerful knowledge is with respect to its educational outcomes. How well does a given study extend our understandings of its topic? Does a study help us name the unspoken? Does it allow us to see and hear what we would otherwise miss? This is a particularly important criterion because, as Robert Donmoyer (1990) points out, multiple perspectives and multiple ways of knowing are often the most powerful means of broadening our understandings of the worlds in which we live.

A final note on transactive knowledge concerns the expression that I have used: "saying yes to the world." This "yes" should not be mistaken for naive optimism or a rosy view of schools and classrooms in particular. To twist a current slogan, transactive knowledge does not "just say yes." To do so would be the same as insisting that artists seek only beauty in the world, turning a blind eye to whatever we find repugnant or unpleasant. This narrow view denies that some art is valued for the very reason that it helps us better see and understand the world's horrors. Researchers too need not avoid the serious problems of contemporary education. Saying yes even to the supposedly protected worlds of childhood may take us to dark places.

EDUCATIONAL CRITICISM: BEYOND ETHNOGRAPHY

> I believe it is far more liberating to live in a world with many different paradigms and procedures than in one with a single version of the truth or how to find it. (Eisner, 1998, p. 48)

Elliot Eisner's name is perhaps more closely associated with my next topic, educational criticism, than it is with any other past development in qualitative research. Eisner developed educational criticism as a particular form of qualitative work. Moreover, because educational criticism has developed as a distinctive approach, it provides the field with a specific and concrete example of how qualitative research in education now draws on traditions outside the social sciences per se. The value of educational criticism in this context is even more important today than it has been in the past. Before turning to its contemporary significance, however, let me briefly sketch out some of the distinguishing features of this approach.

Eisner has developed educational criticism as a form of qualitative research that takes its lead from the work of critics in fields such as literature, film, drama, music, and the visual arts.[3] In these fields criticism serves as a way of inquiring into the qualities and meanings of works of art. The function of criticism is to further our understandings of these works and the genre they represent. In an important sense, however, the critic's job is also to facilitate our use of art as a means of education. Dewey (1934) viewed art and artistic criticism specifically in these terms. He argued that one of the primary functions of art is to enhance our powers of perception. And criticism, from Dewey's perspective, simply furthers this aim. Through criticism we learn about art; through art we learn about the worlds in which we participate and our ways of participation. The worlds of teaching and learning offer an abundance of opportunities for criticism because these worlds include "works" of education (lessons, curriculum materials, assessment practices, and the like) that people have created and in which they take an abiding interest.

Eisner's efforts, moreover, have not stopped with this analogous way of thinking about research. Rather, he goes on to specify four dimensions of criticism and their applications to education in particular. These dimensions include description, interpretation, evaluation, and thematics. I will briefly summarize each in turn.

Description represents the first step in making public what an educational critic has learned from his or her observations. The aim of description is not to record events in a mechanical sense, but to re-present the particulars of an educational "work" or experience. As in art, the particulars of an educational work are the primary carriers of its meaning, and to help others experience these particulars is crucial to understanding the meanings of schools and classrooms. Furthermore, the particulars of a given case are what allow us to determine how it fits within a broader context; that is, description helps us answer the questions of to what types of situations we can generalize. In this respect, the importance of description is common across all forms of qualitative research, not just for educational criticism. However, because researcher-critics act in the service of art rather than in the service of science, they may seek to portray qualities that cannot be

---

[3]Chapters on educational criticism can be found in *The Educational Imagination* (all editions), *The Enlightened Eye* (1991), and *The Art of Educational Evaluation* (1985).

captured by explicit propositional statements or by the other common conventions of research reporting. For this reason, critics often turn to expressive forms of description, including those forms that convey implicit meanings through the analogic features of language. In addition to metaphor, these features include qualities of language such as its tone, cadence, rhyme, iteration, alliteration, onomatopoeia, and quiescence.

Interpretation, the second dimension of criticism, overlaps with description on this very point. And although both terms are used flexibly in this approach, each word conveys a different emphasis. Eisner (1998) puts it this way: "If description can be thought of as giving an account *of*, interpretation can be regarded as accounting *for*" (emphasis in the original) (p. 95). The intent of interpretation is to make sense of what one has described. Critics, like other researchers, can do this in a variety of ways. One common approach in scholarly forms of criticism is to use theories as conceptual tools by which the critic is able to make connections between the particulars of a given case and the categories to which these particulars belong. Human beings always seem to be making such connections at a tacit level of understanding, but the aim of criticism is more explicit. When Howard Becker (1982), for example, writes of "art worlds," he uses that concept to examine art as a form of social organization, and thereby foreground characteristics of art that would otherwise remain hidden.

Evaluation is the third dimension of criticism. This dimension overlaps with the first two dimensions because critics would not usually take the trouble to describe and interpret what they regard as trivial to begin with. However, evaluation involves more than simply determining what counts as significant. It also involves situating the particulars of a given case and its interpretation within a normative framework. Normative frameworks are unavoidable in applied fields. In education, one of the main reasons for doing research is to use its results for preparing future teachers and administrators. In turn, the point of such preparation is to help these professionals be better at what they do. The evaluative dimension of criticism facilitates this aim because it represents an effort to disclose the qualities of goodness as they are understood within a given framework. Assessment specifically for the sake of enhancing practice has its precedent in the concept of formative evaluation (Scriven, 1967).

The fourth element of educational criticism is *thematics*. Like evaluation, this dimension too is grounded in the notion that research should produce some type of educational outcome. In particular, the thematics of a study are its broader lessons or recurrent messages. Theses lessons are what we learn *from* rather than *about* a given situation. We read Theodore Sizer's *Horace's Compromise* (1984), for example, not to learn about Horace but to learn from him. The individual character in this case is less important than what he teaches us about the demands of teaching to which others are largely indifferent. Understanding something about this indifference and its toll on the profession is among the enduring outcomes of Sizer's work.

Albeit briefly, I have outlined these four dimensions to suggest how educational criticism contributes to the field as an artistic and scholarly form of research. With its lineage rooted in the arts and humanities, criticism offers perspectives that differ from more conventional forms of qualitative research such as ethnography and sociological case studies. The importance of this distinction today is augmented by the most recent incarnation of efforts to make science-based research our only option. As O. L. Davis, Jr., (2002) argues, the foreseeable future has been shaped by conservative federal policies that urge researchers to define the quality of their work exclusively on the basis of its scientific rigor. Hearing this call, mainstream researchers have closed ranks. Unlike the past, however, they have closed their ranks to include rather than exclude qualitative research as long as it is loyal to the scientific method. The danger of this response is that it blindly accepts commensurability, or at least commensurability between quantitative research and the "right kinds" of qualitative research.

The potential loss of genuine alternatives is more than a matter of excluding those who do not speak the received languages of science. Instead, the loss is that of a worldview. Science treats the world as a laboratory; art (and criticism) treats the world as a studio. Whether commensurable or not, studios and laboratories produce different types of "educating" materials, and each teaches us in a different way. As alluded to earlier, laboratories produce reports of propositional knowledge about the world. Studios produce expressive works of knowledge in the world. They produce images of the possible, and visions of what we can yet become. At the present time, a time during which the most imaginative plans for educational reform stop short of school vouchers and national standards, laboratories alone are not likely to give us all that we need to know.

EPISTEMIC SEEING AND THE SUBJECT MATTERS OF CLASSROOM RESEARCH

> The eye is not only a part of the brain, it is part of tradition.
> (Eisner, 1998, p. 46)

Because qualitative investigations rely so heavily on direct observation, researchers working in this broad category of research face the difficult challenge of noticing what they do not expect to see. Eisner (1998) locates this difficulty in what he calls the "liabilities of antecedent knowledge" (p. 66). Although often taken for granted, the knowledge that we bring to a given situation is represented in the vast array of labels, metaphors, associations, stereotypes, and lay theories that we acquire through our acculturation. These conceptual tools not only focus our attention, they also shape the qualities and features of a situation that we believe are perceivable to begin with. In short, we look for what we expect to find and what we believe can be found. The dilemma of our knowledge is that perception itself is dependent on a process whereby to know something about an experience is achieved only by ignoring much of what that experience has to offer. Wherever you build a window, to paraphrase Eisner (1985, pp. 64–65), you have also built a wall.

Antecedent knowledge, however, may also take the form of "epistemic seeing," or informed perception. In this case, knowledge serves as a virtue. Our understanding of an artwork, for example, may be enhanced by knowing something about the work's genre, history, author, and means of production. Eisner (1985, 1991, 1994) calls this type of knowledge *connoisseurship*. It contributes to epistemic seeing by allowing a researcher-critic to see a given case "as" or in relation to various other members of the class to which the case belongs. The 1952 film *High Noon*, for example, can be viewed as part of a class, the Hollywood western. As such, it represents a particular "grammar" for filmmaking. In the case of westerns, this grammar includes the portrayal of a masculine hero who epitomizes chivalry, valor, and rugged individualism.

In education, do we have similar "grammars," or more general structures that characterize different types of classroom experience? In response to this line of thinking, Eisner (1988) proposes that educational interests can be viewed broadly along five dimensions, which he collectively calls "the ecology of schooling."[4] The first dimension of this ecology is the *intentional*. This dimension concerns the goals and aims of education. Rooted in educational philosophy, it also reflects traditions of scholarship that range from Bloom's *Taxonomy* to the objectives movement of the 1960s and 1970s. The *structural* dimension of schooling refers to organized patterns of time, space, students, teachers, and even how schools structure knowledge itself. The *curricular* dimension focuses on what schools teach, including both the explicit and implicit messages that students take away from their school experience. The *pedagogical* dimension is represented in broad traditions of teaching, in the ways in which lessons unfold, and in the wide range of skills required by what we expect teachers to do. The final dimension is the *evaluative*. This dimension focuses not only on testing, but also on the increasingly diverse set of activities through which students and teachers seek to appraise their work.

As a conceptual framework, the value of Eisner's school ecology is twofold. First, it suggests that the topics open to classroom research are genuinely broad. Almost nothing is off limits as long as it has meanings significant to those involved in education. Second, Eisner's ecology does not look to any one discipline. Rather, it looks to the day-to-day practices of teaching and learning. Recent developments in the field seem to have made some headway against the reputation of research as being irrelevant

---

[4]P. Bruce Uhrmacher (2001) sees this ecology as only one of two major foci for educational critics. The other is a school's curriculum ideology. Eisner (1992) outlines a range of ideologies in his contributed chapter to the *Handbook of Research on Curriculum*.

to practice. Further strengthening those conceptual tools that help tether research to the workings of schools and the lives of students may help protect these gains.

IN CONCLUSION

In summary, I have addressed three ways in which Eisner's work contributes to educational research. The first is through transactive knowledge, a theoretical basis for arguing that there are multiple worlds to know and multiple ways in which to know them. Perhaps Dewey (1934) summarized this perspective best when he wrote of "a world so multiform and so full that it contains infinite variety" (p. 324). Dewey went on to conclude: "A philosophy of experience that is keenly sensitive to the unnumbered interactions that are the material of experience is the philosophy from which the critic may most safely and surely draw inspiration" (p. 324). The second contribution, an embodiment of this philosophy, is educational criticism. This form of research seeks transactive knowledge through modes of expressive description, scholarly interpretation, formative evaluation, and thematic generalizations. Epistemic seeing, the third contribution, is a type of informed perception. In particular, it is perception informed not just by the rigors of disciplinary knowledge but by the rigors of practice as well. These rigors include, for instance, intentional, structural, curricular, pedagogical, and evaluative components. Epistemic seeing is the means through which we come to view our worlds in new ways and from fresh perspectives. Its promotion more broadly among the policy-makers and practitioners of education may be one of the most enduring outcomes of educational research.

In addition, I have suggested that Eisner's contributions can help us fruitfully understand the continuing debate over commensurability (or incommensurability) of research categories. Transactive knowledge represents the tensions of this debate in several respects. It says yes to the world, thus affirming its postulated existence, for example, but does so without an appeal to absolute truths. A similar tension is found in educational criticism's rejection of positivist criteria while asserting its own visions of rigor in the form of structural corroboration, consensual validation, and referential adequacy. Epistemic seeing raises tensions by asking what are the types and qualities of human experience that extend our powers of perception. To ask this another way: How do we best come to see, hear, and appreciate multiple worlds? In raising these issues, the tensions inherent in commensurable and incommensurable perspectives seem to have been good for the field. As it turns out, Eisner's ideas are particularly good at setting problems rather than solving them. He raises questions rather than answers them. And by asking rather than deciding, he presses the need for further scholarship. These are the hallmarks of innovation.

REFERENCES

Arnheim, R. (1969). *Visual thinking*. Berkeley: University of California Press.

Becker, H. (1982). *Art worlds*. Berkeley: University of California Press.

Cassirer, E. (1960). *The logic of the humanities*. London: Yale University Press.

Davis, O. L., Jr. (2002). Educational research in the foreseeable future: The times they are changing. *Journal of Curriculum & Supervision, 17*(4), 277–282.

Dewey, J. (1934). *Art as experience*. New York: Perigee Books.

Dewey, J. (1938). *Experience and education*. New York: Macmillan.

Donmoyer, R. (1990). Generalizability and the single-case study. In E. W. Eisner & A. Peshkin (Eds.), *Qualitative inquiry in education: The continuing debate* (pp. 175–200). New York: Teachers College Press.

Eisner, E. W. (1985). *The art of educational evaluation*. Philadelphia: Falmer Press.

Eisner, E. W. (1988). The ecology of school improvement: Some lessons we have learned. *Educational Leadership, 45*(5), 24–29.

Eisner, E. W. (1991). *The enlightened eye: Qualitative inquiry and the enhancement of educational practice*. New York: Macmillan.

Eisner, E. W. (1992). Curriculum ideologies. In Philip W. Jackson (Ed.), *Handbook of research on curriculum* (pp. 302–326). New York: Macmillan.

Eisner, E. W. (1994). *The educational imagination* (3rd ed.). New York: Macmillan.

Eisner, E. W. (1998). *The enlightened eye* (2nd ed.). New York: Macmillan.

Feuer, M. J., Towne, L., & Shavelson, R. J. (2002). Scientific culture and educational research. *Educational Researcher, 31*(8), 4–14.

Gombrich, E. H. (1969). Visual discovery through art. In J. Hogg (Ed.), *Psychology and the visual arts* (pp. 215–238). Middlesex, England: Penguin Books.

Goodman, N. (1978). *Ways of worldmaking*. Indianapolis: Hackett.

Kuhn, T. (1962). *The structure of scientific revolutions*. Chicago: University of Chicago Press.

Langer, S. (1976). *Problems of art*. New York: Scribner's.

Noddings, N. (1995). *Philosophy of education*. Boulder, CO: Westview.

Peshkin, A. (1985). Virtuous subjectivity: In the participant observer's I's. In D. Berg and K. K. Smith (Eds.), *Exploring clinical methods for social research* (pp. 267–281). Beverly Hills: Sage.

Polanyi, M. (1958). *Personal knowledge: Toward a post-critical philosophy*. Chicago: University of Chicago.

Scriven, M. (1967). The methodology of evaluation. In R. Tyler, R. Gagne, and M. Scriven (Eds.), *Perspectives of curriculum evaluation* (pp. 39–83). Chicago: Rand McNally.

Sizer, T. (1984). *Horace's compromise: The dilemma of the American high school*. Boston: Houghton Mifflin.

St. Pierre, E. A. (2002). "Science" rejects postmodernism. *Educational Researcher, 31*(8), 25–27.

Uhrmacher, P. B. (2001). Elliot Eisner. In Joy S. Palmer (Ed.), *Fifty modern thinkers on education*. New York: Routledge.

12

Depicting What Goes On in the World of Educational Practice

Who Does So? For Whom? And to What End?[1]

Philip W. Jackson
University of Chicago

*I*n their chapter entitled "Arts-Based Educational Research," which appears in the second edition of *Complementary Methods for Educational Research* (Jaeger, 1997), Tom Barone and Elliot Eisner identify two major kinds of "educational inquiry that draws its sustenance from the arts" (p.80). One of them they call educational criticism; the other, narrative storytelling. As one of two examples of such research they include a brief excerpt from a chapter in a book of mine entitled *Untaught Lessons* (Jackson, 1992). In that chapter I reflect on my sense of indebtedness to my former high school algebra teacher. My account, Barone and Eisner say, constitutes a "mix" of the two kinds of "arts-based" inquiry that they proceed to explicate.

Though naturally pleased at having had something I had written some years ago so favorably acknowledged, I must admit that, while I was writing the account to which they refer, I did not for a minute think of myself as engaging in arts-based educational research. Indeed, I did not think of myself as engaged in educational research of any kind, at least not research with a capital *R*. All I was trying to do at the time was to illustrate a general principle, which is that, by reflecting on one's former teachers, one might possibly learn something about teaching. I chose my old algebra teacher as the subject of my reflection simply because she was so memorable. Though many years have passed since my high school days, I still can picture her vividly and recall in some detail what went on in her classroom.

Now, however, thanks to Barone and Eisner, I come to find out that in the process of describing Mrs. Henzi, for that was her name, I was

[1]The preparation of this article was supported in part by a grant from the Spenser Foundation.

additionally and quite inadvertently engaged in something called "arts-based educational research." That depiction of my activity made me feel a bit like Molière's M. Jourdain, who famously delighted in the discovery that he had been speaking prose all his life without knowing it. All joking aside, I must say that Barone and Eisner's characterization of what I had written provided just the stimulus I was looking for as I prepared my contribution to this volume. It sent my thoughts racing in three directions at once.

It first caused me to reflect on the many ways there are of talking about teaching and schooling and of otherwise depicting their reality, which is a subject I have often pondered in the past. This time I concentrated on trying to identify the major forms that such depictions take and the likeliest reasons for each one of them. I next thought about the various methods employed in generating such talk. I wondered how essential such methods are in helping someone decide what to depict. Thirdly, I got to thinking about my own efforts to say something about teaching over the years, not solely in the form of reflecting on my own experience, as in my essay about Mrs. Henzi, but in other ways as well.

The first two lines of thought jointly led to a singular conclusion, one that I had initially reached some years ago. In essence, what I had then concluded was that decisions concerning what method or methods to employ in the conduct of educational inquiry (or research, as some prefer to call it) are neither as important nor as interesting to think about as are questions having to do with why the inquiry is being undertaken in the first place and what audience is being addressed. Though I had arrived at that conclusion some years past, as has just been said, reaching it yet again was gratifying all the same, for it helped to reaffirm that earlier conviction. The third line of thought, the one involving my own work, proved to be even more gratifying to me personally than having old convictions reaffirmed, for it shed fresh light on the cohesiveness of the questions about teaching that I have sought to address over the years. It helped me see them more holistically than before.

For both of those welcome results I remain indebted to the double stimulus provided by the invitation to join in honoring Elliot by contributing to his festschrift and by my having read and enjoyed, quite accidentally and at just the right moment, the chapter that he coauthored with Tom Barone.[2] My way of partially repaying that debt while at the same time fulfilling the invitation to contribute to this volume will be to

---

[2] I am indebted to Elliot in many more ways than can be acknowledged here. His friendship has been a source of great pleasure for me over many years. His staunch defense of the arts and their place in human affairs, his crusade on behalf of qualitative research of all kinds, and his passionate concern for the improvement of education have all contributed to my sense of indebtedness. Even when we have disagreed, as we have at times, I have never for a moment questioned his utter sincerity and goodwill.

retrace in outline the route by which I arrived at the aforesaid conclusions. Perhaps readers who join me in that effort will share my good fortune and be led as I was to fresh conclusions of their own. To increase the chance of that happening, let's then return to square one of my own journey and begin again.

The topic to be addressed concerns the universe of descriptive and evaluative accounts of what goes on in schools and classrooms. Our first task will be to confront the mind-numbing variety of those accounts and bring some order to it. Consider, as a start, the variety per se. It includes everything that has ever been written, said, or graphically portrayed about what goes on in schools and classrooms. It leaves out nothing. It covers all of educational research; all newspaper, mass media, and governmental reports on the status of schooling; all novels, movies, television shows, cartoons, and comic strips having to do with teachers and teaching; all textbooks used in education courses; all speeches given at teacher conventions and graduation ceremonies at teachers colleges; all of the advertisements used in teacher recruitment drives; all of the gossip shared in teachers' lounges; all of the tales told out of schools by students, teachers, or classroom observers of whatever kind—plus much more. To say exactly what that "much more" might contain defies description.

Fortunately, we can safely leave that task to others. For what we are after is not a complete catalog of every item contained in that total universe of discourse, which would resemble in its detail an astronomer's map of the heavens. What we want instead is a rough and ready way of grouping those diverse elements somewhat more systematically than I have just done— something akin, in other words, to a tracing of the major constellations in the winter sky as seen by the naked eye. To undertake that task with as few intellectual encumbrances as possible, I propose arranging the diversity of items principally by the dominant purpose and secondarily by the nature of the primary audience each presumably serves. Why I choose those two criteria will soon become evident.

Notice that I write "dominant" purpose and "primary" audience rather than either *purpose* or *audience* pure and simple. This is because many such accounts serve more than one purpose. It may even be that most do. Likewise, many could possibly be of interest to more than one audience. An account of schooling that is fundamentally entertaining, let's say, and addressed to the public at large could also be incorporated into a teacher education program and thus serve an instructional purpose for that narrower and more specialized audience. When enjoyed for its own sake, one purpose (entertainment) is dominant; when inserted within an educational setting, the same account serves a quite different purpose (pedagogical instruction). For the time being, however, I shall ignore such complexities. All I seek at the start is the simplest of schemes for bringing a reasonable amount of order to the multiplicity of phenomena under consideration.

To maximize that simplicity, I propose using a very small number of categories. I posit only five of them and, as already said, they all pertain primarily to purpose and secondarily to audience. Four of the five are fairly easy to name and to describe. The fifth, however, proves to be a bit more difficult to nail down conceptually. Consequently, I will save it for last. Two of the four easy-to-explain categories have already been mentioned, though not formally introduced. They were, as named, enter- tainment and pedagogical instruction. The remaining two I will call sys- temic reform and public information. Arranged as headings with key words capitalized and presented in the order in which they will be dis- cussed, we have: Entertainment, Public Information, Systemic Reform, and Pedagogical Instruction. After a brief description of what each category includes, plus a few examples of each, I will offer some passing comments about the set of four before turning to the more elusive and yet-to-be-named fifth category.

ENTERTAINMENT

As already intimated, one clear answer to the question of why someone might provide descriptive and evaluative accounts of what goes on in schools and classrooms lies in the fact that such accounts, when artfully presented, can be downright entertaining. There is no shortage of good examples. Consider the description of Mr. Gradgrind in Dickens's *Hard Times* (Dickens, 1845/1958), or the novel *The Prime of Miss Jean Brodie* (Spark, 1962), or the films *Goodbye, Mr. Chips* (Ross, 1969) or *Blackboard Jungle* (Brooks, 1955) or *Stand and Deliver* (Menendez, 1988) or *Dead Poets Society* (Weir, 1989). Recall the now long-defunct television series of *Our Miss Brooks* (Lewis, 1956) or *Mr. Peepers* (Cox, 1955). Think of all the *New Yorker* cartoons set in classrooms. The list could go on and on. Its length points to the fact that classroom life has drama worth sharing, both comic and tragic. All it takes is the eye or the pen of an artist to bring it out.[3]

Who makes up the audience of such accounts? At whom are they directed? "The public at large" seems to be the answer. And, all things con- sidered, at least from the standpoint of the person making the offer—the author, the artist, the filmmaker—the larger that public, the better.[4]

---

[3]That conclusion reminds me of an assertion made long ago in my presence by the literary critic Renato Paggioli. Paggioli declared that though there might be "interesting" or even "good" novels about teaching, there could never be a "great" one. His explanation: Teaching did not contain enough intrinsic drama. He defied those present to nominate an exception. No one offered to do so.

[4]Here, by the way, are what might truly be called "arts-based" accounts of schooling, though not any that would normally qualify as research and therefore do not fall within the purview of the category being considered in the Barone and Eisner chapter.

PUBLIC INFORMATION

A closely related reason for offering descriptive and evaluative accounts of what goes on in schools and classrooms is not simply to entertain, but to inform the public about current conditions within a particular school or set of schools and classrooms. The content of such reports is often negative, their avowed purpose being to arouse concern and spread alarm. Examples that come quickly to mind include the many muckraking accounts of schooling that are almost constant fare in the public press. These range from the spate of criticism that burgeoned in the late sixties to the continuing book-length critiques from writers such as Jonathan Kozol and the more ephemeral blasts from journalists in our major newspapers. In fairness, it must be said that positive accounts aimed at a general audience are by no means unknown. Newspaper accounts, for example, sometimes laud individual teachers and specific practices. My impression, however, is that the latter are far less common than are those of a muckraking variety.

Like the accounts presented as entertainment, public information accounts are also aimed at a broad audience. Teachers and other professional educators may of course be among that general audience, since most everyone reads the daily paper and attends the same movies, even though the account as such is not specifically aimed at them.

SYSTEMIC REFORM

This category includes a lot of what is commonly called educational research, though not by any means all if it. Such accounts aim at being of help to those responsible for the maintenance and improvement of the educational system as a whole or significant parts of it, from the level of individual school buildings to the nation's schools overall. They commonly exclude, however, what goes on within individual classrooms. The chief audience of such accounts is thus made up of educational administrators, policy-makers, legislators and their staffs, and subgroups within the research community who compile the evidence and critique its significance. Examples would include studies that ask how a voucher system might affect the demographics of education in our large cities, or whether attendance in Head Start has enduring effects, or whether the practice of social promotion might be detrimental or advantageous for students. The official publications of the American Educational Research Association are replete with such accounts.

It is worth repeating that systemic reform accounts are not usually addressed to classroom teachers or to those who prepare them for teaching. They are addressed instead to managers of the system and to those who supply management with the information it requires.

PEDAGOGICAL INSTRUCTION

These accounts constitute the bulk of the material that gets put to use in programs of teacher education. They thus are addressed specifically to audiences of teachers and teacher educators. They focus for the most part on particular ways of teaching, on how to present material to students, on how to evaluate, how to organize the classroom for effective instruction, how to prepare daily lessons and larger units of instruction, and so forth. In short, they principally help teachers deal with the specific portion of the curriculum for which they are responsible. They thus include most of what is read and talked about in so-called "methods courses."

A course on how to teach reading to beginning readers would contain many examples of such accounts. All of the textbooks and video presentations used in such courses would fit within this category. Likewise, instruction in general pedagogical skills, such as computer literacy, developing Web pages, conducting parent conferences, and so forth. All deal with what one might call the nitty-gritty of teaching, looked upon as a clearly defined and rigorously prescribed instructional process. The practical nature of such accounts is one of their most distinguishing features.

COMMENTARY ON THE FIRST FOUR PURPOSES

Let's suppose that our system of four categories satisfies the requirements set for it. It allows us, at least imaginatively, to sort a goodly number (perhaps even the vast bulk) of the almost innumerable accounts of teaching and schooling into four separate piles, each sufficiently distinctive to stand apart despite a number of marginal cases that may be hard to decide. For the most part, however, the task of deciding what goes where looks to be doable and even fairly easy. Let's now pause briefly to think about what the exercise has so far revealed.

Because the thought experiment is conceptual, rather than empirical, it certainly tells us nothing about the relative size of the four piles. Perhaps the entertaining accounts of what goes on in schools and classrooms far outnumber the accounts aimed at systemic reform. Or maybe the reverse is true. We just don't know. And, for our purpose, such quantitative differences are not important.

What the experiment does, most of all, is draw our attention to the fact that there are readily discernible differences between and among accounts, based principally on the *purpose* they are designed to serve and the *audience* to which they are directed. Those differences become most manifest in the distinction between entertainment and public information accounts on the one hand and systemic reform and pedagogical instruction accounts on the other. The former are chiefly addressed to the public at large; the latter are aimed at professional educators. Within those accounts directed principally to professional educators there is another fairly sharp distinction between those aimed primarily at school administrators, policy-makers, legislators, and the educational research community at large, on the one hand, and those directed primarily, if not exclusively, at teachers and teacher educators, on the other. The fuzziness of these major distinctions in individual cases does not diminish the usefulness of the categories as tools of thought.

Consider now how those four categories stand with respect to whatever method might be used in generating each kind of account. For the person starting out to author any of the four kinds of accounts, the question of top priority has to be "What am I trying to accomplish and who am I trying to address?" rather than "What method shall I use?" Let's now have the person say, "I don't want to write an entertaining novel or short story about educational matters, nor do I want to write a newspaper account that will inform the public about what's happening in our schools. I want to contribute to the systemic reform of education. I want to do educational research." *Now* does the question of method become relevant? Hardly.

All we know so far is that the person wants to study educational affairs in some fashion and wants to do so in a way that will be helpful to those who manage the system. We still do not know what aspect of the system the person wants to study nor do we know what prior skills and information he or she brings to the task. Would not the choice of method be largely foreclosed by the problem being studied and the skills and understandings the researcher brings to the task? I feel sure it would be, which is why I said at the start that I find the question of method to be relatively unimportant and to rank far below the questions of purpose and audience.

But suppose our hypothetical researcher says, "Well, I've been trained as an historian and I want to study education, so I guess I'll use the historical method." Are we getting closer to the point at which thought about method begins to pay off? Not really, for we still don't know what skills the historian brings to the task (there being no such thing as the "historical method"), nor do we know whether the problem that has been selected (since one can't just study "education") is amenable to inquiry through the use of those skills and understandings. It may be, for example, that the historian will have to acquire entirely new skills to wrestle with the problem under investigation. It was precisely that point (or a variant of it) that I was out to illustrate in my essay on Mrs. Henzi. I was trying to show that one's memories of one's former teachers provide a fertile subject of investigation when one is out to explore some of the more enduring effects of teaching.

In sum, what method shall the researcher employ? The only answer that makes sense to me is: the method the question calls for, which means the one that best fits the problem and promises to yield the most interesting results. I know no better answer than that. But notice how far along in thought one must be before method, as such, becomes even a remotely interesting question.

THE FIFTH CATEGORY

This brings me, at long last, to the fifth category of my proposed taxonomy, the one yet to be named. To get us thinking about its content, let's return to the beginning of our thought experiment and try to imagine all the items left behind, once we have sorted as many as possible into the first four categories. To aid in our doing so, recall the array of examples listed at the start to illustrate the mind-numbing variety of the accounts about schooling and teaching. That totality includes, I said, everything that has ever been written, said, or graphically portrayed about what goes on in schools and classrooms. It leaves out nothing. It covers all of educational research; all newspaper, mass media, and governmental reports on the status of schooling; all novels, movies, television shows, cartoons, and comic strips having to do with teachers and teaching; all textbooks used in education courses; all speeches given at teacher conventions and graduation ceremonies at teachers colleges; all of the advertisements used in teacher recruitment drives; all of the gossip shared in teachers' lounges; all of the tales told out of schools by students, teachers, or classroom observers of whatever kind—plus much more.

As we go through that list, I think we now can see that our first four categories cover the beginning items quite well. It is not until we reach "all speeches given at teacher conventions" that we begin to have difficulty. From that point on, the items become an odd assortment whose individual members do not fit any of our four categories very neatly. But if we study them carefully, we might be able to discern a common thread running through them.

They all have to do in some fashion with teachers and students (mostly the former) and they all suggest (some more directly than others) that there is more to be said about teaching (and about going to school) than can fit comfortably within the framework of either school reform or pedagogical instruction per se. What they imply, in other words, is that teaching involves far more than instructing.

Convention speakers addressing audiences of teachers know the above to be true, so do the advertisers trying to recruit teachers, so do teachers exchanging experiences in the teachers' lounge, not to mention the classroom observers who come to visit, and the students who tell tales out of school. So did I, I might add, when I wrote the essay about Mrs. Henzi.

Does knowing that there is more to be said about teaching than can fit within Systemic Reform or Pedagogical Instruction suggest a name for the unnamed category into which all those teacher-related items might be placed? I think not. Unless, that is, we wanted to call it something like "More" or "Other" and mean by it "all the other things there are to say about teaching and schooling that are not included in the other categories." The trouble with general appellations like "Other" or "More" is that they do not help us think about the contents of that category in any principled way.

It is at this point that I must turn to my own work and to how my thinking about it has been furthered by my reading of Barone and Eisner's chapter.

Recall that in offering an excerpt from one of my essays as an example of the particular way of studying schools and teaching that they were out to explicate, they characterized what I had written as an instance of "arts-based educational research." Though grateful for having my work acknowledged, I felt uncomfortable with the accolade. In disavowing it I went on to explain that all I was trying to do in my Henzi essay was to illustrate a general principle, which was that "by reflecting on one's former teachers one might possibly learn something about teaching."

But it was clear that in hoping to learn something by reflecting on Mrs. Henzi, I obviously wasn't trying to learn how to teach algebra. I was seeking to uncover something far more basic than that, something about the curious contradictions and paradoxes that lie at the heart of teaching. The fact, for example, that I remember my former teacher's manner quite vividly but recall next to nothing of what she explicitly was trying to teach. Moreover, when I reflect back on other projects I have undertaken over the years, I see at once that most of them have had to do with similar puzzles. They all have been attempts to learn something about teaching that eludes easy description. Yet when I try to place those efforts into any of the four categories that we have so far discussed, they are like fish out of water. All of which returns me to the question of what to name the fifth category.

It was as I was thinking along these lines, while also looking over what I had written so far, that I caught what seemed to be a contradiction in my use of terms. Earlier on I had said that many accounts of school life may serve more than one purpose and may be of interest to more than one audience. I used the example of an account of schooling that was fundamentally entertaining and aimed at the general public being incorporated into a teacher education program and thus serving an instructional purpose for that narrower and more specialized audience. I said that when such an account is enjoyed for its own sake, one purpose (entertainment) is dominant; when inserted within an educational setting, the same account serves a quite different purpose (pedagogical instruction).

But note that I there was using the term *pedagogical instruction* in a far broader sense than when the same term was subsequently introduced as the heading of our fourth category. Within the latter context Pedagogical Instruction referred principally to teaching teachers how to teach. Yet when one makes use of an entertaining book or film as part of a teacher education program or even when one includes such material in a graduate course in a school or department of education, the goal of doing so is seldom to illustrate this or that with respect to specific teaching techniques. More commonly, it is to augment a lecture or discussion that treats broad principles of teaching or that seeks to attain a deepened appreciation of some of teaching's complexities. In a technical sense, however, such goals and purposes certainly qualify as being both pedagogical in their focus and instructional in their intent, which accounts for my use of the terms in the former context.

This suggests that the heading Pedagogical Instruction needs to be changed. It either has to be done away with entirely and replaced by a heading whose application to technical matters is more explicit or, if it is to stand, it needs be made supra-ordinate to two subordinate categories, both of which remain to be named. Either way, we now have two categories in need of names: one to be renamed, the other to be named for the first time.

As a first step, I propose renaming the fourth category Pedagogical Know-How, a heading that explicitly highlights the technical and instrumental side of teaching. This allows us to retain Pedagogical Instruction as an umbrella term. But it still leaves open the question of what to call those accounts of teaching and schooling that deal directly with the depiction of classroom affairs but that have little or nothing to do with how to teach this or that. It was at this point that I began to see my own past efforts in a fresh light.

I saw that they were not just attempts to reveal the complexities of teaching, for surely what I am now calling pedagogical know-how covers material that is sufficiently complex to tax our best efforts at explication. Rather, the aspects of teaching that I have felt drawn to as an investigator typically have had more to do with what teaching and learning are like as lived experiences, what they embrace conceptually in their totality. I also saw that with respect to that totality, as sensed or comprehended by teachers or students, my goal has usually been to see how it might be extended or expanded to include aspects of teaching and learning that presently might be ignored or overlooked by many practitioners for one reason or another. To say that I saw these things for the first time while in the process of writing this essay would not be true. I had come to similar conclusions in the past. This time, however, those prior understandings emerged with renewed force and clarity.

I realize that the expressions "what teaching and learning are like as lived experiences" and, even more, "what they embrace conceptually in their totality" are vague if not downright obscure. Moreover, I lack the space to say much more about them in this essay, certainly not enough to make their meaning clear. I would, however, like to give at least a crude indication of their meaning as a way of rounding out the present discussion and coming up with a label for the final category of the rough and ready taxonomy that has been the subject of these remarks.

A commonplace of phenomenology as the study of human consciousness, which is how it is usually defined, is that we each inhabit, as it were, a unified world of objects, events, and things, including such internal happenings as ideas, volitions, purposes, and the like. We do so both consciously and unconsciously. For each of us that world is uniquely our own in its detail, yet it is also shared in important respects with the consciousness of others. It is at once, therefore, an individual reality and a social one. It is also fluid in that its contents may change over time, both momentarily, as when we shift our attention from one object to another, and more enduringly, as when we develop new habits of perception, thought, and action. The shared components of these individual worlds allow us to speak of the quasi-separate worlds of subgroups of people and even to compare their similarities and differences. Thus, we may speak of the world of the Kansas farmer, let's say, and wonder how it differs from the world of the New York drug dealer. Likewise we easily might posit the existence of something we would want to call a teacher's world, or a student's world and proceed to explicate and discuss its presumed structure and content. It makes a big difference, however, whom we conceive the recipients of those explications and discussions to be. Do they live in the world being discussed, or do they dwell elsewhere?

Picture someone discussing the world of the Kansas farmer before a New York audience and then imagine the same or a similar discussion being held in Kansas before an audience of the farmers themselves. In the first instance, the account is impersonal with respect to its audience. It resembles what we have here been calling Public Information accounts. The subject under discussion is presented in the third person. Kansas farmers are "they." In the second instance, the account's subject has to be addressed in either the first or second person, depending on who is presenting the account. Kansas farmers spoken to in Kansas become either "you" or "we," but never "they."

This seemingly trivial grammatical point is immensely important, however, not just because it dictates the proper form of address, which in itself is of small consequence, but because it leads to an obvious question when those being addressed already inhabit the world being discussed. The question, in short, is: Why bother? Why speak to Kansas farmers, for example, about the "world" of Kansas farmers, or to teachers, for that matter, about the world of teaching? Isn't either exercise a waste of time and energy? Isn't it rather like bringing coal to Newcastle?

The reasons why such seemingly foolish practices might not be so foolish after all are far too numerous to discuss here in any detail. Chief among them, however, is the possibility that persons who inhabit particular worlds may be only partially aware of the worlds they daily inhabit. Indeed, they may even be totally blind to features of those worlds. Think of how one comes to overlook or totally ignore pictures or photographs that have hung too long in the same place. They may also lose sight of their world's teleological features, especially its higher goals and purposes, in favor of concentrating exclusively on the immediate task at hand.

Additional examples of such shortsightedness are easily produced. I call attention to them because I have lately come to see how so many of my own efforts have not only tended to focus on what might be called the teacher's world but have been principally addressed to audiences of teachers and teacher educators, rather than to the general public or even to educational administrators and policy-makers. In most cases my goal has been to call attention to aspects of teaching that may, for various reasons, be currently unattended by teachers themselves.

Here comes the final twist that brings me to the proposed name for my yet-to-be-named fifth category. My first inclination was to call it the teacher's world for reasons that by now should be obvious and also, less consequentially, because the word *world* appears in the title of these remarks and I thought it would be appropriate and even a nice touch aesthetically to reintroduce the term near their close. Upon further reflection, however, I decided against that course of action. Let me explain why.

Recall that what is to be included under this heading are accounts addressed principally if not exclusively to audiences of teachers and teacher educators. Yet the heading The Teacher's World sounds as though it would contain accounts that would chiefly be of interest to people who are not themselves teachers but are interested in learning something about what today's teachers are like or about the conditions they face in today's schools, the kind of audience addressed in Public Information accounts. As I pointed out earlier, such accounts would address the subject matter of teaching in the third-person mode rather than the first- or second-person. So instead of adopting the teacher's world I tried to think of alternatives that sounded less third-person-ish yet still connoted the all-inclusiveness that the word *world* implied.

The heading I have finally settled upon is The Whole of Teaching. My chief reason for choosing it is that it does indeed retain the notion of all-inclusiveness, yet manages to do so in a way that does not explicitly look at teaching from afar as does the teacher's world. I also like the way it contrasts with the heading of the fourth category: Pedagogical Know-How. The Whole of Teaching all but proclaims that there is more to teaching than know-how.

Readers of a logical bent may complain that I have erred by making Pedagogical Know-How and The Whole of Teaching coordinate in my small taxonomy. The latter category, they might point out, actually subsumes the former, since Pedagogical Know-How is quite obviously included within The Whole of Teaching. They are logically correct, of course. However, the scheme I have presented is immune to such a lapse of logic. As announced at the start, it aspires to be nothing more than a crude but useful way of bringing some order to the multiplicity of accounts that seek to depict what goes on in the world of educational practice. Within that manifold, those accounts that focus on Pedagogical Know-How stand out with sufficient clarity, through their sheer abundance, to be worthy of a category all their own. Whether that category is subordinate or coordinate with the accounts that get grouped under The Whole of Teaching is for my purpose of little consequence.

I have no difficulty subsuming many of my own writings under the rubric: The Whole of Teaching. In fact, I am pleased to have settled upon that heading, for it not only covers a lot that I have written in years past, it also helps me to think about what still needs doing. As a rallying flag, The Whole of Teaching invites and shelters such explorations.

But what of the other items included in my earlier list of candidates for the unnamed fifth category? What about the speeches given at teachers' conventions, the advertisements used to recruit teachers, the gossip shared in teachers' lounges, the tales told out of school? Are they also appropriately placed under the banner: The Whole of Teaching? They certainly are so in the sense of addressing aspects of teaching that go beyond Pedagogical Know-How. They also have teachers as their primary audience rather than the public at large on the one hand or educational administrators or policy-makers on the other. In those two respects they seem perfectly at home there. There is a deeper affinity of placement, however, for at least two of those items—the speeches given at teachers' conventions and the advertisements used to recruit teachers. They each explicitly appeal to the self-image of teachers, to how they see themselves and what they want to become. Self-image as a teacher, which could also be called pedagogical self-consciousness, is what The Whole of Teaching is all about. It is what each teacher conceives teaching to be for himself or herself. It is not, however, something set in stone. It is plastic, malleable, changeable, at least in part, as every convention speaker and teacher recruitment advertiser knows.

I realize that much remains to be said to make The Whole of Teaching more than a serviceable rubric that draws together a bunch of disparate accounts aimed principally at teachers and teacher educators. That task, however, must await another occasion. At present I can only say that I find the rubric useful in the short run and heuristic in the long run. I hope others do as well.

Finally, to make the circle complete, let me return briefly to Barone and Eisner's depiction of my Henzi essay as an example of "arts-based educational research." They were right, of course, in one sense, but wrong in another. They correctly saw that what I had done was closer in style to the writing of a story than to the usual piece of educational research. For that reason, I suppose, they thought of it as being "arts-based." I understand their reasoning, even while demurring at having my essay described in those terms.

What they overlooked, quite understandably given the purpose of their chapter, was what I was trying to do and whom I was trying to address, which at the time seemed to me of far greater moment than a label that stood for whatever method I might have been using. As explained at the start, I was trying to enter the teachers' world through the backdoor of recollecting my former teacher. I sought to describe what I found there to an audience of teachers and teacher educators. I can see why Barone and Eisner might want to call that "arts-based educational research." They have a right to their own terminology. For myself, however, I prefer to think of it in rather more clumsy terms as an instance of Depicting What Goes On in the World of Educational Practice—Category Five: The Whole of Teaching.

REFERENCES

Barone, T., & Eisner, E. (1997). Arts-based educational research. In R. M. Jaeger (Ed.), *Complementary methods for research in education* (pp. 75–116). Washington, DC: American Educational Research Association.

Brooks, R. (Director). (1955). *Blackboard jungle* [Motion picture]. United States: Turner Home Video.

Cox, W. (1955). *Mr. Peepers, a sort of novel*. New York: Simon & Schuster.

Dickens, C. (1958). *Hard times for these times*. New York: Rinehart. (Original work published 1845)

Jackson, P. W. (1992). B(e)aring the traces: Reflections on a sense of being indebted to a former teacher. In *Untaught lessons*. New York: Teachers College Press.

Jaeger, R. M. (1997). *Complementary methods for educational research* (2nd ed.). Washington, DC: American Educational Research Association.

Lewis, A. (Director). (1956). *Our Miss Brooks* [Television series]. United States: Warner Home Video.

Menendez, R. (Director). (1988). *Stand and deliver* [Motion picture]. United States: Warner Studios.

Ross, H. (Director). (1969). *Goodbye, Mr. Chips* [Motion picture]. United States: Warner Studios.

Spark, M. (1962). *The prime of Miss Jean Brodie*. New York: Lippincott.

Weir, P. (Director). (1989). *Dead poets society* [Motion picture]. United States: Touchstone Video.

13

Teaching Qualitative Inquiry

How Elliot Eisner "Makes Sense"[1]

Denise Pope
Stanford University

When I was an undergraduate at Stanford University, a friend of mine who worked as a student reporter at the *Stanford Daily* newspaper offered some useful advice on how to remember key points in our professors' lectures. "Take quotes, not notes," he said, "just write down the good stuff." I took this advice and have been recording memorable quips, phrases, and aphorisms ever since. In this chapter I highlight a few significant quotes from my courses with Elliot Eisner. Many educators are familiar with Dr. Eisner's writings on qualitative research, but few may have had the privilege to learn the craft of qualitative inquiry directly from the man who has had so much influence in the field. I was fortunate enough to study with Dr. Eisner as my advisor and mentor for six years, and to work as a teaching assistant and lecturer in his department. Today, as I conduct my own qualitative research and teach courses to prepare graduate students to be both effective "consumers and doers" of this kind of research, I draw extensively from my experiences with Elliot Eisner. I write this chapter as a form of appreciation for Eisner's wisdom and advice. In it, I hope to disclose some of his key assertions about qualitative research and to discuss implications for preparing future researchers.

The first quotation I address has become somewhat of a mantra for me. Professor Eisner often reminded his students of the need to do research "*where the rubber hits the road*." In our field of education, the rubber hits the road in the classroom—that is, in the relationships and experiences of the students and teachers. Eisner emphasizes the importance of looking carefully and critically at schools and classrooms and examining the educational experiences of the students and teachers working within them.

---

[1]An earlier version of this paper was presented at the American Association of Teaching and Curriculum (AATC) conference in Alexandria, Virginia (October 2000).

He writes in his book *The Enlightened Eye* of the need to "attend to the particulars" in classrooms: "To know what schools are like, their strengths and their weaknesses, we need to be able to *see* what occurs in them" (Eisner, 1991, p. 22, emphasis in the original).

How can we know how to improve schools without examining what is actually going on behind closed doors? How can we know if the curriculum is effective if we do not look carefully at how it is enacted and shaped in the context of a classroom?

Several of my colleagues from Stanford have heeded Eisner's advice. In fact, a quick scan of dissertations written by Elliot's students in previous years shows this kind of in-depth classroom research taking place in a variety of settings: For example, Sam Intrator (1999) seeks experiences of engaged learning in an innovative high school English classroom, Simone Schweber (1998) looks closely at four different classrooms implementing Holocaust education units, and Ira Lit (2003) examines the consequences of a voluntary transfer program on students in kindergarten classes. And the list goes on.

Eisner's words continue to inspire me as well. For instance, in my dissertation, I chose to do in-depth research on the students' experiences of the high school curriculum (Pope, 2001). As I reviewed the literature on adolescents and secondary schools, I noticed that few studies addressed students' educational experiences from the points of view of the students themselves. How ironic that we require students to attend high school, and yet we know relatively little of what they make of their school experiences. Adopting a strategy Eisner used in his study of schools in 1986 (see Eisner, 1986), I chose to shadow five high-achieving adolescents for several months, closely observing their behaviors in classrooms, accompanying them to all school-related events, and interviewing them at length over the course of the study. I was interested in their perspectives of their lives as students, which educational endeavors, if any, were meaningful to them, and how they made sense of their classroom curricula.

During my field work I was reminded of another significant Eisner quote, this one borrowed from a school administrator with whom Dr. Eisner worked years ago.[2] The administrator urged Elliot to look around and notice that "*there are very few soft surfaces in school.*" When Professor Eisner told this story in class, I was struck. The stiff-backed chairs, the hard tile floors, the harshness of the fluorescent lights, the steel rims of the chalkboards and teachers' desks—indeed, schools do not offer many soft surfaces, and it is this kind of appreciation to detail that Eisner urged us to seek. He asked: What are the consequences to students, teachers, administrators, and parents for instance, when the architecture of schools affords so little comfort? And what other aspects of the school are similarly hard and harsh?

---

[2]Eisner also tells a version of this story in *The Enlightened Eye* (1991, p. 206).

For Eisner, one of the most critical and difficult tasks of a qualitative researcher is to learn to see what we have learned not to notice in schools (Eisner, 1991). This act of appreciation, the ability to make fine-grained discriminations among complex and subtle qualities, embodies Eisner's conception of educational connoisseurship (Eisner, 1991). To learn to see, to develop a perceptivity based on experience, both past and present, is to be able to notice the fine details of the many dimensions that comprise what Eisner calls the "ecology of schooling"—dimensions such as the curricular, the pedagogical, and the structural that demand the researchers' close attention.

In my own work, I strive to achieve this kind of appreciation for details, subtleties, and nuances. In the study I mention above, for example, I came to see that the high-achieving high school students spent very little time thinking about the content of their courses or delving into projects and assignments. Instead they spent the majority of their time and energy learning to "do school"—honing strategies that would help them achieve high grades and test scores, such as multitasking, forming classroom treaties and alliances, and becoming "squeaky wheels" to contest certain grades and decisions. I had learned to see beyond the students' depictions of success, the facades they created to appear well prepared and on task even when they were not. I was working hard to see what many others had failed to notice, and in the process, I noticed the phenomenon of "doing school."

In *The Enlightened Eye*, Eisner advocates that teachers of qualitative research spend considerable time helping students to develop this kind of perceptivity. One strategy he encourages is for educators to play videotapes of classrooms in real time. Videotapes can convey the complexity of classroom life and allow students to practice the art of classroom observation. Unlike live observations, videotapes can be replayed for close analysis and discussion. In the course I took from Eisner years ago, I still remember the "Popcorn Video." We were assigned to watch a video of an elementary classroom lesson where the teacher and students sat in a circle and popped a kettle of popcorn without a lid. After a few minutes of hearing the sounds of sizzling oil and some faint crackling of kernels, the students were bombarded with loud popping sounds and the sight of freshly popped corn flying all over the classroom. The teacher artfully incorporated math and writing lessons into the experience, as students measured the flight distance of individual kernels and wrote stories about what they saw, smelled, heard, and eventually tasted that day.

I still remember the difficult process of watching the video and striving to see nuances in the lesson. I remember wondering, "What exactly am I supposed to note about this lesson, this teacher, these kids? What am I supposed to see here?"—questions that my own students often ask as well. But after multiple viewings and class discussions, the students get a "feel" for the lesson (Keller, 1983). They learn that much of what we see depends on how we view the world; it depends on our own subjectivity, our past experiences,

our expertise with the subject matter, our research questions, and our varying abilities to make fine-grained distinctions.

   Of course, we must also practice our perceptivity in live classrooms. As
Eisner reminds us: "Nothing replaces being there" (Eisner, 1991). In my own
courses on qualitative research, I design several exercises to help students learn
to see. In one exercise I have students work in small groups to do practice
observations of settings around campus for 15 minutes at a time. The students
choose a spot as a group and are simply told to observe and take notes. After
7 minutes or so, the students are given a lens, such as "teaching" or "gender"
or "equality"—depending on the research interests of the group. For the rest
of the exercise, students are to use this lens to focus their observation. Back in
class, we discuss the differences in the observations of the group members; we
discuss the usefulness of having multiple pairs of eyes observing the same phenomenon; we discuss the pros and cons of doing focused observations with particular lenses, and debate if it is ever possible—or necessary, for that
matter—for a group to agree on what had transpired in the observation. These
exercises with video and live experiences help prepare students for the difficult
job of doing observations in real schools and classrooms. They emphasize the
complexity of seeing educational phenomena and of grappling to make sense
of what has been perceived.

   But, learning to see is only half the battle. Eisner also asserts the
importance of re-presenting what has been perceived in order to educate
others of our findings. He refers to this development of the skills of representation as "educational criticism," or the art of disclosure that gives connoisseurship a public face (Eisner, 1991). Through the act of criticism, the
researcher describes, interprets, evaluates, and forms generalizations about
a phenomenon, so that the reader may participate vicariously in the event
and may gain a deeper understanding of the experience. Eisner reminds us
that "the medium is part of the message," and—a classic Eisnerism—"*that
forms of representation both reveal and conceal*" (Eisner, 1993, 1994, 1997). I first
heard this line in a class on qualitative inquiry where Elliot asked us to try to
describe one of our most memorable meals. As I struggled to convey the
complex tastes of a warm chocolate soufflé, I was reminded that we are limited both in our capacity to capture qualities of experience and in our ability to convey all that we perceive.

   This is, in part, why Eisner makes the case for alternative forms of data
representation (Eisner, 1997). Eisner believes that "there are multiple ways in
which the world can be known: Artists, writers, dancers, as well as scientists,
have important things to tell about the world" (1991, p. 7). And he emphasizes that "educational inquiry will be more complete and informative as we
increase the range of ways we describe, interpret, and evaluate the educational world" (p. 8). In one of his more famous speeches, his presidential
address at the 1993 meeting of the American Educational Research Association, this line of thinking leads Eisner to ask, "What would an entirely new
array of presentational forms for research look like? What might we learn

about a school or a classroom, a teacher or a student, a form of teaching and a style of learning, through an integration of film, text, photo, and poem?" (1993, p. 10). In this same speech he sets the stage for great debate and controversy when he says he is "optimistic" about the possibilities for a novel to be accepted as a dissertation.

Ah, the great novel debate. It has filled conference halls and journal pages for almost 10 years now. Of the kinds of alternative studies Eisner advocates, people, including Eisner himself, have asked, "Yes, but is it research? Is it science? Is it valid? Is it even art?" And the debates continue to rage in journal pages, in Eisner's classrooms, and in my courses on qualitative research as well. This quarter, for example, Elliot Eisner and Ray McDermott are currently teaching a course entitled Emerging Conceptions of Qualitative and Ethnographic Research. In the first part of the course, students learn the concept that "form shapes feeling and insight" (Eisner & McDermott 2001). They translate haikus into collages and read various styles of reporting life in schools, such as a short story, a poem, and a measurement scale. The hope is for students to understand precisely that the medium is part of the message, and that qualitative researchers ought to pay great attention to the forms of their representations.

Similarly, in my classes, we compare very different narrative pieces such as David Cohen's (1990) case of Mrs. Oublier, and Ray McDermott's (1993) "Acquisition of a Child by a Learning Disability." We juxtapose these pieces that rely on diverse stylistic devices with qualitative research articles from journals that read very similarly to traditional quantitative reports, complete with sections on methods, findings, results, and conclusions. We ask, always keeping in mind the intended audiences: What are the strengths and limitations of each piece in light of these decisions on form and structure? What do they reveal? What do they conceal? And how do we as budding researchers make the difficult decisions on how to present our own research in various forms to different audiences and for different purposes? To keep us honest and somewhat humble, we also read Geertz's assertion in *The Interpretation of Cultures:*

> In short, anthropological writings are themselves interpretations, and second and third order ones to boot. …They are, thus, fictions; fictions, in the sense that they are "something made," "something fashioned"—the original meaning of fiction—not that they are false, unfactual, or merely "as if" thought experiments. (1973, p. 15)

I assign this chapter on thick description, and this passage in particular, to convey to students the importance of the fashioning of their work, and to remind them that at best, they are fashioning interpretations—not conveying Truth with a capital *T*. This is a tough point to make. Many students come into my classes with a conception of research as objective and fixed. They assume that the goal of research is the uncovering of truth or the depiction of reality. Geertz reminds us that we can "never get to the bottom"—and that the deeper our analysis, the less complete it is. For Geertz and for Eisner, the goal of qualitative research is not getting to the bottom—uncovering truth; rather, the goal is to bring us in touch with the lives of others and to deepen our understanding of the world around us.

My students struggle with this point. They are not necessarily comfortable with a goal of "understanding." They ask: If this is the goal, then how do we know if we have achieved it? How do we know we have done quality work? The question leads me to another classic Eisner quote—and that is "*the proof is in the pudding.*" Even if you hone your skills of perception, look closely at a phenomenon, reach a plausible and perhaps important conclusion, it won't mean a thing, if your presentation fails to resonate with your audience. Eisner often reminded me to write from my heart with passion and verve, to convey my research on students' experiences in school with a sense of detail and vivid description that would encourage others to see what I saw and to have a sense of empathy for the students' situations. He urged me to conceptualize my findings in ways that would be accessible to others in the field and those outside of the field, and to write in ways that reveal the larger themes that extend beyond the particular students and situations I observed.

I will never forget in my practice dissertation defense (something Dr. Eisner arranges for each of his students) when he asked me, "What would you want someone in the United States Senate to think of your dissertation? What's the point here, Denise, when we get right down to it—the implications for practice and educational policy?"[3] The question captures Dr. Eisner's commitment to the primary function of research as "educational" (Eisner, 1991, p. 121); that is, according to Eisner, good qualitative research, and research in general, ought to increase our perception and deepen our understandings to help improve schools and the process of teaching and learning. According to Eisner, it is through qualitative inquiry that we literally "make sense" (p. 21). As researchers, we have a responsibility to "make sense" of what is going on in our schools and to conduct studies with some ameliorative value, studies that folks in the U.S. Senate and in our local communities would be able to use.

This point brings up sticky issues of generalization and validity in qualitative research. Can we in good faith generalize our findings from an N of 10 or 5 or 1, for that matter? And, to echo my own students, how do we know when or if we have done good work? Eisner and McDermott's syllabus from their Emerging Conceptions of Qualitative and Ethnographic Research course alludes to these issues:

> Can cases generalize? At one level of analysis, everything is different
> with each new glance. Heraclitus had it that no person can step into the
> same river twice, because everything changes between the first and

---

[3] I reconstruct this quotation from memory. The words are not exact, but the sentiment behind the question rings true to Eisner's original intention.

second try. At another level of analysis, everything is relentlessly the same. Step in one river, and you have stepped in them all. And so it seems, at the first level, that nothing we describe carefully and in depth generalizes easily to other circumstances, at least not without distortion, without violence. ... And so it seems also, at the second level of analysis, that everything is so patterned, structured, rule bound, determined that a description of any representative sample tells the full story. Just place your bets. If these are the only two choices, we go with the first; only twentieth century social science has been silly enough to think otherwise. This course seeks a third alternative. No person, said Gregory Bateson, can step into the same river twice, not because everything is changing, but because everything is well organized. ... Vibrant people can produce deadening results because the world is well organized. Live researchers can produce deadening results because the world is well organized. What is the possibility of using the varied ways in which people are alive to figure out how they might change their circumstances? What is the possibility of using the varied ways in which people learn to imagine how they might be better educated to create a better world? What would the problem of generalization look like in such a world? What would educational research look like in such a world? This course is given in the hope that we might answer this question. (Eisner & McDermott, 2001)

I quote the syllabus at length to show the complexity of the thinking exemplified here. McDermott and Eisner don't pretend to have the answers for their students. Instead, they articulate some of the current views in the field and seek a "third alternative." They wonder aloud how to avoid the often "deadening results" of research and invite another conception of educational research to create a better world. They offer the course as a way for themselves and their students to pursue answers to these kinds of sticky questions together in class.

Such is the case with many questions regarding qualitative research. Researchers in the field have yet to come to any agreement on questions of generalizability, validity, appropriate and effective forms of representation, matters of ethics, procedures for data collection and analysis, to name but a few (Denzin & Lincoln, 2000; Patton, 2001; Taylor & Bogdan, 1998). We agree that the research must be rigorous and robust, but we disagree about how to achieve these results. Just as we teach our students of the complexity and ultimate impossibility of fully capturing experience—a moving target— we must recognize the complexity of teaching qualitative research when the field itself is and will continue to be a moving target. What is our responsibility to our students, then? Can we teach methods with any sense of certainty that we are preparing our students well for future work? What is the best way to address these sticky matters without presenting a conception that "anything goes" in the world of qualitative research?

Dr. Eisner said once that he "does not believe in last words, only better conversations," and, in part, it is through these conversations that we build a community of researchers and a basis for teaching the practice of research.

As such, Dr. Eisner works hard to create a close community of qualitative researchers at Stanford University and beyond. When you study with him, in his words, *"you join a special kind of family,"* committed to ongoing conversations about the process of doing research and improving schools. To invite this kind of collegiality, Dr. Eisner regularly asks groups of students over for dinner, hosts weekly gab sessions about current research progress, and holds special meetings where students present tentative findings and analyses and can critique one another's work. Even after graduation, many of us keep in close contact with each other and with our mentor and come together at conferences to continue our conversations and hone our research skills. At the faculty level, Eisner further encourages this kind of collegiality— hosting "Half-Baked Idea" sessions where faculty members can discuss research in progress with their peers. These informal gatherings and relationships with other researchers inform both practice and teaching. Through these live conversations as well as conversations Eisner promotes in journal articles, books, and lectures, we can work together to pursue the complex, unanswered questions in the field. As Denis Phillips (1995), one of Eisner's favorite sparring partners, asserted a few years ago:

> If such things can be quantified, over the past quarter-century or so my colleague Elliot Eisner has produced more excitement, stimulus, discussion, discomfort, and chagrin than perhaps any other academician writing about educational research and curriculum issues. So he must be doing something right. (p. 71)

This chapter and others in this volume attest that Eisner *is* doing something right and something extremely valuable. He helps us learn to see the world anew, to convey these sights in meaningful ways, to expand our conception of knowledge and intelligence, and to contribute to the improvement of education. The conversations he provokes continue to push our thinking and will spur us toward better research and practice in years to come.

REFERENCES

Cohen, D. (1990). A revolution in one classroom: The case of Mrs. Oublier. *Educational Evaluation & Policy Analysis 12*(3), 311–329.

Denzin, N., & Lincoln, Y. (Eds.), (2000). *Handbook of qualitative research* (2nd ed.). Newbury Park: Sage.

Eisner, E. W. (1986). *What high schools are like: Views from the inside*. A report to the Stanford School of Education, Stanford-in-the-Schools Project: Curriculum Panel Report. Stanford, CA: Center for Educational Research at Stanford.

Eisner, E. W. (1991). *The enlightened eye: Qualitative inquiry and the enhancement of educational practice*. New York: Macmillan.

Eisner, E. W. (1993). Forms of understanding and the future of educational research. *Educational Researcher, 22*(7), 5–11.

Eisner, E. W. (1994). *Cognition and curriculum reconsidered* (2nd ed.). New York: Teachers College Press.

Eisner, E. W. (1997). The promise and perils of alternative forms of data representation. *Educational Researcher, 26*(6), 4–10.

Eisner, E. W., & McDermott, R. (2001). Syllabus for Education 321A, Emerging Conceptions of Qualitative and Ethnographic Research, Stanford University.

Geertz, C. (1973). The *interpretation of cultures*. New York: Basic Books.

Intrator, S. (1999). *Spots of time that glow*. Unpublished doctoral dissertation, Stanford University.

Keller, E. (1983). *A feeling for the organism*. New York: Freeman.

Lit, I. (2003). *The bus kids*. Unpublished doctoral dissertation, Stanford University.

McDermott, R. (1993). Acquisition of a child by a learning disability. In S. Chaiklin & J. Lave (Eds.), *Understanding practice* (pp. 269–305). Cambridge: Cambridge University Press.

Patton, M. Q. (2001). *Qualitative research and evaluation methods* (3rd ed.). Newbury Park: Sage.

Phillips, D. C. (1995). Art as research, research as art. *Educational Theory, 45*(1), 71–79.

Pope, D. C. (2001). *"Doing school": How we are creating a generation of stressed out, materialistic, and miseducated students*. New Haven: Yale University Press.

Schweber, S. (1998). *Teaching history, teaching morality: Holocaust education in American public high schools*. Unpublished doctoral dissertation, Stanford University.

Taylor, S., & Bogdan, R. (1998). *Introduction to qualitative research methods* (3rd ed.). New York: John Wiley & Sons.

14

A Vision of Possibilities

D. Jean Clandinin
University of Alberta

I stand in front of my students
telling them about sentence fragments.
I ask them to find the ten fragments
in the twenty-one-sentence paragraph on page forty-five.
They've come from all parts
of the world—Iran, Micronesia, Africa,
Japan, China, even Los Angeles—and they're still
eager to please me. It's less than half
way through the quarter.

They bend over their books and begin.
Hamid's lips move as he follows
the tortuous labyrinth of English syntax.
Yoshie sits erect, perfect in her pale make-up,
legs crossed, quick pulse minutely
jerking her right foot. Tony,
from an island in the South Pacific,
sprawls limp and relaxed in his desk.

The melody floats around and through us
in the room, broken here and there, fragmented
re-started. It feels mid-eastern, but
it could be jazz, or the blues—it could be
anything from anywhere.
I sit down on my desk to wait,
and it hits me from nowhere—a sudden
sweet, almost painful love for my students.

"Never mind," I want to cry out.
"It doesn't matter about fragments.
Finding them or not. Everything's
A fragment and everything's not a fragment.

Listen to the music, how fragmented,
How whole, how we can't separate the music
From the sun falling on its knees on all the greenness,
From this movement, how this moment
Contains all the fragments of yesterday
And everything we'll ever know of tomorrow!"

Instead, I keep a coward's silence.
The music stops abruptly;
they finish their work,
and we go through the right answers,
which is to say
we separate the fragments from the whole.

Algirdas Zolynas (1996)

This fragment from a poem opens up my wonderings about the work of Elliot Eisner. It creates a space, an opening, for me to speak about Eisner's work in at least three ways. Firstly, Eisner is an artist, a painter, someone who paints his knowing with words into our lives as Zolynas does. Secondly, the poem opens a way to talk about educational connoisseurship, a way of thinking about inquiry that is uniquely Eisner's development in qualitative inquiry. Eisner's methodology is how he engages in his educational life—that is, as a connoisseur. And thirdly, the poem speaks of staying silent. Eisner lives a life in the research community where he does not stay silent; he does not "keep a coward's silence." He lives a life of asking researchers to wonder again, to reimagine how we might engage in thoughtful educational inquiry. It is these three topics I want to address as I reflect on Eisner's work in educational inquiry.

NARRATIVE BEGINNINGS AS A VISUAL ARTIST

In my work with Michael Connelly, we have come to understand experience narratively—that is, to see our lives as narrative life compositions. Understanding ourselves and our worlds narratively, our attention is turned to how we are engaged in living, telling, retelling, and reliving our lives within particular social and cultural plotlines (Clandinin & Connelly, 1998, 2000). Thus, as I read Eisner's work, I see it as a narrative expression of what he knows, of who he is. And he is, as he often reminds us in his work, a visual artist. I find references to his narrative beginnings in words such as the following:

All written works, but especially books that attempt to open some new ground, have an autobiographical character. This book is no exception. In it I have attempted to draw on a background in the visual arts that has, as long as I can remember, been an important part of my life. From my earliest recollections as a child in Chicago, art was always important to me and has continued to be a major interest. It is from this interest and professional involvement in art and art education that I have drawn many of the assumptions on which this book is based. The uses of art for dealing with the problems of designing and evaluating educational programs has not been a characteristic of educational inquiry, particularly in the United States. The traditions that we have drawn from are neither aesthetic nor artistic; they are scientific and technological. (Eisner, 1979, p. vii)

In this quotation from a book written almost 25 years ago, Eisner narratively positions himself as artist, as someone who continues to view himself and his landscapes from the place of artist. It is his lived and told story of being an artist and of being involved with art that has both shaped who he is in educational inquiry and how he sees the field of educational inquiry. As he positions himself in his own story, he also positions himself in the field of educational inquiry as coming from a stance of wanting to see educational inquiry in different terms from those commonly accepted. He imagines new traditions of educational inquiry grounded in the aesthetic and artistic, grounded where he narratively grounds himself.

The early training that I received as a graduate student in education virtually ignored the art of teaching, not to mention the possibility of using artistic assumptions to think about the study of education. The exclusive mode for research was a scientific one, although between the lines one could get a sense of the artistry with which my teachers conceptualized and analyzed education problems, with which they interpreted data, and perhaps most of all with which they taught. (Eisner, 1979, p. vii)

Here he speaks narratively of his experience in graduate studies, an experience in which he could find no place for the artistic in the educational research discourse, no place to ground himself, no place to stand. However, as he studied with his graduate instructors, he understood their research and teaching practices as artistic ones. As a narrative inquirer I read him as seeing his teachers' practices through his narrative of experience as a visual artist. This focus on the artistic in the practices of inquirers continues throughout his career as he reconnects to this narrative thread in a recent *Curriculum Inquiry* article (Eisner & Powell, 2002).

Twelve years after the publication of *The Educational Imagination*, when *The Enlightened Eye* (1991) was published, he more forcefully claims his story of himself as a visual artist and names how his narrative beginnings shape what he sees and writes in educational research.

The title of this book, *The Enlightened Eye*, is intimately related to my life as a painter, and my life as a painter is intimately related to the ways in which I think about inquiry. Although I haven't painted for more than a quarter of a century, my engagement in the visual arts from age six onwards and my studies at the School of the Art Institute of Chicago and later at the Illinois Institute of Technology's Institute of Design did much to shape the ways in which I think about seeing and solving problems. If the visual arts teach one lesson, it's that seeing is central to making. Seeing, rather than mere

looking, requires an enlightened eye: this is as true and as important
in understanding and improving education as in creating a painting.
(Eisner, 1991, p. 1)

While the first two excerpts above are taken from *The Educational Imagination* and the third from *The Enlightened Eye*, I could have selected excerpts
from other places (Eisner, 2002), where he also names himself a visual artist
and tells his narrative of experience as a person who is an artist who has
come to live a life in educational research.

This explicit self-telling of his story with its beginnings as an artist is
not the only way that Eisner's life as an artist has shaped his work. In all of
his books he draws heavily on the arts to shape the conceptualizations that
he is developing. For example, in *Cognition and Curriculum* (Eisner, 1982) he
draws on his experiential knowledge as an artist as he writes, "Consider the
task of the painter" (p. 47), and goes on to draw on his knowing of the visual
arts to develop the ideas in the chapter, "Forms of Representation." For
example, he writes:

> In the first place, no painting or musical composition, no dance or poem
> is governed by rules wherein each element and combination among
> them is so specified that, by applying the rules to the performance or
> object made, one can without ambiguity determine if the performance or
> object is correct or incorrect. ... For that achievement, there are no rules.
> (Eisner, 1982, p. 65)

Here he draws on his knowledge of the arts—painting, musical composition,
dance, poetry—to make the point that there are different ways of representing experience, of coming to know. I think about Eisner as I read the fragment
of the Zolynas poem with which I began. I see him in Zolynas's classroom,
seeing what Zolynas sees: the assigned task and the children from home places
from around the world who bend to the assigned task. Zolynas sees himself
as teacher and the children in artistic terms: as joined by a melody, by the
colors of green and yellow, by scene, by metaphor. This is a teacher's story that
Eisner would see in his own and other teachers' practices when he attended to
them as a researcher. Seeing and representing, in artistic terms, the teacher's
and children's experience within the context of an institutional story of school
is what Zolynas offers. While some might reject the educative possibilities for
Zolynas's poem, Eisner offers us ways to see what Zolynas is doing as a way of
representing and knowing experience. Zolynas's poem is a possible starting
point for engaging in the way Eisner sees qualitative inquiry—that is, as
pervading "human life" (Eisner & Peshkin, 1990, p. 367).

RESEARCH AS CONNOISSEURSHIP

Eisner, in his development of qualitative inquiry, particularly connoisseurship
as a way of engaging in research and evaluation, provides a way of seeing and
representing classrooms as Zolynas does. Eisner writes:

> The word *connoisseurship* comes from the Latin *cognoscere*, to know. In
> the visual arts, to know depends upon the ability to see, not merely to
> look. Criticism refers to the process of enabling others to see the quali-
> ties that a work of art possesses. (Eisner, 1991, p. 6)

These words, for me and for many other scholars of qualitative inquiry,
created a space to reconsider how we saw our work as educational inquirers.
Eisner offered the possibility, as did Dewey (1934), of conceptualizing the
experiences of those who live in classrooms as works of art. We could, as we
read Eisner, reconsider experiences in classrooms not as sets of tasks being
done or time spent on task but as works of art. The experiences of those in
classrooms, indeed classrooms themselves, could be apprehended and
understood in inquiry as works of art. This shift to what we could see when
we looked in classrooms resonated with me as I reflected on how Michael
Connelly and I see curriculum:

> It is a very different thing to say the word "curriculum" and then have
> a textbook flash to mind or a teacher lecturing flash to mind or an eval-
> uator measuring intended outcomes flash to mind than it is if the total
> picture of a classroom, preferably one with which you are familiar,
> flashes to mind. ... Your picture is important to understanding this
> book. (Connelly & Clandinin, 1988, p. 7)

Our intention was to enable teachers and others to see curriculum in classrooms as narrative constructions, as children's and teachers' life stories
being composed and lived out within particular stories of school. Eisner's
work drew our attention more particularly to seeing these lives, these classrooms in the making, as works of art. He called us, as educational inquirers,
to see, to apprehend, to know them as such.

   This is no easy undertaking. It is not the way most of us learned to see
our experiences in classrooms, nor is it the taken for granted way of seeing
classrooms in educational inquiry. We needed to learn, with careful study
and with imagination, to see and to know classrooms differently. This
requires restorying of the stories we have learned to live and tell of classrooms in educational research terms (Connelly & Clandinin, 1999). We
needed to step into other ways of seeing, other ways of knowing classrooms.
This restorying is difficult work, for as Eisner reminds us:

> There are no algorithms, no statistical significance tests for qualitative
> studies, that most exquisite of human capacities must come into play:
> judgment. But good judgment is not a mindless activity. It depends
> upon attention to detail, sensitivity to coherence, appreciation of innu-
> endo, and the ability to read subtext as well as text. (Eisner & Peshkin,
> 1990, p. 12)

Learning to see classrooms in this way requires new ways of seeing and
knowing, new skills and new judgments, new stories to live by set within new
plotlines of educational inquiry.

> We need not only to see what we look at, we also need to interpret it.
> This interpretation requires a willingness to listen deeply to what peo-
> ple have to say, to see beyond what they do in order to grasp the mean-
> ings that their doings have for them. (Eisner, 1988, p. 7)

I see this in what Zolynas writes. He sees, listens deeply, to the teacher's
experience. He tells the experience from the position of teacher with a
diverse group of students, students diverse in culture, ability, gender.
But he also situates his story as teacher within the classroom within the
institutional narrative of how to teach English. We see the nestedness of
stories within stories. While he struggles to attend to the children's lives
in the midst of the institutional narrative as he knows it, we feel with
him. We are pulled into the story. Even after we learn other ways of
seeing—that is, seeing life in classrooms as artistic works—we need to
enable others to also see in artistic, aesthetic terms. Zolynas has found a
way to express what he sees and how he interprets a teacher's experience
in an artistic form.

Zolynas's poem shows what Eisner tells—that is, the need to create
forms of representation that enable others to see in artistic ways.

> Our telling is a way of making public what we have come to know.
> (Eisner, 1991, p. 68)

Some might interpret Eisner as calling for us to become artists, to create art
forms, as our forms of representation of educational inquiry. For example,
perhaps he wants all of us to become artists, poets, as Zolynas is. Perhaps
this is his call. However, I do not see his call in this way. I see him asking
educational inquirers to learn other ways of seeing and then to experiment
with forms of representation that are expressive of what we see. Our forms
of representation would be guided by aesthetic principles but would not
themselves be first and foremost works of art. We do not need to become
artists to be educational inquirers. To do so would require rather more
than what most educational inquirers can do. However, Eisner does ask us
to open our minds, to reimagine other forms such as visual forms, narrative forms, poetic forms, and so on that might express our knowing of
what we see in ways that speak to audiences. One of the arguably most
referred to debates at AERA was a debate between Gardner and Eisner in
which they debated the question of whether a dissertation could be a novel.
While Eisner took the side that a dissertation could take a novel's form,
he was not saying that all forms of representation of research must be a
work of art. He suggests, however, that our forms of representation be
guided by a sense of the aesthetic.

At conferences and workshops, I have watched Eisner guide audiences through videotapes taken of classroom teaching, another account
of life in a classroom. As a guide, he engaged in "reading" the video
account in order to help other researchers see the classroom in artistic

terms. In another way, I can imagine Eisner engaging with the Zolynas poem to help researchers see it both as Zolynas's poetic account of his experience and as a representation of what might have been Zolynas's inquiry into his teaching.

Both the seeing and the ways we represent what we see are part of the work of educational inquirers, of connoisseurs. As Eisner wrote:

> In fact, educational connoisseurs attend to everything—almost. That is, they must attend to everything that is relevant either for satisfying a specific educational aim or for illuminating the educational state of affairs in general. (Eisner, 1991, p. 71)

This wide awakeness to everything that we see in classrooms in artistic terms is what Eisner asks us to do as educational inquirers. This is difficult, challenging work and for those of us first educated and continually immersed in other ways of seeing and knowing schools, the challenge is ever present. Even when we learn to engage in the ways Eisner calls us to, we find ourselves caught in other institutional stories of what counts as research, as what really matters in understanding schools. Eisner, however, has not shied away from the conversations where what counts as research is discussed. He makes spaces to engage others in discussing other ways of knowing.

NOT STAYING SILENT

At the end of the Zolynas poem, the teacher chooses a coward's silence, chooses to stay within the institutional plotline of teaching English in that particular high school. It is the comfortable known plotline, one that does not require that he live on the threshold of liminality (Heilbrun, 1999), with a plotline of uncertainty, of not knowing, of composing a new story.

In educational research in the 20th century, Lagemann (1996), an educational historian, tells us that Edward L. Thorndike won and that John Dewey lost. Michael Connelly and I wrote about it this way:

> We see the competition between Dewey and Thorndike as competition between two stories of how to do social science research. The story scripted by Thorndike became so pervasive, so taken for granted, as the only valid story, that we call it a "grand narrative" of social science inquiry. (Clandinin & Connelly, 2000, p. xxv)

The plotline for educational inquiry became one that valued a quantitative plotline for educational research. If Eisner had kept a coward's silence, he could have stayed within the plotline of educational inquiry that was set in Thorndike's work. It was the taken for granted story of research. He did not. Eisner, more than any other educational researcher, created a new plotline, drew on narrative threads in Dewey's work, a plotline that others like myself can follow. As he created these more divergent inquiry paths to include the artistic and aesthetic as ways of engaging in educational inquiry, he did not ignore the dominant narrative of educational inquiry. He worked all his life to ensure there was a conversation with those who knew schools in more quantitative ways.

> In the encounter between quantitative and qualitative researchers, albeit a lopsided one favoring the former, the politics of method emerged that continues robust but unabated to the present time. It involves, as politics always does, power, resources, control, policy making and personnel. (Eisner & Peshkin, 1990, p. 2)

He recognized that in order for more qualitative forms of inquiry, particularly those such as connoisseurship rooted in the arts, to become viable alongside the more dominant form, there would need to be many conversations. As his life progressed he began to see change.

> Not only is the contemporary interaction between quantitative and qualitative researchers less lopsided, it is increasingly less an encounter and more and more an interface. (Eisner & Peshkin, 1990, p. 3)

Knowing that he was calling for a new story of educational inquiry, he became a tireless worker for enabling others to find ways to engage in their work.

RESEARCH FOR EDUCATIVE INTENTIONS

As a former teacher and now teacher educator, curriculum theorist and educational inquirer, I care deeply about what it is that I do. My care is grounded in my concern for the children that Zolynas writes about, for the kinds of spaces that we create in schools as educative spaces for children, for teachers, for parents. It is my passion for holding myself accountable to those who live their lives in schools that guides me in my work. I share this passion with Eisner, who writes:

> The intent of all this, lest we forget, is to enhance what we do in our scholarly pursuits, so that, in turn, we can enhance the educational process. In the end the differences we seek to make are located in schools, those social institutions in which children and adolescents spend so much of their lives. (Eisner & Peshkin, 1990, p. 368)

It is the spaces we create for Zolynas's children—for Hamid, for Tony, for Yoshie—that, for me, matter. What knowing are they composing as they spend time with various subject matter? Does it matter that the kind of space created for them in their classroom separates the whole from the part? What view of subject matter do we teach? What story of school do we create as a milieu for that classroom where they live? Are there ways to compose a curriculum of life that honors multiple, changing, diverse lives in schools and classrooms? It is these questions that burn for me as I enter into schools as an educational inquirer, as I try to see in ways that attend to lives being lived and to see each life as an artistic composition. As Eisner writes:

> The work of art is a process that culminates in a new art form. That art
> form is the re-creation of the individual. (Eisner, 2002, pp. 240–241)

And yet I know, in part because of Eisner and his work, how important it is
to speak not only to teachers but also to other researchers and to policy-
makers about what matters in educational inquiry. Eisner has helped me
realize that if I want to make a difference in the lives of children and teachers and parents, then I need to be in conversation with other researchers
and policy-makers. Even when I tire of trying to be heard, Eisner has
shown me, and others, that we need to stay in the conversation so that we
can continue to move forward. We cannot take the coward's silence.

> We believe the nature of that dialogue will create a legitimate plurality
> of methods that will shed greater light on educational matters than any
> single set of methods can provide. (Eisner & Peshkin, 1990, p. 11)

Eisner's courage lights a path for others like myself to follow.

FUTURE POSSIBILITIES

As I reflect on the path that Eisner has created, is creating, for us as qualitative inquirers, I am drawn to think about the people who walk with me on the
path. I walk alongside children, teachers, parents, researchers, and others in
this life composition. When I enter a school I enter into the midst of many
stories—children's stories, teachers' stories, school stories, stories of school,
stories of subject matter, and so on. I enter in the midst of living and telling
my own stories. As I think about the multiple lives in progress, I want to see
these interwoven lives from multiple vantage points, through the eyes of
multiple connoisseurs. I wonder about the possibility of seeing through the
eyes of all participants in more relational ways. I wonder about how to negotiate relationships in which the seeing and knowing of multiple people, multiple connoisseurs, of diverse lives in school are honored. Each of us have
different stories to tell of our lives in school and surely we can imagine ways
to both see and represent from the midst of multiple stories lived and told
from multiple positions on the landscape of schools. This honoring of multiplicity is a challenge as inquirers step into the liminality beyond the path that
Eisner has created for us.

Ethical tensions and dilemmas in qualitative inquiry also seem apparent
in new shades as we step off the path for more relational forms of inquiry. We
need to imagine an openness to a continual renegotiation of research relationships among all participants so that questions are always being asked and
re-asked, shaped and reshaped. Ethical issues around narrative smoothing,
narrative secrets and silences, are issues to reimagine in these research relationships where we honor multiple connoisseurs of lives in school. Issues of
confidentiality and of opting out also emerge in new ways within these more
relational forms of research.

It is in how we represent this relational work that I also note significant differences. It is not one person whose judgment, whose life, is at issue. Rather it is the lives, the judgment, of a group of individuals who are trying to work together to represent their experiences in telling ways, ways that offer each participant a space in which to tell his or her story and to have themselves and his or her work represented. As we step off the path Eisner has created, reimagining how to engage in ways that honor the relational, the context dependent, the multiplicity of diverse lives in school is a challenge. Eisner offers us hope as he writes:

> My hope is that the leads offered in the foregoing chapters are sufficiently attractive to encourage at least some of us to chart the waters of these new seas and to see what the winds are like. (Eisner, 1991, p. 246)

And for those of us who take up Eisner's work, we need to continue to create a path that takes us beyond the charts that Eisner has left for us.

REFERENCES

Clandinin, D. J., & Connelly, F. M. (1998). Asking questions about telling stories. In C. Kridel (Ed.), *Writing educational biography: Explorations in qualitative research* (pp. 245–253). New York: Garland.

Clandinin, D. J., & Connelly, F. M. (2000). *Narrative inquiry: Experience and story in qualitative research*. San Francisco: Jossey-Bass.

Connelly, F. M., & Clandinin, D. J. (1988). *Teachers as curriculum planners: Narratives of experience*. New York: Teachers College Press.

Connelly, F. M., & Clandinin, D. J. (1999). *Shaping a professional identity: Stories of educational practice*. New York: Teachers College Press.

Dewey, J. (1934). *Art as experience*. New York: Minton.

Eisner, E. W. (1979). *The educational imagination: On the design and evaluation of school programs*. New York: Macmillan.

Eisner, E. W. (1982). *Cognition and curriculum: A basis for deciding what to teach*. New York: Longman.

Eisner, E. W. (1988). Foreword. In F. M. Connelly & D. J. Clandinin, *Teachers as curriculum planners: Narratives of experience* (pp. ix–xi). New York: Teachers College Press.

Eisner, E. W. (1991). *The enlightened eye: Qualitative inquiry and the enhancement of educational practice*. New York: Macmillan.

Eisner, E. W. (2002). *The arts and the creation of mind*. New Haven: Yale University Press.

Eisner, E. W., & Peshkin, A. (1990). *Qualitative inquiry in education: The continuing debate*. New York: Teachers College Press.

Eisner, E. W., & Powell, K. (2002). Art in science? *Curriculum Inquiry, 32*(2), 131–159.

Heilbrun, C. (1999). *Women's lives: The view from the threshold*. Toronto: University of Toronto Press.

Lagemann, E. C. (1996). *Contested terrain: A history of education research in the United States, 1890–1990*. Chicago: Spencer Foundation.

Zolynas, A. (1996). Love in the classroom. In C. Milosz (Ed.), *A book of luminous things* (pp. 193–194). New York: Harcourt Brace.

PART 4

School Reform, Teaching, and Teacher Education

15

Preserving the Beauty of Learning

The Qualities of an Aesthetic Curriculum

Sam M. Intrator
Smith College

*D*eep in the heart of Texas, a friend taught Shakespeare to fifth graders in a gritty inner-city school. His students read, discussed, and enacted great scenes from the plays, and he spoke of these projects as the heart of his teaching because it was "an amazing, joyful experience for the kids, the audience, and myself." After his school became designated a "low-performing" school because of low test scores on the Texas Assessment of Knowledge and Skills (TAKS), he was pressured to dump the theatre arts focus of his language arts curriculum and install a curriculum relentlessly and narrowly focused on preparing students to take the exam. He lamented in his teaching journal that "the school's heart has been given over solely to the TAKS, and the test is heartless. Its soil is too shallow to support the root of dreams. We are starved for beauty here, for the beauty of learning, the joy of it" (Stromberger, 2002, p. 164).

My friend's demoralizing experience with Texas's educational reform agenda has become an alarmingly familiar and bitterly ironic occurrence for many of our public school teachers. Ironic because many of our teachers believe that the cherished gifts they bring to their work—their creative discretion, their ability to forge caring relationships with youth, and their ability to conjure up artistic approaches to the disciplines they teach—have little worth if these gifts don't translate into unambiguous test score gains.

Importantly, teachers like my friend do not discount the importance of teaching basic and essential skills, but they aspire to more. They long to ignite their students' imagination, excite their passion for learning, and deepen their experience of living. They value imagination, critical dialogue, and other habits of thinking that can't be readily measured or calculated by the exams that now count for so much in our schools. Resisting ideologies that would denude humane approaches to teaching, learning, and thinking is one of Elliot Eisner's most compelling contributions to American education. He warns us that, "the durable outcomes of schooling are not to be found in short-term, instrumental tasks. Such outcomes must penetrate deeply. When school programs neglect attention to the aesthetics of shaping form, they neglect the very satisfactions that reside at the core of education" (Eisner, 1984, p. 35). In the spirit of Eisner's argument, this chapter contends that schools should be places where the quality of experience undergone by students and teachers matter. It advocates for school curricula that emphasize the aesthetic by cultivating delight and developing receptivity to experiences that expand our consciousness.

Importantly, the *aesthetic* curriculum is not the sole province of the arts, but the province of all human experience. It is a vision of teaching and learning devoted to refining our senses so that our interactions with our qualitative world yield cognitive and aesthetic return. The aesthetic curriculum strives, across disciplinary boundaries and age groups, to engage students in educational activities that provoke them to experience a state of keen, focused attention, described by Maxine Greene as "wide-awake" (Greene, 1978). The aesthetic curriculum can be more fully understood by briefly considering its two less-compelling siblings.

The *anesthetic* curriculum refers to a curriculum delivered so erratically or mechanically that it deters students from ever securing insight or producing artfully made work. The anesthetized curriculum never invites experiences that unfold and run a course to fulfillment. Instead, students and teacher will careen from one disconnected, fragmented activity to the next or proceed so monotonously that all vigor will be siphoned off from the transaction. A student whom I interviewed for a study evoked the deadening spirit of a classroom where the teacher adhered to the history textbook as if it were a script. He said, "Sitting in a bad class is like being in the car with your parents on a vacation. It numbs you."

A closely related form is the *monoaesthetic* curriculum, which refers to those experiences that limit our perceptive faculties by focusing relentlessly on developing only narrow modes of knowing and representing the world. One of the student teachers I have worked with captured the relentless and singular rhythm of a monoaesthetic curriculum after observing her supervising teacher for a month: "All we do in our class is practice the MCAS essay [MCAS is the Massachusetts standardized high-stakes exam]. After every story we read, this teacher gives the students an essay modeled on an MCAS question. That's all we do: practice the winning formula. We don't write autobiography, we don't write poetry, we don't write personal essays." When I asked the student why she thought the teacher didn't provide opportunity to explore other facets of writing than the MCAS-essay, the student told me, "The teacher says that stuff is extra. You can do that writing when you get this other stuff down."

In other words, the art form of Seamus Heaney, Maya Angelou, and Pat Conroy has been reconstituted as formula-driven so that students can perform it on an exam. The aesthetic features of writing that include playing with words, trying out different organizational formats, taking risks with style, and experimenting with images are not only discouraged but also seen as potentially damaging to writing that counts.

The rest of this chapter seeks to explore an alternative to this calculating and efficient conception of what students should be doing and learning in the educational setting by describing the dimensions and characteristics of an aesthetic curriculum. I describe four features of an aesthetic curriculum and illustrate them in action by using ethnographic classroom data from a yearlong research project that I conducted in an 11th grade English class taught by a veteran teacher named Mr. Quinn. The class I researched was at Stanton High School, a large, comprehensive high school located near a large West Coast city. Mr. Quinn's junior English class was ethnically diverse (60% white and 40% nonwhite) and possessed a range of abilities (17 read below grade level and 15 above grade level). During a school year, I observed 124 classes and collected a vast archive of classroom data. The lesson I highlight as possessing attributes of the aesthetic curriculum was designed by the teacher to introduce students to John Steinbeck's use of description in his writing.

THE FEATURES OF THE AESTHETIC CURRICULUM

Mr. Quinn began class by telling students, "We're going to continue today on our quest to understand how poets, artists, and scientists experience and remake the world, but instead of doing it here amidst the desks and fluorescent lights, we're going out to the baseball field, and once we get there we will engage as if we were Steinbeck. Let me reread the passage I want us to be thinking about":

> Cannery Row in Monterey in California is a poem, a stink, a grating noise, a quality of light, a tone, a habit, nostalgia, and a dream. Cannery Row is the gathered and scattered, tin and iron and rust and splintered wood, chipped pavement and weedy lots and junk heaps, sardine canneries of corrugated iron, honky tonks, restaurants and whore house, and little crowded groceries and laboratories and flophouses. (Steinbeck, 1945, p. 1)

After reading the passage, Mr. Quinn stopped, put his arms on his hips, and surveyed his students. They sat there looking both bemused and curious as to what Mr. Quinn would have them do. He continued:

> Keeping this quote in mind, what I'd like for you to do is find a place anywhere on the grass in the baseball field or Washington Park and sit there for the period and write about what you see in your immediate domain. The purpose is to think like Steinbeck. What biologists, writers and artists do is observe. They simply look at the world really closely. They look very, very carefully. Sometimes we think we see, *but we don't*.

Much happened for students during this period in the park that embodied the features that comprise what I call the aesthetic curriculum.

Feature One: An Aesthetic Curriculum Teaches Students to Make Meanings of Their Worlds by Engaging Their Senses

Our senses serve as the primary means through which we know the qualities of our world. We, as Eisner has repeatedly argued, can only secure meaning from the world when our senses successfully get in touch with the qualities of our environment. We expand the depth and breadth of our experience when we learn not just to look and listen, but also to taste, smell, and feel. When we operate the full network of our sensory apparatus and engage the world with our visual, gustatory, olfactory, tactile, and auditory systems, the range of meanings we can secure is substantially deepened and expanded (Eisner, 1984).

In some manner, the core of the aesthetic curriculum involves teaching us to expand the prowess of our senses. Senses, developed to be more acute, allow us to cast a wider, more nuanced net into the world. For Eisner, this is no small accomplishment. He writes: "Hearing … is an achievement, not simply a task. To *hear* the music, to *see* the landscape, to *feel* the qualities in a bolt of cloth, are not automatic consequences of maturation. Learning how to experience such qualities means learning how to use your mind" (Eisner, 1998, p. 118).

During this lesson, Mr. Quinn worked hard to both instruct and model for students a variety of approaches they could experiment with that would allow them to deploy their senses with intelligence. He told them: "Notice what Steinbeck observed, 'a grating noise, a quality of light, corrugated iron, honky tonks.' Steinbeck tunes in with all his senses. He knew Monterey with more than his eyes." Later in the instructions, before they headed out to the park, he told them, "Dig down between the grass. Peer down and see, hear, smell what kinds of things can be found there." The instructions conveyed an important belief: Students' perceptual acuity is not solely biological or hard-wired. Aesthetic capacity is not merely a gift or an inborn talent, but a habit, a skill, or a mode of using our minds that can become more refined when supported by careful teaching.

Once the information is procured, making sense of what we have collected—whether it is a sentence of prose, a melody, or the texture of a sculpture—is itself an act of discrimination, a fine-grained, sensitively nuanced, selective process that requires a fully engaged mind. Thus, when Mr. Quinn's students run their fingers through the grass in an attempt to secure the character of insight constructed by Steinbeck, their engagement in sensory experience represents an achievement of mind that yields both insight and emotion.

Learning how to use our minds and expand the acuity of our senses represents a primary agenda of the aesthetic curriculum. Done well, it provides students with an increasingly refined ability to experience the qualities of the world we inhabit.

Feature Two: Engagement in the Aesthetic Curriculum Provokes Imaginative Thought and Enables Us to Secure Meaning Beyond the Merely Literal

To be imaginative means to fashion thoughts and feelings in our minds. It means that we take what we know as real and literal and invent concepts of what ought to be or what might be. Imagination liberates us to think beyond what is merely prosaic and eventual and it enlarges, as Maxine Green tells us, our "sense of the possible" (Greene, 1995, p. 38).

As I watched Mr. Quinn's students settle down in the outfield, they exhibited a serene focus that I had only witnessed a few times during my year with them. Interviewing them afterward, they described their delight in engaging in an experience where their literal understandings became a launching pad for thinking about what will be and what should be in their lives and world. Tony told me that the experience was kind of weird:

> Sort of like staring at one of the fuzzy designs at the mall that you have to keep on looking at before it suddenly clears up. At first, I looked at the grass and saw grass. Big shit. I looked again and saw grass and then I started to see different things, hear different things, and then smell things that I never noticed before. I noticed like the grass blade gets thicker towards the bottom and then I started to see these weeds, which stood out like loners in the school. Sometimes I feel like that here at Stanton, which is why I'm transferring next year.

Several things happened for Tony. His initial account of "looking at the grass" and "seeing grass" resulted in merely cataloging the qualities of the empirical world; however, the experience became more significant when he moved through the literal and into a more expansive and imaginative reflection. When Tony linked the weeds to loners at school and considered the implications of loneliness as the impetus for his impending transfer, he was actively making projections and securing insight into his life. His imagination was robustly engaged.

A curriculum rich with opportunity for students to practice, engage with, and experience the insights that come when we wrest meaning from the environment is an aesthetic curriculum.

Feature Three: In the Aesthetic Curriculum, Students Learn to Secure Meaning From a Variety of Media and Forms

William Blake's great line, "to see a world in a grain of sand and heaven in a wild flower," evokes the central idea of this principle (Blake, 1946, p. 150). In the aesthetic curriculum, students become practiced in reading a broad array of forms, such as poetry, film, novel, expository text, visual art, sculpture, and the natural world.

In their study of *Cannery Row*, Mr. Quinn's students encountered a broad array of media. They read a plot of grass, first as a biologist concerned with clinical observation, then as a writer-poet. They read the novel *Cannery Row*. They read and analyzed Philip Levine's poem, "Work," in regard to how it could illuminate the characters of the "Row." They listened to and critiqued the reflective writings they had each produced about their experience on the grass. They viewed and discussed visual images of Monterey and studied photographs of the Depression.

Each form encountered possesses different qualities and syntactical features that express unique nuances and features of meaning. Eisner describes forms of representation as the varied modes that humans use to make public what they understand about their experience. "They are the vehicles through which concepts that are visual, auditory, kinesthetic, olfactory, gustatory, and tactile are given public status. This public status might take the form of words, pictures, music, mathematics, dance and the like" (Eisner, 1994a, p. 39). Each form of representation expresses unique meanings, and by providing opportunity for students to encounter multiple forms of representation, Mr. Quinn enlarged the channels through which students could secure understanding about the world they studied.

Students were reading *Cannery Row* in the context of a larger unit investigating the history of California. As I watched them encounter a broad array of "texts" that included visual art, expository essays, photographs, music, or sculpture, it was apparent that significant meanings were secured from each form of "text" studied. "I'm not really a reader," said one student. "But when I saw the photographs [Dorothea Lange] of the Depression I could see what Mack and the boys looked like sitting there in the vacant lot amidst all the junk like the old boilers." Another student described how reading about the history of Monterey and the fishing economy helped "give me an understanding of how the characters in the book faced so few economic options." Mr. Quinn devised opportunities for students to access the special contributions that distinct forms of representation offer. They learned to "read" art, poetry, music, film, and other forms and in doing so expanded their cognitive capacity to intelligently "read" the multiple forms of "text" humans use to express what they know.

Feature Four: Aesthetic Curricula Broaden the Modes of Representation We Have Available to Make Public What We Know

A central challenge of living a full and complete life hinges on our capacity to represent our experiences to others. Schools should be places that enlarge our capacity to share what we know by providing opportunities to learn about and practice a wide variety of representative forms. We can live a fuller, more robust life if we can harness the powers of writing, speaking, painting, poetry, and dance to express to others what we know. Eisner tells us that "learning how to represent what we have experienced is a primary means for contributing to the expanded consciousness of others. Thus, a culture or a school program that dulls the senses by neglect or disrespect thwarts the development of human aptitude and undermines the possibilities of the human mind" (Eisner, 1994b, p. 297). One of Mr. Quinn's students offered this reflection on her experience:

> We went out to the baseball field and everyone was sitting on the grass. I chose to sit on the dirt or on the border of the dirt and the grass and I wrote "Moving across the middle of the plot was a six-legged insect." It sounded like a lab report. But then I asked myself: How would John Steinbeck see this? What would he write? I had written *pretend-poetry* before in middle school, you know, like "Roses red, crimson," but I had never had written any *poetry* before. But then I wrote this:
>
>> Each pebble, each stone
>> With a different story to tell
>> Some mud red, others as pale as bone
>> The entire ground glows
>> Underneath the soil gets darker and moist
>> Like cutting into an unripe orange

Lilia's poem ended up being very much a novice's effort, but what was significant was the process. As she looked at that space, she realized that her conventional modes of representation were not adequate to convey what she was thinking. Months after that lesson, she told me, "I learned something really important that day. I mean I learned I could write poetry and say things poetically, but I also learned how to look at things differently." Mr. Quinn's curriculum invited Lilia to treat what she knew in a different medium. Her attempt to express herself poetically provided opportunity for her to discover for herself one of Eisner's most cherished principles: "Each form of representation has a special contribution to make to human experience. We see this daily in our own culture: we use different forms to say different things" (Eisner, 1994a, p. 19).

I began this chapter by sharing my friend's lament at the loss of beauty and joy. What a terrible and perverse prospect. We must resist forces that would suffocate curiosity, creativity, imagination, and delight. These qualities, in the end, give meaning and excitement to our lives. Cultivating these qualities as habits of our interaction with our world and refining them through practice is the heart of an aesthetic curriculum.

REFERENCES

Blake, W. (1946). "Auguries of Innocence." *The Portable Blake* (pp. 150–154). Selected and arranged by Alfred Kazin. New York: The Viking Press.

Eisner, E. W. (1984). Aesthetic modes of knowing. In E. W. Eisner (Ed.), *Learning and teaching the ways of knowing* (pp. 23–36). Chicago: University of Chicago Press.

Eisner, E. W. (1994a). *Cognition and curriculum reconsidered* (2nd ed.). New York: Teachers College Press.

Eisner, E. W. (1994b). *The educational imagination: On the design and evaluation of school programs*. New York: Macmillan.

Eisner, E. W. (1998). *The kind of schools we need: Personal essays*. Portsmouth, NH: Heinemann.

Greene, M. (1978). *Landscapes of learning*. New York: Teachers College Press.

Greene, M. (1995). *Releasing the imagination: Essays on education, the arts, and social change*. San Francisco: Jossey-Bass.

Steinbeck, J. (1945). *Cannery Row*. New York: Viking Press.

Stromberger, C. (2002). So sweet it made me jingled: Offering my own truth within the system. In S. M. Intrator (Ed.), *Stories of the courage to teach: Honoring the teacher's heart*. San Francisco: Jossey-Bass.

16

School Reform and Social Studies Possibilities

Stephen J. Thornton
Teachers College, Columbia University

$\mathscr{P}$erhaps Theodore Sizer best articulated what school reform is about when he spoke of the "dilemma of the American high school" (Sizer, 1984). He was pointing to the disjunction between school institutional organization and curricular-instructional arrangements. Reform of one part of this dualism is insoluble without reform in the other.

In the 20 years since Sizer wrote of this dilemma, school reform has been in high gear. Significantly, however, reformers appear to have delved more deeply into the organization side of the dualism. In contrast, the most central educational question—what should be taught in schools?—suffered relative neglect. Elliot Eisner attributes this neglect to an avoidance of the normative character of curriculum and exaggerated faith in reforming teaching as an alternative to curriculum reform (Eisner, 1997).

But institutional change, for better or worse, has a normative dimension. It is never value-neutral. Similarly, the separate theoretical consideration of teaching and what schools teach creates a disjunction in the union of curriculum and instruction in practice. For example, although the last two decades have witnessed renewed interest in the role of subject matter in teaching by educational researchers such as Lee Shulman, the body of work produced has frequently neglected comprehensive consideration of curricular purposes. A conception of education that stops at what scholars consider the "structure of the disciplines" is too narrow a perspective, as it fails to adequately consider the purposes of general education.

In this chapter, I consider the role of the curriculum in reformed schools. Rather than examine the means (institutional change) by which school reform is accomplished, I look at what kind of school program we would want once school reform had "succeeded." In other words, supposing we had "the kind of schools we need" (Eisner, 1998), what would schools look like from the inside? My answer to this question is necessarily limited by

183

available space so I restrict my answer to one school subject, social studies. If we have to confine our discussion to one subject, arguably the breadth of the social studies curriculum makes it as good a proxy of the entire curriculum as we are likely to find.

"Social studies" is not only broad but also variously understood in education. I mean by it the selection and arrangement of subject matter for instructional purposes drawn from history, geography, and the social sciences, as well as material less beholden to the traditional academic subjects such as current events, service learning, ethnic or gender studies, and environmental or global education. Although creating or finding the "correct" aim for social studies has long constituted a cottage industry in both the United States (Thornton, 1994) and other countries such as England (Marsden, 2001), resolving the definitional dispute is not my concern here. Suffice it to say that I adopt an aim comprehensive enough to hold wide appeal to educators: "to enrich and liberate the more direct and personal contacts of life by furnishing their context, their background and outlook" (Dewey, 1966, p. 211).

WHAT CAN EISNER CONTRIBUTE TO SOCIAL STUDIES?

Social studies is not, of course, what Eisner is particularly known for. Since boyhood, he has been drawn to the arts. In high school he found his academic salvation in a curriculum that offered students significant choices, freeing them to pursue their aptitudes and interests. Art courses were to prove his entry point into the broader life of the mind. He went on to major in art and education in college. While in college, however, he took a job teaching African-American boys in the neighborhood in which he grew up on the west side of Chicago. This experience was to shift his focus from art to art education (Uhrmacher, 2001).

His fascination with the arts helped shape his perspective on and conception of educational theory, research, and practice more generally, a position historically and presently uncommon. Eisner could no longer conceive of the arts and education as separate entities. In this vein, he frequently invokes an admonition by Sir Herbert Read: The aim of education is the preparation of artists (Read, 1943). Read was not referring to painters, musicians, and the like. Rather, he meant individuals who have developed the ideas, the sensibilities, the skills, and imagination to create work that is well proportioned, skillfully executed, and imaginative, regardless of the domain in which one works (Eisner, 2002).

I should confess at the outset that I have, in some respects, made a parallel educational journey to Eisner's. In school and college, I loved the social studies, especially history and geography. Like Eisner, however, becoming an educator changed my perspective on history and geography—I found I could no longer think about them solely as an historian or geographer might. Rather, I gradually found my view of the social studies qua academic subjects fusing with conceptions of educational purpose and organization. This outlook, which blends subject matter and method, made writing this chapter a labor of pleasure.

Returning to Eisner, what can his curricular thought contribute to social studies? When he has turned his mind to social studies, Eisner has characteristically stressed how the arts, music, and literature serve as ways to enlarge human understanding. Some scholars have studied how these ways of "seeing" can make social studies vivid (Epstein, 1994). Seeing is an accomplishment—one can look but fail to see—and is not an automatic product of human maturation. It must be learned. For example, a history teacher could have students look at a Romanesque church and lead them to see the way in which its forms represent a worldview and a way of life (Eisner, 1991).

Seeing turns out to be of crucial importance for social studies education. All seeing is, to an extent, context dependent. While related, seeing a Romanesque church is different from seeing a glacial cirque or a madding crowd. Educating for cultural pluralism, a central social studies aim, requires differential seeing of the world. Monocular vision fails to see cultural pluralism. The social studies curriculum must, in other words, incorporate cognitive pluralism if we are serious about educating for cultural pluralism.

Cognitive pluralism, of course, has not been the dominant view of cognition in the American curriculum. Rather, evaluation of intelligence has been largely restricted to verbal and mathematical reasoning. This drastically understates the range of human cognitive capabilities—the multiple and interconnected ways by which human beings come to know and the forms by which they can express what they have come to know. Policies such as content standards and high-stakes testing have been antithetical to cognitive pluralism. Rather than cognitive pluralism constituting a basis for deciding what and how to teach, dominant policies have nurtured an unbalanced curriculum (Eisner, 1982).

In addition to cognitive pluralism, Eisner's guiding light in education appears to have been progressivism, especially as exemplified by John Dewey. That is to say his view of an ideal curriculum includes it being problem-centered, individualized, and in significant measure, teacher-created. As may be apparent, these ideas fit comfortably with cognitive pluralism. Experience also shows that constructing a sound curriculum, even in good schools, is more of an ongoing journey that serves as a source of professional growth than a final destination that is eventually reached (King, 1991; Lightfoot, 1983). Reformed schools should not be confused with perfect schools. Thus, Eisner never seems to have been afraid, rightly to my mind, to acknowledge that sometimes a half-loaf is better than none. This perspective often manifests itself in generous rather than stingy appraisals of educators working in imperfect circumstances.

Thus far I have suggested that if schools were reformed, then Eisner's curricular thought, heavily influenced by the arts, could make a particularly valuable contribution to the enhancement of social studies programs. In the remainder of this chapter, I explore what such an enhanced curriculum might look like. More specifically, I apply two of the key principles that Eisner considers essential to a sound curriculum to contemporary social studies curriculum. Finally, I suggest that even reformed schools are unlikely to develop exemplary social studies programs unless teacher education is also overhauled.

SOCIAL STUDIES POSSIBILITIES

The quality of American education is currently gauged by shallow and crude benchmarks of how well schools are doing, most particularly test scores. School reform demands more adequate criteria to determine how well schools are doing. What a child *can* do is not necessarily the same as what he or she typically *will* do. It's what students do with what they learn when they can do what they want to do that is the real measure of educational achievement (Eisner, 2001). This requires rethinking the models of mind, method, and knowledge that now dominate in American schools (Eisner, 1998).

But once these new models are embraced, what would the social studies curriculum actually look like? Although I cannot give a comprehensive answer to this question here, I outline two important elements of such a curriculum. Rather than confine my discussion to abstractions, I describe approaches to actual subject matter and instructional arrangements.

More specifically, I look at ways of treating the social studies concept of "internationalism," the principle of cooperation among nations for the promotion of their common good. Internationalism should be an idea with wide applicability, as it has been, in one form or another, a staple of the curriculum in countries around the globe for generations. These nations include Australia, Canada, England, and Japan as well as the United States.

Internationalism appears in standard American social studies courses such as global history, economics, world geography or world cultures, and perhaps civics or government in both elementary and secondary schools. It also appears in special programs that are sometimes part of the curriculum, such as "Model United Nations" or "International Education and Resource Network" (iEarn). (In the latter, schoolchildren in different nations are connected by technology to engage in collaborative projects on topics of shared concern, such as the environment and world peace.) Finally, the topic of internationalism will surely arise sometimes in discussions of current events.

Let us now turn to the first application of Eisner's principles to contemporary social studies.

THE POWER OF IDEAS: IN ART

A first principle concerns the role of ideas in the social studies curriculum (hereafter, *curriculum*, unless otherwise stated). What is the intellectual significance of the ideas that youngsters encounter? Do the ideas go someplace

(Eisner, 2001)? While this is a central question in any school subject, it may have special meaning in social studies. It is frequently claimed that social studies overly relies on the transmission of information at the expense of critical thinking (Thornton, 2001d).

Perhaps the most revealing glimpse of what role Eisner believes ideas should play is a curriculum he and a team developed at Stanford University in the 1960s. It is an art curriculum for elementary schools called the Kettering Project, which included curriculum materials for a more than two-year sequence of elementary school art instruction (Eisner, 1985).

The Kettering Project grew out of concern that art education was being neglected in the national curriculum reform movement then under way. Eisner was concerned that neglect was likely to marginalize further the role of art in elementary school programs. Art was already a low-status subject, receiving scant attention relative to subjects widely perceived as more "academic," such as mathematics and language arts. Ironically, the lack of attention to art reinforced the perception that it did not warrant a basic role in the curriculum.

The low status of art education posed additional challenges for curriculum reform. Elementary school teachers were accustomed to the relegation of art to the margins of the curriculum. Art was taught, if at all, in the time left over from the basic subjects. Compounding this grim picture was that relatively few elementary teachers had substantial preparation in the teaching of art and itinerant art specialists were scarce at the elementary level.

Given this state, teacher beliefs, and teacher preparation, the Kettering Project was developed to be user-friendly. Seven units were selected for the development of lessons. Using these units, the developers produced 67 lessons and about 700 specifically designed instructional materials that accompanied the lessons in the units. The materials developed and the process of teachers working with them were intended to both encourage art instruction and serve as a form of in-service education.

Although it may be considered strange from many perspectives, providing to teachers a curriculum they will be expected to implement is relatively uncommon. Such work is undervalued relative to one-shot workshops, which seldom appear to significantly improve practice. In-service education devoted to curriculum implementation, however, may be the most valid form of teacher education since all teachers serve as curricular-instructional gatekeepers (Thornton, 1991). As gatekeepers, teachers make the day-to-day decisions concerning both the subject matter and the experiences to which students have access and the nature of that subject matter and those experiences.

The character and arrangement of the ideas in the Kettering Project reveal Eisner's curriculum ideology. Three characteristics of the curriculum package seem particularly noteworthy. First, it was designed to be a comprehensive curriculum incorporating what were considered to be the three main domains of art education: the productive (helping children acquire necessary skills for making art), the critical (for seeing and responding to art), and the historical (concerning the cultural context within which the art was made). Second, the curriculum was organized so that learning activities were sequential, because existing elementary school art programs often failed to provide for continuity of subject matter. Third, a wide variety of visual resources were provided that were intended to be directly related to tasks and objectives that appeared in the written curriculum guide.

A concept from psychology was the curriculum's pivot: "visual differentiation." The learning activities were sequentially designed to allow students to refine gradually their abilities to see visual images. Thus, theory concerning a desirable educational goal—visual differentiation—and how it can be effectively learned provided direction to the practical work of curriculum making.

THE POWER OF IDEAS: IN SOCIAL STUDIES

At the same time that the Kettering Project was attempting to redress the balance in elementary curriculum between art and "academic" subjects, dozens of social studies projects were completed or nearing completion (Risinger & Radz, 1971). These projects, which became collectively known as the New Social Studies, were mostly in the social sciences as distinct from history and geography. As with the Kettering Project, New Social Studies developers were mostly interested in ideas and skills rather than fixed bodies of scholarly information (Price, Hickman, & Smith, 1965).

For all the time, energy, and educational imagination expended on the New Social Studies projects, few of them found a lasting home in most American classrooms. The materials developers appear to have misgauged how their products would be received by the average classroom teacher (Goetz, 1994). In part, this may be because the materials broke with established curricular-instructional arrangements. Further, developers' estimations, conscious or unconscious, of how school organization and instructional arrangements might be managed so that teachers could function optimally often proved too optimistic. As some observers concluded in examining how educational change occurs, teacher participation in curriculum development may need to be considered a variable. Rather than regarding it as some fixed right or duty, this kind of teacher participation may depend on the talent and enthusiasm of individual teachers and the ability of administrators to capitalize on this competence (Noddings, 1979).

Whatever stumbling blocks were encountered, the New Social Studies projects still have something to offer to today's educators (Noddings, 2001). Of course, much of the content of the projects is now dated, but many of the educational ideas themselves are still wonderful. Although their imaginative ideas may have had disappointing impact on teaching practices, the reformers were surely right that existing emphases upon the transmission of information had long had a stifling effect on critical thinking in social studies.

Then and now, a great deal of time and effort goes into arguing whether the curriculum should contain more of topic X and less of (or even eliminating) topic Y. These debates are often resolved by adding X *and* retaining Y unchanged. The predictable result is an ever more crowded curriculum in which the treatment of all topics suffers from superficiality. Instruction becomes a race through too much material and students may be turned off from engagement with all of the material. Advocates for both X and Y too infrequently ask, Does it really matter what the curriculum contains if students aren't learning it (Thornton, 2001c)?

Harold Rugg (1939) long ago recognized the connections among superficial coverage, student disengagement, and the failure to treat significant social studies concepts in meaningful depth. He noted that, with more than 70 countries in the world—there are now about three times as many—time did not permit meaningful study of them all. But, in any case, exhaustive coverage ought not be the first curricular priority. Rather, we should first select and arrange major explanatory concepts for social education purposes. This selection could then guide which countries in South America, for example, should be included in the curriculum (Rugg, 1939). Unless we wish to perpetuate superficial coverage that fails to engage young people and leads to the disappointing educational outcomes so often (and so long) lamented, some version of what Rugg called "understanding units" is just as necessary today as it was in his time (Thornton, 2001b).

To their credit, the New Social Studies reformers, as did Rugg, recognized the same problematic pairing of coverage and lifeless instruction. They stressed significant concepts and inquiry skills. Critical thinking, not mere memorization of information, was a central aim. Of course, this aim contrasts with today's lists of information purporting to deliver "cultural literacy" or raising "standards" through microspecification of information. The reformers participated in an important tradition. The philosopher Alfred North Whitehead advised: "Let the main ideas which are introduced into a child's education be few and important, and let them be thrown into every possible combination" (Whitehead, 1967, p. 2). What might this approach look like today teaching internationalism?

Internationalism arises in required topics in the secondary school curriculum, such as world trade in economics and Woodrow Wilson and the League of Nations in American history. At the elementary school level, internationalism arises with material such as how the United States cooperates with its hemispheric neighbors (e.g., Mexico, Canada). Opportunities to introduce internationalism will also arise naturally with almost any topic in the social studies curriculum. Sometimes these may be cases where international cooperation has had some success, such as restrictions on fishing in certain waters to restore global fish stocks and marine habitats. In other cases, an act of national self-interest and international cooperation may coincide, such as American adoption after World War II of the Marshall

Plan for the reconstruction of war-devastated Europe. This could be contrasted with U.S. refusal to participate in the principal internationalist effort after World War I, the League of Nations.

More generally, the sometime failure of nations, including the United States, to engage in urgent internationalist efforts should also be discussed and possible courses of action considered. In the already overburdened school curriculum, Dewey (1991) contended, a significant place for "the social studies" cannot be justified if it is taught "simply as information about present society." Rather its justification rests upon "the extent to which the material of the social studies, whether economics or politics or history or sociology, whatever it may be, is taught ... in connection with things that are done, that need to be done, and how to do them" (p. 185).

For example, conflict between Israel and its Arab neighbors has served to undermine international cooperation on the worsening problems of the degradation of water sources in the Jordan River valley upon which the entire regional population vitally depend. In the case of the United States, students might consider the causes and effects of our recent reluctance to participate in some internationalist efforts. This stance on the jurisdiction of international courts and fossil fuels emission controls to protect the global environment, for example, has put the United States out of step with many other nations, among which are some of our closest allies.

In summary, let's look at a unit on deforestation in a geography course to illustrate how the New Social Studies may still be relevant. Perhaps we would first consider what concepts in addition to deforestation would need to be introduced in this unit. These would likely include the greenhouse effect, global warming, soil erosion, and making distinctions between types of logging that are sustainable and those that are not. Next, bearing in mind that concepts and critical thinking outrank loading on superficial information, we might consider which examples best illustrate what we want to get across, selecting from, say, the U.S. Pacific Northwest, Hawaii, Borneo, and the Amazon Valley. We would also want to consider how to organize instruction so that a significant amount of the learning about these topics comes from students' own investigations.

This last point about student investigations, however, suggests a possible limitation of the New Social Studies from the perspective of progressive education. The problems that students investigated in the inquiry-oriented projects of the 1960s were in some ways too piecemeal and too removed from the lives children led outside of school (Eisner, 1974). In these projects, topics for inquiry were more likely to have been selected for their contemporary scholarly relevance than whether they provided for continuity of subject matter or were useful to children's life beyond the school.

In the next section, we will look at a more "interactive" view of curriculum designed to remedy the aforementioned curricular shortcomings.

INTERACTIVE CURRICULUM: BY EISNER AND IN SOCIAL STUDIES

Proponents of interactive curriculum regard curriculum not as a body of materials prepared in advance and intended for instruction, but as an *outcome* of the interactions among teacher, curriculum materials, and student (Noddings, 1979). In this scheme it is not just the outcome that counts but also the quality of present experience. Purposes may change and new purposes emerge during learning activities. Since purposes are jointly constructed by student and teacher, the learning activities are tailored to the child's interests and aptitudes (Dewey, 1963). There is "no point in the philosophy of progressive education sounder," Dewey wrote late in his career, than the participation of the learner in forming the purposes that direct his or her activities during the learning process (p. 67).

Eisner observed individualized instruction in the open classrooms of Plowden-oriented English primary schools during the 1970s. As he noted, the spirit of Lady Plowden's report to Parliament is captured in its title, *Children and Their Primary Schools*. Curriculum in these schools was intended to be individualized to a significant degree. For example, the teacher may take the students to visit a construction site. Some students might wish to paint or write about activity at the site. Library research on water supply may ensue, and so forth. Other children may wish to investigate the wages workers make or how water is channeled to the site (Eisner, 1974). As Eisner reported: "The teacher does not know what interests such an experience will generate, but once they emerge, his task is to facilitate their development" (p. 49).

Almost any student participation in selecting how and what to study is unusual in American schools today. This may explain why most young people report a lack of personal significance in and authentic engagement with their school work. They learn, as Denise Pope puts it, to "do school." They learn, in other words, how to cope with school without being significantly touched by it. It is experiences that were personally meaningful, however, that adults remember of their school days (Eisner, 1974). An interactive curriculum can be a powerful counterweight to the dearth of intrinsic motivation that characterizes today's schools (Noddings, 2003).

In spite of its promise, interactive curriculum has often been accused of lacking rigor. Even proponents such as Dewey and Eisner expressed concern that sequential learning may be neglected in practice (Dewey, 1963; Eisner, 1974). But poor implementation does not discredit the idea itself (Noddings & Enright, 1983). Given that low student motivation and engagement have long been reported as central problems in social studies education, the possibility that an interactive approach to curriculum might help redress these problems seems at least worth considering.

Oddly enough, even at the height of the American open education movement in the 1970s, when interactive curriculum received unprecedented attention in both theory and practice, there appears to have been limited attention to it in social studies. But the goals of social studies and of open education are much the same (Berger & Winters, 1973). Both are concerned with people—their individual rights and privileges, their adjustment to each other and to their world, and the working out of mutual problems (pp. 3–4).

It is likely that the potential of interactive curriculum can be most fully exploited when the curriculum is largely determined by the classroom teacher. Here William Heard Kilpatrick's project method is often touted. Students identify an area of social study (e.g., how people dress or make a living, ancient Egypt, the Amazon rain forest, skiing resorts of the world) and the teacher ensures that the topic is properly conceived for a productive investigation and that adequate curriculum materials are available.

These days the teacher's autonomy in curriculum is likely to be constrained. But this is insufficient reason to give up on individualization. Consider that a sixth grade course on the Eastern Hemisphere may require treatment of African grasslands. With some imagination and coordination, it should be possible for the teacher to set up stations where students can approach the topic through various means. For example, one corner of the classroom may hold a television and headsets with video of animal life in the grasslands. Another station could contain trade books or old *National Geographic* magazines about various cultural groups and how they interact with the grasslands. Yet another station might have physical maps documenting desertification, and so forth.

Although it seems that the kinds of learning experiences described here and above (with the role of ideas) are more likely to be found in reformed schools, much of what is described should also be possible, to varying extents to be sure, in more traditional schools. This brings me to the final section of this chapter—that teachers are frequently ill-prepared to enact the kinds of curriculum I have sketched in *both* reformed and unreformed schools.

WHAT KIND OF TEACHER EDUCATION BEST SERVES SOCIAL STUDIES REFORM?

Presently the subject matter and the method preparation of social studies teachers are generally separate undertakings. Methods instructors have little choice but to assume that their students have achieved some level of competence in the social sciences (in which I am including history and geography for the sake of brevity) when they arrive in methods courses. However, whether subject matter competence has been acquired—and then methods instructors teach how to transform subject matter for purposes of instruction—seems questionable.

The social science material that undergraduates encounter may hold only a tenuous connection to the content of the school curriculum (Thornton, 2001a). In New York State, for instance, high school students are required to take a course titled Participation in Government. As the name denotes, this course is intended to be an exercise in civic education rather than a bookish introduction to political science. But the latter is what prospective teachers seem more likely to experience in their college social science courses.

Perhaps even more worrisome is that college social science work is so often compartmentalized. What students learn in sociology is unlikely to be connected (unless students do so on their own for intrinsic reasons) to what they learn in economics or to what they learn in history. Yet, taking the African grasslands example above, it is just the kind of lateral knowledge that extends across and links academic subjects that often proves most valuable in school social studies teaching. How is the housing of the savanna reflective of the natural building materials available? How might modernization and accompanying trade have modified traditional housing practices? What do houses reveal about family structure, gender roles, and work and leisure? What kind of music and art do these people produce? What literature written by them or about them might help bring alive these people for faraway American students?

The distance between social science coursework and the school curriculum suggests that teachers' social science preparation might be properly different from preparing a geography major or an anthropology major (Noddings, 1999). An anthropology major will properly be concerned with a comprehensive examination of contemporary scholarship in the subject. Teachers may benefit more from a synthetic approach to the social sciences, especially an approach coordinated with the content of the school curriculum. Such an approach to subject matter preparation is far from simplistic. Rather, it requires examining fundamental material from a higher standpoint. Such an examination extends beyond competence in the subject itself to additional questions of its suitability and arrangement for purposes broader than subject matter competence—preparing students for the demands of contemporary living.

Methods preparation may also require rethinking. It seems to be widely assumed in the school reform literature that method and subject matter are practically separable. Methods courses often focus on professional competencies such as map and writing skills, classroom management, and how to infuse special subject matters. This focus may be conventional; however, its net effect of separating subject matter and method appears to be unhelpful to teachers (Hertzberg, 1988).

Just as social science preparation should be influenced by the content of the school curriculum, so methods courses should be organized around the major subject matters teachers will be expected to teach. The demands of teaching the American Revolution to fifth graders may be quite different from teaching tenth graders about how Hindu-Muslim relations proceed in contemporary India. Are map skills interchangeable in teaching geography and anthropology? As both the Kettering Project and my own experience in teacher education suggest, moreover, perhaps the most valuable methods of instructional experience may be working through actual curriculum packages and materials.

IN CONCLUSION

Although changing institutional arrangements can (and should) have benefi-
cial effects on the professional and personal lives of teachers and administrators, it is easy to confuse means and ends in school reform. Having a reformed
school *and* an impoverished curriculum is a Pyrrhic victory. Securing the kind
of schools we want will require reforming not just the organization of schools
but also their curriculum and the education of teachers who staff them.

REFERENCES

Berger, E., & Winters, B. A. (1973). *Social studies in the open classroom: A practical guide*.
    New York: Teachers College Press.
Dewey, J. (1963). *Experience and education*. New York: Collier Books.
Dewey, J. (1966). *Democracy and education*. New York: Free Press.
Dewey, J. (1991). The challenge of democracy to education. In J. A. Boydston (Ed.),
    John Dewey: The later works, 1925–1953 (Vol. 11, pp. 181–190). Carbondale:
    Southern Illinois University Press.
Eisner, E. W. (1974). *English primary schools*. Washington, DC: National Association for
    the Education of Young Children.
Eisner, E. W. (1982). *Cognition and curriculum: A basis for deciding what to teach*. New
    York: Longman.
Eisner, E. W. (1985). *The educational imagination: On the design and evaluation of school
    programs* (2nd ed.). New York: Macmillan.
Eisner, E. W. (1991). Art, music, and literature within social studies. In J. P. Shaver
    (Ed.), *Handbook of research on social studies teaching and learning* (pp. 551–558).
    New York: Macmillan.
Eisner, E. W. (1997). Who decides what schools teach? In D. J. Flinders &
    S. J. Thornton (Eds.), *The curriculum studies reader* (pp. 337–341). New York:
    Routledge.
Eisner, E. W. (1998). *The kind of schools we need: Personal essays*. Portsmouth, NH:
    Heinemann.
Eisner, E. W. (2001). What does it mean to say a school is doing well? *Phi Delta
    Kappan, 82*(5), 367–372.
Eisner, E. W. (2002). What can education learn from the arts about the practice of
    education? *Journal of Curriculum & Supervision, 18*(1), 4–16.
Epstein, T. L. (1994). Sometimes a shining moment: High school students' represen-
    tations of history through the arts. *Social Education, 58*(3), 136–141.
Goetz, W. W. (1994). The new social studies: The memoir of a practitioner. *Social
    Studies, 85*(3), 100–105.
Hertzberg, H. W. (1988). Are method and content enemies? In B. R. Gifford (Ed.),
    History in the schools (pp. 13–40). New York: Macmillan.
King, M. B. (1991). Leadership efforts that facilitate classroom thoughtfulness in
    social studies. *Theory & Research in Social Education, 19*(4), 367–390.
Lightfoot, S. L. (1983). *The good high school: Portraits of character and culture*. New York:
    Basic Books.
Marsden, W. E. (2001). *The school textbook: Geography, history, and social studies*. London:
    Woburn Press.

Noddings, N. (1979). NIE's national curriculum development conference. In J. Schaffarzick & G. Sykes (Eds.), *Value conflicts and curriculum issues* (pp. 291–312). Berkeley, CA: McCutchan.

Noddings, N. (1999). Caring and competence. In G. A. Griffin (Ed.), *The education of teachers* (pp. 205–220). Chicago: National Society for the Study of Education.

Noddings, N. (2001). Care and coercion in school reform. *Journal of Educational Change, 2*(1), 35–43.

Noddings, N. (2003). *Happiness and education*. New York: Cambridge University Press.

Noddings, N., & Enright, D. S. (1983). The promise of open education. *Theory Into Practice, 22*(3), 182–189.

Pope, D. C. (2001). *"Doing School": How We are Creating a Generation of Stressed Out, Materialistic, and Miseducated Students*. New Haven: Yale University Press.

Price, R. A., Hickman, W., & Smith, G. (1965). *Major concepts for the social studies*. Syracuse: Syracuse University, Social Studies Curriculum Center.

Read, H. E. (1943). *Education through art*. London: Faber & Faber.

Risinger, F., & Radz, M. (1971). *Social studies projects tour: An informal report*. Boulder, CO: ERIC Clearinghouse for Social Studies/Social Science Education & Social Science Education Consortium.

Rugg, H. O. (1939). Curriculum design in the social sciences: What I believe. In J. A. Michener (Ed.), *The future of the social studies: Proposals for an experimental social-studies curriculum* (pp. 140–158). Cambridge, MA: National Council for the Social Studies.

Sizer, T. (1984). *Horace's compromise: The dilemma of the American high school*. Boston: Houghton Mifflin.

Thornton, S. J. (1991). Teacher as curricular-instructional gatekeeper in social studies. In J. P. Shaver (Ed.), *Handbook of research on social studies teaching and learning* (pp. 237–248). New York: Macmillan.

Thornton, S. J. (1994). The social studies near century's end: Reconsidering patterns of curriculum and instruction. In L. Darling-Hammond (Ed.), *Review of research in education, 20* (pp. 223–254). Washington, DC: American Educational Research Association.

Thornton, S. J. (2001a). Educating the educators: Rethinking subject matter and methods. *Theory Into Practice, 40*(1), 72–78.

Thornton, S. J. (2001b). Harold Rugg, 1886–1960. In J. A. Palmer (Ed.), *Fifty modern thinkers on education: From Piaget to the present* (pp. 10–15). London: Routledge.

Thornton, S. J. (2001c). Legitimacy in the social studies curriculum. In L. Corno (Ed.), *A century of study in education: The centennial volume* (pp. 185–204). Chicago: National Society for the Study of Education.

Thornton, S. J. (2001d). Subject-specific teaching methods: History. In J. Brophy (Ed.), *Subject-specific teaching methods and activities* (pp. 291–314). Oxford, England: Elsevier Science.

Uhrmacher, P. B. (2001). Elliot Eisner, 1933– . In J. A. Palmer (Ed.), *Fifty modern thinkers on education: From Piaget to the present* (pp. 247–252). London: Routledge.

Whitehead, A. N. (1967). *The aims of education and other essays*. New York: Free Press.

17

He Must Not Know That the War
Is Over and the Other Side Won,
Because He Just Keeps Fighting

Elliot Eisner as Advocate for School Reform

Robert Donmoyer
University of San Diego

*C*hange is a constant in the history of American education. My task here is to discuss Elliot Eisner as a promoter of change and advocate for educational reform.[1]

The discussion starts with a kind of "Cooks tour" of the educational reform landscape over the past 100-plus years and then situates Eisner's reform advocacy within this larger context. The discussion also explores why Eisner—and his intellectual allies—have so often been on the losing side when it comes to influencing what actually happens in America's schools and briefly considers what those who share Eisner's views—and want to continue to promote his vision of education—might do to enhance their influence in the future.

REFORM IDEAS AND INITIATIVES: AN OVERVIEW

The Progressive Impulse

Educational reform efforts during the latter part of the 19th and first half of the 20th centuries were part of a much larger progressive reform movement that was oriented toward radically altering various sectors of civic

---

[1] Much of Eisner's writing in areas such as curriculum and arts education has had a school reform message at least implicit within it. These writings will be touched on in this chapter, but, since they are the focus of other chapters in other sections of this book, this chapter will focus primarily on Eisner's discussions of more general reform strategies (e.g., Eisner, 1992a) and his discussions of the contemporary standards and standardized assessment movements (e.g., Eisner, 1992b, 1993, 1994, 1995, 1999). Many—though certainly not all—of these works have been collected in Eisner's recent book, *The Kind of Schools We Need* (Eisner, 1998).

life, including the education sector. Progressive reformers tended to agree, at least at a general level, about both the source of the problem and the solution. The source of the problem was politics and self-interested politicians.[2] The solution was to take power from politicians and give it to certified professionals educated in the tenets of science. Within the education sector, this solution was often expressed as a slogan: Take the schools out of politics![3]

The sticking point for progressive educators, at least, was the emergence of two quite different visions of the role that science should play within reformed schools and school systems. One view was articulated and championed by E. L. Thorndike; John Dewey served as the principal spokesperson for the rival position.

Thorndike's View of Science and Its Role in Education

Thorndike summarized his thinking in the lead article of the inaugural issue of the *Journal of Educational Psychology* that appeared in 1910. "A complete science of psychology," Thorndike wrote,

> would tell every fact about everyone's intellect and character and behavior, would tell the cause of every change in human nature, would tell the result which every educational force—every act of every person that changed any other or the agent himself—would have. It would aid us to use human beings for the world's welfare with the same surety of the result that we now have when we use falling bodies or chemical elements. In proportion as we get such a science we shall become masters of our own souls as we are now masters of heat and light. Progress toward such a science is being made. (p. 6)

This quotation contains a number of subtexts that are, in fact, hallmarks of Thorndike's thinking. These subtexts include the following:

---

[2]This problem was rather obvious in the education field, especially in large urban school districts. Historian David Tyack (1974), for instance, documents the sorts of abuses that might have made even a Tammany Hall politician blush. He describes, for example: teachers buying their positions from political bosses; politically powerful textbook salesmen engineering the hiring of particular school superintendents who purchased the publishers' wares; and unscrupulous representatives from textbook publishing companies using prostitutes to entice school board members into illicit liaisons that could later be used for blackmail purposes.

[3]Operationally, efforts to substitute professional for political control of education took a number of different forms. These forms included vesting greater authority in formally educated superintendents and replacing ward-based election of school board members with an at-large approach. Adoption of an at-large election strategy made it unlikely that representatives of minority groups, which normally were segregated in separate sections or wards within a city, would get elected to boards and more likely that school boards would be composed of members who accepted the progressive storyline about the importance of deferring to scientifically trained professionals.

> Human beings are formed and shaped almost entirely by the external environment rather than through self-initiated activity of their own.[4]

Learning, and the process that promotes it, can be atomized; learning, in other words, can be broken into component parts and these components can be linked, through scientific research, to discrete environmental factors so that, in time, we can understand what factors in the environment cause desired (as well as undesired) effects.

Once we understand cause-effect relationships, we can routinize the teaching and learning process to maximize the outcomes we desire.

Such routinization, of course, requires the use of precise measurement both to develop the highly specific understanding of cause-effect relationships on which the standard operating procedures of teaching and learning are to be based and to determine whether the expected "surety of results" has been produced once the instructional routines have been implemented in schools. (Thorndike, in fact, is considered the father of the standardized testing.)

Dewey's Alternative Vision

Like Thorndike, Dewey believed that science offered a solution to education's problems. However, while Thorndike's focus was on the results that he believed would emerge from scientific research in education, Dewey's primary focus was on the scientific process. Scientists' work, in fact, became, in Dewey's thinking, the prototype for the kind of work students—and also their teachers—should be doing in schools.

This difference in perspective is rooted in Thorndike and Dewey's very different conceptions of cognition. Dewey (1916/1997) in fact, explicitly rejected the externally driven view of learning that Thorndike embraced. According to Dewey, learning is the result of an ongoing transactional process between (a) individuals who actively construct ideas that influence how they engage with the external environment (which, in Dewey's thinking, is very much social as well as physical [Dewey, 1900/1990b]), and (b) the external environment itself, which provides feedback about the adequacy of the thinking that guided the individual's actions. The feedback provided by the external environment provides the impetus for individuals to modify or reconstruct the ideas that guided their initial actions and these reconstructed ideas are then tested through further interactions with the environment.

An individual's current interactions with the environment, in other words, are influenced by his or her prior interactions and, in turn, influence interactions that will occur in the future; Dewey referred to this linkage between past, present, and future experiences as the continuum of experience.

---

[4]Thorndike, in essence, endorsed John Locke's *tabula rasa* or blank slate view of mind. Of course, Thorndike's endorsement of—and efforts to develop—tests that could identify differences in innate intelligence suggests that he believed that some people's blank slates were better than others.

He labeled an experience "educative" if it provided the knowledge, skills, and dispositions that promote further transactions with the environment and "mis-educative" if it, for whatever reason, inhibited ongoing experimentation and, by definition, ongoing growth. (Dewey also suggests that some experiences might neither promote nor inhibit further growth; such experiences he labeled "non-educative.")

Dewey's transactional conception of learning, of course, introduces a wild card into the learning process: the learners themselves, each of whom brings to school experience a somewhat different set of prior experiences. Since, according to Dewey, meaningful learning will happen only when students actively construct their own understandings, test the adequacy of their constructions by interacting with the physical and social environment, and revise their thinking to accommodate the environment's response, the teaching and learning process can never be routinized in the way that Thorndike envisions. Teachers can—and, Dewey emphasizes, must[5]—structure their classroom environments (including their own interactions with students) in ways that make it more likely that students' construction processes will be educative rather than mis-educative or non-educative. If students are to function as miniature scientists in the classroom, however, teaching will inevitably have to be more responsive than directive and more improvisational than systematized.

Although Dewey primarily emphasized the process of science, he does not totally ignore the intellectual products that formal scientific work produces.[6] In *Experience and Education*, for instance, Dewey noted that the academic disciplines—which, he argued, logically organized the results of attempts by society (and, in particular, society's scientists) to solve real-world problems—should function as "ends-in-views" for teachers engaged in structuring classroom environments. Teachers, in other words, should attempt to structure the classroom environment with an eye toward promoting their students' acquisition of disciplinary knowledge. However, Dewey also emphasized that disciplinary knowledge could not simply be transmitted to

---

[5]Dewey, in fact, was quite critical of some of his more laissez-faire followers whose commitment to being child centered led them to ignore the environment part of the transactional relationship. In his little book, *Experience and Education*, written at least in part to correct what he perceived to be misinterpretations of his thinking, Dewey (1938/1963) writes, "I do not know what the greater maturity of the teacher and the teacher's greater knowledge of the world, of subject-matter and of individuals, is for unless the teacher can arrange conditions that are conducive to community activity and to organization which exercises control over individual impulses by the mere fact that all are engaged in communal projects. Because the kind of advance planning heretofore engaged in has been so routine as to leave little room for the free play of individual thinking or the contributions due to distinctive individual experience, it does not follow that all planning must be rejected" (pp. 57–58).

[6]Dewey, after all was a secular Hegelian. He stripped Hegelian philosophy of its metaphysical dimensions but retained Hegel's notions of thesis, antithesis, and synthesis as analytical tools. Consequently, when confronted with an either-or choice such as whether to focus on the process or the products of science, he invariably sought a way to incorporate in a coherent way apparently antithetical choices into a new way of thinking about the issue.

students in its logically organized form, as Thorndike envisioned. Rather, students had to reenact a reasonable facsimile of the real-world problem-solving process that scientists and others had used to construct disciplinary knowledge in the first place. Dewey(1902/1990a) referred to this approach as the psychological as opposed to the logical organization of curriculum.

Dewey also saw a use for the findings of educational research, though their role and function in Dewey's thought are quite different from Thorndike's thinking. In *The Sources of a Science of Education* (1929), Dewey indicated that the findings and theoretical constructs emerging from formal education-related research should function merely as intellectual tools that aid teachers' thinking as they experimented within their classrooms. And the winner is ... So whose ideas triumphed? Which vision of reform ended up influencing education during and after the progressive era?

Historian Ellen Lagemann (2000) has a simple answer to these questions. Thorndike won and Dewey lost, she tells us—and this answer is certainly more correct than incorrect historically and very much on target today. Lagemann's answer, however, is a tad too pithy to do justice to what actually occurred.

For instance, while it is true that Dewey's influence on school practice during the progressive era tended to be limited to small, often private schools and that most public school systems during the progressive era were run in a manner that was more consistent with Thorndike's vision (Tyack, 1974) of education, what happened hardly represents a total victory for Thorndike's thinking. After all, social scientists never did establish the sort of knowledge about causes and effects that Thorndike promised; consequently, it was, paradoxically, the story this man of science told about the teaching-learning process—not actual scientific results—that was the source of Thorndike's influence. Indeed, Thorndike's storyline of teaching and learning as a highly routinized process meshed nicely with imagery provided by the increasingly industrialized society beyond the schoolhouse door and provided academic legitimacy for educational administrators' decision to organize schools in ways that were consistent with the assembly line[7] (Callahan, 1962; Cubberly, 1909). In short, Thorndike's academic writings helped legitimate approaches to school organization and teaching, but most of these approaches would have been implemented in one form or another even without Thorndike's academic justification.

Lingering Legacies

Furthermore, Dewey's ideas did not simply disappear after the progressive era ended. Indeed, Dewey, in time, actually won the rhetoric wars. Although B. F. Skinner—who once said his work was simply a footnote to work done

---

[7]E. L. Cubberly, the so-called father of the educational administration field, for instance, wrote in a 1909 monograph: "Our schools are, in a sense, factories, in which the raw materials (children) are to be shaped and fashioned into products to meet the various demands of life" (p. 338).

by Thorndike—kept Thorndike's vision of teaching and learning viable for a time, we are virtually all constructivists now. Even some leaders in the special education field—the field in which Skinnerian behaviorism has been most influential—have begun to use more constructivist rhetoric.

Furthermore, Dewey's influence has not been merely rhetorical. Dewey's notion that students must engage in meaningful problem-solving, that curriculum must be organized psychologically rather than logically, and that teachers must be reflective practitioners rather than the educational equivalent of factory workers were alive and well in a number of high-profile reform movements that appeared during the latter half of the 20th century. The list includes a substantial portion of the curriculum development initiatives of the 1960s, the open education movement of the late 1960s and 1970s, and the whole-language initiatives of the 1980s and early 1990s.

The actual impact of most of these movements in schools was quite limited, of course, and all of them were short-lived. Much the same thing, however, can be said about later 20th century reform initiatives consistent with Thorndike's thinking—initiatives such as competency-based education, competency-based teacher education, and the behavioral objectives movement. The competency-based teacher education movement, for instance, was undermined, at least in part, by the realization that educational researchers still had not identified the sort of linkages between particular teaching processes and student learning outcomes that Thorndike had promised.[8] The behavioral objective movement simply collapsed under its own complexity. Even one of the gurus of the movement, James Popham, acknowledged in a 1987 article: "We learned an important lesson during the heyday of behavioral objectives. Teachers who are inundated with endless litanies of minuscule instructional targets will pay heed to none" (p. 680).

Even while acknowledging problems with the sort of atomized curriculum and choreographed teaching both he and Thorndike once dreamed of, however, Popham strongly endorses another key component of Thorndike's thinking: standardized testing. Popham, in fact, calls measurement-driven instruction "the most cost-effective way of improving the quality of public education in the United States" (p. 679). He adds: "Those who deny the instructional influence of high-stakes tests have not spent much time in public school classrooms recently" (p. 680). The policy community has embraced this sort of thinking without much reservation, of course, and has made high-stakes testing and measurement-driven instruction key components of the standards movement that is the dominant educational reform initiative within the United States today.

---

[8]There was also a growing realization that such knowledge would never be produced (Cronbach, 1982).

Reforming Education Through Standards and High-Stakes Testing

Indeed, teaching to standards and high-stakes testing are now the law of the land in the United States. Even in the current environment, and even among standards movement partisans, however, Dewey's vision of education still has a certain romantic cachet. The National Science Education Standards document produced by the National Research Council (1994), for instance, presents a series of vignettes that purportedly illustrate what standards-based teaching should look like in the classroom; these vignettes—in which teachers spontaneously take advantage of their students' misconceptions and encourage their students to design and conduct experiments to test their erroneous assumptions—are vintage Dewey.[9] The authors of the report—and many others within the standards movement—also endorse the use of more "authentic" forms of standardized assessment that require students to perform the sorts of problem-solving tasks that Dewey believed should be at the center of school experience. Some leaders in the standards movement have even argued that more authentic tests can be used to drive teaching in a more constructivist (i.e., Deweyan) direction, much as traditional tests led to an emphasis on basic skills (Furhman & Massell, 1992).

Unfortunately, attempts to implement large-scale performance assessments that are sufficiently standardized to pass legal muster demonstrate quite clearly what Dewey knew intuitively: Standardizing authenticity is an oxymoron (Black, 1993; Donmoyer, 1995; Page, 1995). And anyone who has spent time in American schools recently knows that the sort of teaching illustrated in the charming vignettes presented in the National Science Education Standards document mentioned above is rare, at best. Rather, in most schools, teaching and curriculum increasingly mimic not only the content but also the form of standardized tests. In short, in terms of what really matters—impacting what students have an opportunity to do and learn in school—Dewey really has lost and Thorndike, finally, has won the battle for the soul of American education.

---

[9]In one vignette, for instance, an elementary school teacher spontaneously fashions a series of experiences to teach both scientific inquiry and physical property of matter standards from a student's casual observation that the water in the watering can used to water the classroom plants had disappeared over the weekend. When no student admits to drinking or spilling the water, the teacher asks the class to hypothesize what might have happened to the water. One student hypothesizes that Willie, the classroom's pet hamster, must be getting out of his cage at night and drinking the water. The students decide to test this hypothesis by covering the watering can so Willie will not be able to drink the remaining water. When no more water disappears, the students conclude—erroneously, of course—that Willie was, indeed, the culprit. At the urging of the teacher, the students devise additional experiments to assess the adequacy of their conclusion. Each subsequent experiment leads quite naturally—with only the most subtle nudging from the teacher—to careful reflection and additional experimentation.

SITUATING EISNER IN THE LARGER HISTORICAL CONTEXT OF REFORM

So, where does Elliot Eisner's reform-oriented writing fit in the pantheon of ideas and initiatives discussed—admittedly, all too briefly—in the previous section? It is clear, after reading Eisner's writing on educational reform—and much of his other academic writing as well—that he is solidly in Dewey's camp.

Echoes of Dewey in Eisner's Writings About Reform

In his introduction to a collection of articles on performance assessment, which he edited for a 1999 issue of the *Phi Delta Kappan*, for instance, Eisner not only characterizes Thorndike's thinking as passé, saying "The kind of thinking that students are now encouraged to engage in requires much more than what Edward Thorndike, the father of American psychological connectionism, dreamed of "(p. 658)—but he also often sounds like a reincarnation of Dewey (albeit with a more engaging writing style):

> In a sense, all teachers can do is to "make noises in the environment." By this I mean that we have in education no main line into the brains of our students. We are shapers of the environment, stimulators, motivators, guides, consultants, resources. But in the end, what children make of what we provide is a function of what they construe from what we offer. (p. 658)

Eisner also invokes ideas that are more than a little reminiscent of Dewey's thinking in other writing about contemporary reform initiatives. In a 1992 *Teachers College Record* article on school reform, for instance, Eisner reminds us of the importance of allowing students to formulate problems: "Students typically have few opportunities to formulate their own questions and to pursue them," Eisner writes; "the provision of opportunities for students to define at least some of their purposes is arguably an important educational aim and the ability to do so an important educational achievement" (1992a, p. 624). In the same article, he also explicitly rejects the Thorndikian assumption that "curriculum can be followed by teachers as a script" (p. 624).

In some of his other critiques of contemporary efforts to reform schools, Eisner's comments are reminiscent of what Dewey said about the continuum of experience. In a 1995 *Kappan* article about the standards movement, for instance, Eisner reminds us that students bring different sets of experiences to schools and that "the reality of differences—in region, in aptitude, in interests, and in goals—suggests that it is reasonable that there be differences in programs" (p. 762). Three years earlier, in another *Kappan* article about national standards, Eisner (1992b) also emphasized that we should expect—and value—different outcomes: "Why do we believe that the most important aim of education is to get everyone to the same destination at the same time?" (p. 722) he asks in an article criticizing federal reform policies.

Explicit Acknowledgements of Dewey's Influence

The resemblance between Eisner's and Dewey's thinking alluded to above is not coincidental. In fact, throughout his career, Eisner has frequently made his intellectual indebtedness to Dewey explicit. In the 1995 article on national standards discussed in the previous paragraph, for example, Eisner quotes at length from Dewey's *Art as Experience* (1934/1980) in the process of (a) differentiating between applying a standard, on the one hand, and using criteria, on the other, to assess educational success, and (b) arguing that, in education, as in art, the latter approach is more appropriate than the former.

Eisner has also invoked Dewey's standard/criteria distinction—along with Dewey's more general views of art and education as experience—in explicating and justifying the notions of educational connoisseurship and criticism and arts-based research (Eisner, 1976, 1991). In 1973, for instance, Eisner actually did a study of British Infant Schools that bore at least a family resemblance to his educational criticism evaluation model and the genre of research that he would later dub "arts-based." But it was not until he drew upon the ideas of Dewey and others (e.g., the ideas of the aesthetician Susanne Langer) that he articulated a theoretical foundation for—and the aesthetic dimension of—the evaluation and research approaches he initially dubbed "educational criticism" and now calls "arts-based educational research."

Eisner also made the link between his thought and Dewey's thinking explicit in his early writing on curriculum. In a monograph entitled *Instructional and Expressive Educational Objectives: Their Formulation and Use in Curriculum*, for instance, Eisner (1967) makes the case for what he referred to, at the time, as expressive objectives (and later renamed, at one point, expressive activities, and, more recently, expressive outcomes[10]) as a necessary complement to behavioral objectives in designing curriculum. While instructional or behavioral objectives precisely specify in advance what students will learn (and be able to do) after a particular piece of curriculum is delivered, an expressive activity is a rich educational encounter—for example, a school trip to the zoo, a student production of *Romeo and Juliet*—that can produce quite different, often unexpected outcomes because different students bring different sets of experiences to the encounter. In his analysis, Eisner links instructional/behavioral objectives with technological and industrial metaphors of education and associates them with the thinking of E. L. Thorndike. By contrast, he grounds the notion of expressive activities/outcomes in Dewey's growth-focused biological metaphor of human development.

---

[10]See the three editions of *The Educational Imagination* (1979, 1985, and 2002).

Caveats

Thus Dewey's influence is apparent and at times even explicit in Eisner's writing about school reform and his work in other areas as well (e.g., curriculum design and research methodology). Consequently, there can be no doubt about whose side Elliot Eisner is on in the historical battle among educational reformers for the field's soul. Having said this, however, I must quickly add that I do not wish to portray Eisner merely as an intellectual clone of Dewey. Such a characterization would be inappropriate for a number of reasons.

First, Eisner, on occasion, has been Dewey's critic as well as his champion. In the second (1985) edition of *The Educational Imagination*, for instance, Eisner criticizes not only E. L. Thorndike but also John Dewey for overemphasizing the contributions science can make to the education field. He notes, for example, that Dewey did not get around to even considering the significance of aesthetics until he wrote *Art as Experience* (1934/1980) at the age of 74.[11] Second, Eisner's contributions are not limited to academic-oriented advocacy for the reform of schools, curriculum, and educational research methods. He has also produced more descriptive work that consciously eschews advocacy, even of an academic sort. A prime example of this is *Conflicting Conceptions of Curriculum* (1974), a book he coauthored with Elizabeth Vallance. In this book, Eisner and Vallance articulate—and provide illustrations of—five quite different ways to think about and construct curriculum. Dewey's influence is apparent in some but certainly not all of the curriculum perspectives discussed by Eisner and Vallance, but all of the conceptions reviewed are treated with an even hand.

Third, in his own curriculum development work in the area of arts education, Eisner has displayed a healthy eclecticism (Schwab, 1969). One can certainly see the influence of Dewey in Eisner's (1987, 1990) contributions to the Getty Foundation's Discipline-Based Art Education reform initiative, especially in his writings about the "disciplines" of art criticism and studio work. But there are other components of Discipline-Based Art Education— for example an emphasis on teaching art history—that do not seem especially Deweyan but reflect more of what Eisner and Vallance refer to as the academic rationalist conception of curriculum. Indeed, if one uses the five-part schema articulated in *Conflicting Conceptions of Curriculum* to analyze both Eisner's contributions to the Getty initiative and his earlier arts curriculum design work (Eisner, 1975), one sees a number of quite different conceptions of curriculum informing Eisner's approach to curriculum development.

Finally, even when he is functioning as an academic advocate for Dewey's vision of educational reform, Eisner's work is not merely derivative. Rather, Eisner reconstructs Dewey's thinking in much the same way that teachers transform subject matter when they create what Shulman calls pedagogical content knowledge. Dewey, after all, was first and foremost

---

[11]Eisner seems even more critical of the education field for generally ignoring what he refers to as Dewey's *magnum opus* when it finally did appear.

a philosopher; he used education—especially early in his career—as a means to accomplish his philosophical ends. Eisner, by contrast, is an education scholar who uses philosophy and the products of other intellectual traditions to construct processes and procedures for educating students (and also for studying educational process). Because educational concerns are in the foreground in Eisner's work, he has been able to make truly innovative contributions (e.g., the notion of expressive objectives/activities; the procedures of educational criticism and arts-based research) that educators (and educational researchers) have found exceedingly useful. These ideas almost certainly would never have occurred to the philosophy-oriented John Dewey.

WHY NOT VICTORY?

With the subtleties and nuances duly noted in the above list of caveats, I can now return to portraying the Eisner/Dewey relationship with relatively broad brushstrokes and consider the final questions to be discussed in this essay: Why have Eisner and others who share Dewey's vision of education—including Dewey himself, for that matter—so often been on the losing side in the battle to reform American education and what can those who wish to hoist the Dewey banner in future skirmishes do differently so the past is not prologue? These questions must be considered in two different domains: (1) the policy context that has enthusiastically embraced Thorndike's emphasis on standardized testing, and (2) the contexts of teaching and schooling, contexts whose members seldom embraced Dewey's vision of educational practice (even though they often employed Dewey's rhetoric) during the period when high-stakes testing was not the law of the land and teachers and schools functioned in what organizational theorists (e.g., Weick, 1976) referred to as a loosely coupled system. I will begin by focusing on the teaching/school context.

Accounting for and Responding to School-Level Resistance

Actually, Eisner (1992a), himself, in an article entitled "Educational Reform and the Ecology of Schooling," does a pretty good job of articulating reasons for resistance at the school and classroom levels. To be sure, Eisner, in this article, is talking about resistance to reform in general; much of what he says, however, can be applied to reforms of a Dewey/Eisner sort. Eisner begins his explanation with the observation that "schools are robust institutions whose very robustness provides a source of social stability" (pp. 610–611). He then goes on to list nine factors that, he argues, contribute to maintaining the status quo. Heading the list of factors—and among the more compelling factors Eisner discusses—are factors related to characteristics of teachers. Eisner, for instance, writes:

> Teachers are often reluctant to relinquish teaching repertoires that provide an important source of security for them. New content areas might require new pedagogical routines. Given the overload that teachers

typically experience in school—large number of students and many courses or subjects to teach—economy of effort is an important value. Familiar teaching repertoires provide economy of effort; hence changes in schools that require new content and new repertoires are likely to be met with passive resistance by experienced teachers who have defined for themselves an array of routines they can efficiently employ. To make matters even less promising for school reform, few efforts at reform in the United States have provided time for teachers to develop mastery of new content or skills required for new forms of teaching. (p. 612)

Of course, when the "new forms of teaching" are of a Dewey/Eisner sort, the problem is not temporary and cannot be solved simply by giving teachers more time to develop new routines to substitute for old ones. Teaching a curriculum that is organized psychologically rather than logically and structuring learning around expressive activities that, by design, generate idiosyncratic responses from students who inevitably bring different experiences to the classroom require the sort of pedagogical improvisation that is the antithesis of routine and standardization (Donmoyer, 1983). This fact, possibly more than any other, explains why Dewey's ideas got implemented primarily in small, private schools with a limited number of students per classroom, and why, even in these ideal situations, Deweyan approaches to teaching often could not be sustained over an extended period of time. It also helps explain teachers' reliance on textbooks and teachers' manuals that choreograph the teaching-learning process. Classrooms are complex, and teachers must find ways to simplify the complexity to survive.

If the above analysis is at all on target, what those of us who wish to hoist the Dewey/Eisner banner in the future must do seems rather obvious: We must find ways to simplify and, dare I say, routinize, to the extent possible, the Eisner/Dewey vision of education. The most obvious way to accomplish this task is to develop curriculum materials (possibly even textbooks) that structure the teaching process for the teacher, at least to some extent, and to translate Dewey's ideas into standard operating procedures that at least partially choreograph teachers' work. This will not be easy, especially for academics socialized to value logical consistency. The notion of a Deweyan textbook, after all, is a bit of an oxymoron, and the idea that a curriculum manual could choreograph a series of Eisner's expressive activities designed to produce expressive—that is, idiosyntratic—outcomes seems like a contradiction in terms. One is reminded of Cremin's (1964) criticism of William Heard Kilpatrick, one of Dewey's students who also attempted to "translate" Dewey's ideas into a form teachers could use. Cremin argued that Kilpatrick's pedagogical translation of Dewey's thinking exaggerated the significance of method and, consequently, deviated in fundamental ways from Dewey's vision of education in the process.

Yet, unless we are willing to embrace contradictions and engage in the intellectual tightrope-walking act such embracing requires, the Dewey/Eisner vision of educational reform will almost certainly exist only in reform rhetoric and in the minds of educational academics who, from their perch in the ivory tower, have the luxury of dreaming about things that cannot be. Busy teachers charged with managing incredibly complex classroom environments are in no position to construct curriculum totally from scratch out of the interests and needs of their students, and, unless there is a massive reallocation of resources within school districts, the sort of collaborative collegial planning Dewey (1929) envisioned—and Eisner(1992a) alludes to in his list of factors inhibiting reform—is unlikely to occur in most United States schools.

Of course, even if we make the sorts of compromises alluded to above, there is no guarantee that the watered-down version of the Dewey/Eisner vision of education will get enacted in United States classrooms. After all, many of the curricula that resulted from the curriculum development movement of the 1960s—curricula such as Man: A Course of Study, and the Elementary Science Study curriculum—had a decidedly Deweyan tilt and could be viewed as examples of the sort of compromises called for in the above paragraphs. Yet most of these curricula either never took hold or, in the limited number of places where they were implemented, faded away in a relatively short period of time. Despite this legacy, however, I suspect that those of us who want to carry into the future the banner of educational reform first carried by Dewey, and later shouldered by Eisner, will have to continue to experiment with the sorts of tactics employed by many of the curriculum developers of the 1960s until we get things right—or at least less wrong. If the vision of education put forth by Dewey and Eisner has any chance of existing and flourishing in classrooms—even in a somewhat altered state—we have little choice but to mine this less than fertile field. One way or another the complexity of classrooms must be accommodated.

Convincing the Policy Community

Of course, even if we succeed in modifying Dewey and Eisner's ideas so they are functional for teachers to implement, there is still the policy community to contend with. Eisner makes it clear that he has little patience with members of this community. In one article on the federal effort to reform schools, for instance, after peppering the reader with a barrage of questions that clearly are rhetorical and designed to function as criticisms of the federal reform effort (e.g., "Why do we think that all students should be measured by the same yardstick?" [Eisner, 1992b, p. 722]), Eisner writes the following:

> These are some of the questions that puzzle me. What puzzles me even more is that such questions seem to puzzle policy makers so little. Indeed, the federal approach to school reform … seems oblivious to such considerations. (Eisner, 1992b, p. 723)

I suspect we need to adopt a somewhat different tack: Rather than glibly writing off policy-makers' ideas as silly and superficial, we should adopt the mind-set of the anthropologist studying an alien culture. Anthropologists start with the assumption that the unusual (and seemingly absurd) beliefs and practices they observe are functional within the cultural context in which they operate, and they accept as their primary task understanding why this is so. Thus, if we take our cue from the anthropologists, we will start with the assumption that policy-makers' ways of thinking and acting are functional within the policy "culture" and attempt to understand policy-makers' thinking and their actions from their "cultural" frame of reference. When we do this, I suspect we will see that ideas that can appear nonsensical to us are not really illogical in the different cultural context in which policy-makers live and work. Once we understand this fact, we may, once again, be able to do something similar to what I suggested must be done to make the Dewey/Eisner vision of educational reform palatable for teachers: develop and propose compromises that may have a chance of being accepted and implemented.

We will almost certainly never convince policy-makers to totally reject standardized testing, for example—as one policy-maker once told me, policy-makers need the equivalent of the Dow Jones averages to do their work—but we may be able to convince them that standardized tests are such a gross indicator of what we care about that their use should be limited to assessing whether minimum levels of learning have been achieved and to alert us to students, schools, and school districts that are in a crisis situation. This case will be even more palatable if we develop other, more site-based accountability mechanisms that accountability-oriented policy-makers will find appealing.[12]

We might also approach the problem from a different angle by studying outlier schools that manage to produce impressive test results without making curriculum and teaching mimic the content and form of tests. The qualitative methods Eisner has championed are ready-made for studying such outliers.

IN CONCLUSION

Once again, I know the strategy I am recommending will not be easy to implement. I have spent a career interacting with members of the policy community and understand quite well that there is a certain incommensurability between the thinking of policy-makers, on the one hand, and the educational vision of scholars like Eisner and Dewey, on the other. Consequently, the compromises one must make to appease the policy community are often less than satisfying for anyone who shares the Eisner/Dewey vision of ideal educational practice.

Still, in an era when national magazines such as the September 6, 1999, issue of *Newsweek* promise on their covers to provide "The Truth About Testing," when parent groups are so opposed to standardized tests that they

---

[12]For an indication of what I am talking about, see my study of the implementation of a deliberative approach to evaluation (Donmoyer, 1991).

refuse to let their children take them, and when there is increasing evidence that improved performance on high-stakes tests does not improve performance even on other standardized tests, policy-makers may be more receptive to our arguments than they have been in the past. Even if this turns out not to be the case, those of us who want to promote the vision of reform championed by Dewey and Eisner can hardly refuse to engage with the policy community, just as we cannot ignore the legitimate concerns of teachers who must negotiate complex classroom environments. Dewey has articulated a beautiful vision of education and Eisner has both rearticulated this vision in a more engaging and compelling way and reconstructed it in a form that makes abstract philosophy tangible for educators. Unless that vision is further tweaked in ways that make it more palatable to policy-makers and more possible for practitioners to implement, however, Thorndike will continue to win and Dewey—and Eisner—almost certainly will continue to lose the battle to influence the lives of students.

REFERENCES

Black, P. (1993, April). *Performance assessment and accountability: The Great Britain experience*. Invited address at the annual meeting of the American Educational Research Association, Atlanta.

Callahan, R. (1962). *Education and the cult of efficiency*. Chicago: University of Chicago Press.

Cremin, L. (1964). *The transformation of the schools*. New York: Knopf.

Cronbach, L. (1982). Prudent aspirations of social inquiry. In W. Kruskal (Ed.), *The social sciences: Their nature and lines* (pp. 42–54). Chicago: University of Chicago Press.

Cubberly, E. (1909). *Changing conceptions of education*. Boston: Houghton Mifflin.

Dewey, J. (1929). *The sources of a science of education*. New York: Liveright.

Dewey, J. (1963). *Experience and education*. New York: Collier Books. (Original work published 1938)

Dewey, J. (1980). *Art as experience*. New York: Perigee Books. (Original work published 1934)

Dewey, J. (1990a). *The child and the curriculum*. Chicago: University of Chicago Press. (Original work published 1902)

Dewey, J. (1990b). *School and society*. Chicago: University of Chicago Press. (Original work published 1900)

Dewey, J. (1997). *Democracy and education*. New York: Free Press. (Original work published 1916)

Donmoyer, R. (1983). Pedagogical improvisation. *Educational Leadership, 40*(1), 39–43.

Donmoyer, R. (1991). Postpositivist evaluation: Give me a for instance. *Educational Administration Quarterly, 27*(3), 265–296.

Donmoyer, R. (1995). The rhetoric and reality of systemic reform. *Theory Into Practice, 34*(1), 30–34.

Eisner, E. (1967). *Instructional and expressive educational objectives: Their formulation and use in curriculum*. ERIC document (ED028838).

Eisner, E. (1971). *English primary schools: Some observations and assessments*. ERIC document (ED093471).

Eisner, E. (1975). Curriculum development in Stanford University's Kettering Project: Recollections and ruminations. *Journal of Curriculum Studies, 7*(1), 26–41.

Eisner, E. (1976). Educational connoisseurship and criticism: Their forma and function in educational evaluation. *Journal of Aesthetic Education, 10*(3/4), 135–150.

Eisner, E. (1987). *The role of discipline-based art education in America's schools*. Los Angeles: Getty Center for Education and the Arts (BBB23373).

Eisner, E. (1990). Discipline-based art education: Conceptions and misconceptions. *Educational Theory, 40*(4), 423–430.

Eisner, E. (1991). *The enlightened eye: Qualitative inquiry and the enhancement of educational practice*. New York: Macmillan.

Eisner, E. (1992a). Educational reform and the ecology of schooling. *Teachers College Record, 93*(4), 610–627.

Eisner, E. (1992b). The federal reform of schools: Looking for the silver bullet. *Phi Delta Kappan, 73*(9), 722–723.

Eisner, E. (1993). Why standards may not improve schools. *Educational Leadership, 50*(5), 22–23.

Eisner, E. (1994). Do American schools need standards? *School Administrator, 51*(5), 8–11, 13, 15.

Eisner, E. (1995). Standards for American schools: Help or hindrance? *Phi Delta Kappan, 76*(10), 758–764.

Eisner, E. (1998). *The kind of schools we need*. Portsmouth, NH: Heinemann.

Eisner, E. (1999). The uses and limits of performance assessment. *Phi Delta Kappan, 80*(9), 658–670.

Eisner, E. (2002). *The educational imagination* (3rd ed.). Upper Saddle River, NJ: Prentice Hall.

Eisner, E., & Vallance, E. (Eds.). (1974). *Conflicting conceptions of curriculum*. Berkeley, CA: McCutchan.

Furhman, S., & Massell, D. (1992). *Issues and strategies in systemic reform* (CPRE Research Report Series RR-025). New Brunswick, NJ: Consortium for Policy Research in Education.

Lagemann, E. (2000). *An elusive science: The troubling history of educational research*. Chicago: University of Chicago Press.

National Research Council. (1994). *National science education standards*. Washington, DC: National Academy Press.

Page, R. (1995). Who systematizes the systematizers? *Theory Into Practice, 34*(1), 21–29.

Popham, J. (1987). The merits of measurement-driven instruction. *Phi Delta Kappan, 68*(9), 679–682.

Schwab, J. (1969). The practical. *School Review, 78*(1), 1–24.

Thorndike, E. (1910). The contribution of psychology to education. *Journal of Educational Psychology, 1*(1), 5–12.

Tyack, D. (1974). *The one best system*. Cambridge: Harvard University Press.

Weick, K. (1976). Educational organizations as loosely coupled systems. *Administrative Science Quarterly, 21*(1), 1–19.

PART 5

Reflections

18

Elliot Eisner as Educator

Howard Gardner
Harvard University

*E*lliot Eisner is an educator. Indeed, he is one of the few *genuine* educators that I know. In this essay, I want to explain this claim. In addition, I want to pay tribute to a person from whom I have learned much and whose company I have enjoyed for 30 years—ever since we first rubbed shoulders as advisors to a Television Arts Project.

When I speak of an educator, what do I mean? An educator is not the same as a teacher, nor an expert on educational policy, nor a disciplinary scholar who happens to teach at a School of Education. Rather, an educator is a person who has deep and rounded knowledge of the processes of education and who embodies that knowledge in his or her own professional life. Fundamental to being a good educator is being a good teacher in the classroom. With his deep knowledge of several subjects, his interdisciplinary cast of mind, his extraordinary eloquence, his capacity to engage students in dialogue, and his concern about the development of his students, Elliot Eisner is an exemplary teacher.

However, an educator's skills go beyond expertise in the classroom. An educator needs to be knowledgeable about three disparate areas of knowledge. The educator needs to understand the nature of the learning process: how the human mind develops, what its potentials are, and how it can be fashioned along certain lines. Turning from the learner to the teacher, the educator must understand the nature of pedagogy, the development of curriculum, and the ways in which learning can be assessed. Finally, an educator needs to be cognizant of the larger forces that affect any educational system beyond home schooling: the political currents, the economic constraints, the processes at work in the broader society, the ambient culture, and the global context. Among those of us who populate the world of education, Elliot Eisner stands out for his extraordinary grasp of these various facets and how they work—or, all too often, fail to work—together.

Of course, even a polymath like Elliot Eisner must have areas of special expertise. Since I first encountered Elliot in the area of arts education,

I tend to think of his focus as the arts, and particularly the visual arts. (But right away I remember how well he has written about literature and about hybrid arts, like the movies.) Yet a case could be made that Elliot is equally focused on curriculum, on pedagogy, and on qualitative assessment; and that he approaches educational issues with the analytic skills of the philosopher, the rhetorical skills of the lawyer, the sensitivity of the artistic connoisseur, and a "knowledge at his fingertips" (*Fingerspitzgefuehl*) of the relevant social science literature—psychology, sociology, cultural anthropology. And while the mind of educator looms large in these various settings, Elliot can more than hold his own in company where no one knows (or even cares) about educational issues.

Though our education and our styles are quite different, I find myself in agreement with 95% of what Elliot has said and written in the area of education. Typically, he was there first. He has always been sensitive to the different ways of knowing of which human beings are capable. He has understood equally well the role of different kinds of culturally devised symbol systems in capturing knowledge and truths about the world. He has been skeptical of the scientism and quantification that is imposed, often inappropriately, on the curriculum and the classroom. He has appreciated the role of connoisseurship in evaluating classrooms, curricula, and the cultures of school. And he has been perhaps the leading figure in the world in arguing for the legitimate role of artistic expression and knowledge in the classrooms and the experience of each child. We might say that he has mastered the language of Susanne Langer, given John Dewey his due, and extracted what is good from the often-opaque Nelson Goodman.

Not surprisingly, I remember vividly two areas in which we have disagreed. Interestingly, both of the areas of our disagreement have centered on the role of the disciplines in the arts; and both have had their paradoxical facets. Elliot has been more of an enthusiast than I for an arts education that is discipline-based—the form of arts education that was promulgated for two decades by the Getty Center for Education in the Arts. My hesitation with this program had to do with its recommendation that children study the disciplines of art history, art criticism, and aesthetics. My own feeling has been that, before college (or senior high school), the precious time allowed for the arts should be reserved primarily for activities that are distinct from the verbal-analytic bias of school—the making of art. The paradox here is that Elliot began life as a painter, where my involvement in all arts save music has been chiefly as an audience member. Moreover, in most of my writings, I have been an ardent defender of the traditional discipline, while Elliot is more sympathetic to postmodern skepticism about disciplinary boundaries.

The second area has been our disagreement about the requirements for a doctoral dissertation in education. Elliot has been open to the idea that educators should be allowed to submit works of art—and, specifically novels—as a fulfillment of the requirement for the doctorate. I have resisted this idea.

I argue that the doctoral degree is an academic achievement and that the dissertation should be an instance of an academic discipline—usually an analytic discipline like philosophy or one of the social sciences. I have argued, further, that the criteria for evaluating a novel are necessarily different from those entailed in evaluating a piece of scholarship—we can't block a well-researched novel just because we don't like its aesthetic properties, nor should we award a degree to a novel that is artistically effective but based on faulty logic or inaccurate data. (For Elliot's side of the story, see his essay titled *Viewpoints: Should Novels Count as Dissertations in Education?* in *Research on the Teaching of English*, December 1996.) But again, there paradox lurks. In his view of arts education, Elliot defends the disciplines. And it is I, with my theory of multiple intelligences, who might be expected to be more sympathetic to a work of art as a culminating performance in graduate school.

I have a word of advice for those who would disagree with Elliot. Get your arguments straight and practice your rhetoric! Elliot is expert on both dimensions. I have no doubt that if he had decided to be a lawyer, he would be able to bill hours at an astronomic rate. Whether on the strength of his arguments, or in spite of their flaws, Elliot always wins the debates. I must add that he is very gracious—and that I would rather lose a debate to him and learn something, than have the opposite outcome with a less able adversary.

I trust it is clear that I hold Elliot Eisner in extremely high regard as a colleague and friend. I recommend him on both counts. But in saluting Elliot Eisner, I have in mind a broader message for all of us who elect to traffic in the world of education. The field of education cannot and should not be restricted to classroom teachers; nor should it be restricted to those who have mastered a discipline but happen to have found themselves in a Department or School of Education. Just as those who are in public policy or public health should exhibit a special blend of skills and knowledge, so, too, those who call themselves educators should be in possession of a unique set of skills and a defined area of knowledge. Elliot Eisner belongs to that small group that fully merits the descriptor *Educator*. His inspiring example has already swelled the ranks of educators and will continue to do so for many years to come.

19

An Interview With Maxine Greene

Jonathan Matthews

P. Bruce Uhrmacher

Jonathan: Tell us how long you've known Elliot. Do you remember where and when you first met?

Maxine: I've known him more than 20 years. I was at Teacher's College when I first met him. I don't remember why he was in town, but what I do remember was he seemed to have a dash of philosophy of education in his curriculum talk, and I had that funny feeling you get when you want to protect your baby. I thought, "What is he doing talking philosophy?"

We've done a number of gigs together at AERA, over the years. I can't say we agree on everything because we don't. But I can say that we both share a passionate belief in the importance of the arts in education. And of course I love that. Still, I believe that our differences are significant. I believe that Elliot is interested in art in education, which some people say with a small *a*, and I'm interested in Art in education with a big *A*.

Jonathan: Can you talk about that distinction?

Maxine: [At AERA one year, Tom Barone read a fictional essay about education.] Is it right to say that if Tom Barone writes a fiction about a classroom, that we should call it art simply because he used fiction? I impolitely pointed out [at AERA] that Tom Barone is not Leo Tolstoy. You can use the form of fiction, but to say something is a work of art is another cup of tea.

Jonathan: Okay, that's an interesting distinction. So, you feel that art is more of an achievement, perhaps, and Elliot is saying it's a way of knowing or asking?

Maxine: That's really the difference. In my case, aesthetic education has to do with the kind of encounters that Dewey talks about when a work of art becomes an object of your experience and transforms your experience and makes you see things in your

219

experience and in the world you never saw before. And I think that to get people to attend that way, to get involved that way, to get their lives, their energies into the veneer of a painting by Monet or a novel by Tolstoy, they have to be helped to see. And regardless of this, it's not for us to impose interpretations, but to help students see the differences that are there. For instance, in Matisse's painting, *The Piano Lesson*, I'd like to help students notice the shape of the metronome in contrast to the sensual figure. To point to these things is probably more important to me than it is to Elliot.

I'm interested in what are called works of art and all their diversity, and Elliot is interested, as he said, in the kind of perceiving and kind of feeling and the kind of meaning you get from involving yourself in art media.

Jonathan: But I don't think that Elliot disagrees with you about the aesthetic experience. He's very much into Dewey, also, and the true value of a fine work of art and the kind of experience you can have with it, but I think he's trying to broaden the utility. What do you think he's trying to do?

Maxine: I certainly agree with him on that. He's trying to deal, in part, with the problem of representation and our overdependence on technical means of describing, measuring, and representing. In that sense I think we agree with each other. The reason I'm a big supporter of Elliot's, for all of our differences, is that he's a wonderful advocate for something that's all too often ignored, the special kind of capacities and sensitivities neglected by so many educators—partly because they never felt them themselves. And I rather agree with him on the way curriculum and assessment plans, too often, exclude what's impossible to measure—art experience.

In Elliot's new book, *Art and the Creation of Mind*, he writes that an artist starts out with a purpose, with some idea of what he's going to create in the course of his painting. I really disagree with that, if I'm reading him right. Nobody can ever say how a work of art is going to end up. And the other thing I think we disagree on is his concept of the creation of mind. Have you seen his new book? I don't believe that mind is created. I think it develops. I think it develops as a response to inner and outer forces. And I see mind as Dewey did. Dewey said mind is a verb and not a noun. It's a way of acting and a way of feeling. If you look at it that way it's hard to say it's created. We could have a big discussion about that.

Jonathan: He says that the schools help in that creation of mind, right? Would you disagree that, based on the experiences a person

has, his or her mind is created one way or another, depending
upon those experiences?

Maxine: *Created* sounds like a transitive verb. I would say that mind
emerges from certain kinds of experiences, or something like
that. Art is not an agent; it creates. Maybe I'm just quibbling.

Another disagreement that I have with Elliot is that I say he
doesn't allow enough for the mystery of the unanswered question,
the dimension of the unutterable that's in all art. He says that my
criticism is unfounded, but I believe that he hasn't answered it
well. Although he acknowledges the importance of imagination,
I probably put more stress on imagination than he does.

Jonathan: Perhaps we could now explore something that may be related
to your criticism. Elliot is one of the primary thinkers behind
the broadly influential reform movement known as Discipline-
Based Art Education. Some people, though they are relatively
few, criticize it as emphasizing a kind of knowing that is more
like traditional schooling and less like what happens in the
whole imaginative, creative side of art. Where do you see him,
how do you see that whole?

Maxine: DBAE seems to have been a reaction to a romantic period,
expressive approach to the arts. Anything you made was beautiful, as long as it was spontaneous. There was even a kind of
pseudo-Freudian approach for little kids, you know; it came out
of their ignorance/innocence, so it had to be valued. I think the
people who developed DBAE were saying that we lose the work
of art, or we forget a very important part of the artistic process,
if we emphasize only feeling and spontaneity. I object to DBAE,
because, first of all, I think it was too highly cognitive. In the
last analysis, art becomes a discipline like every discipline, and
there is a kind of hierarchy that I never cared about. Again, I
feel that the work of art, and art itself, sort of gets laid aside or
forgotten. When DBAE reached real popularity, I think it was
associated with what they call cultural literacy. Remember that?

Jonathan: Yes, coming from E. D. Hirsch.

Maxine: Cultural literacy, to me, was a conservative way of thinking of
literacy. It was too often read to a kind of mystification that
domesticated the consciousness. Its people, like the beloved rule
of Bennett, wanted to press everybody's literate self into one
mold. I think I worried about that, but in the last couple of
years, when Elliot and I did our soft shoe together, that never
came up as an issue of disagreement.

When you transcribe this, will you say that that I'm speaking
out of an honest and long-term friendship and regard for Elliot?

Like all judgments, mine can be faulty. And like all memory, mine can be incomplete. I don't want people to think I got the last word. I'm talking about my responses over the years on art to a comrade, I guess you would say. Our positions aren't identical at all. And one of the reasons is the distinction that I make: "I'm in aesthetic education; I'm not in art education."

Jonathan: What makes up this distinction? What does it mean for you?

Maxine: It means I focus in my classes on the ways of apprehending or perceiving a painting, for example. And I am very liable to use existential literature, like Merleu-Ponty writing about Cézanne. My hope is that some students, anyway, will find themselves reading the paintings in such a way that some windows open in their own experiences and in their own imaginations. And maybe I downplayed the doing part, the craft part, the expressive. I keep saying the value of learning how to paint, or how to use watercolors, helps you get the feel of what a Cézanne watercolor is. I painted a little with oil and watercolors and that just added a kind of modality to my looking at art. That part is art education. My practice of aesthetic education has been influenced by working for 25 years at Lincoln Center Institute. They used me as a source of doctrine no matter how I protested. My view is very much affected by Dewey and also by existential thinkers like Sartre and Merleu-Ponty. I put a lot of emphasis on a kind of freedom that becomes possible when you hold open many options for life and being. And some of that grows from my feelings about what is still incomplete, what still has to be—that's an existential view. At the end of the documentary about me, I say, "I am what I am not yet." And that's existential. And the arts play into that for me. Because I'm always in process of creating something in myself.

Jonathan: I'm intrigued by this. I'm hearing this emphasis on imagination and freedom, and in contrast, at least for the purpose of this discussion right now, Elliot seems to try to establish for the aesthetic or for arts education a cognitive footing.

Maxine: I think he puts stress on it. I've talked to many of my colleagues at Lincoln Center. I'm likely to say reflectiveness or thoughtfulness rather than cognition. That makes a difference, you know. And I suppose Elliot would agree with me. I'm very, very opposed to dualisms, to the idea that the subject and object are totally separated. I always think in terms of a transaction. For example, I'm influenced by Wolfgang Iser, who talks about the aesthetic object like the painting that is to be set on the wall. That's the aesthetic pole. At the other pole is the person who's going to experience it. But what I'm interested in is the space in between. It's a kind of space that grows in so many fascinating ways. When I look at a painting, I'm experiencing not the painter's view or my view, but something that happens between the two of them. It never happened before, I tell students. It never happened in the world before now because I've never before seen Vermeer at this moment in the world. So something new happens for everybody.

Jonathan: Why do you think that Eisner maybe wanted to emphasize the cognitive? Is it because he's trying to appeal to folks who are not in art education or not in the arts?

Maxine: And then he gets phenomenological. I hope, like the good phenomenologist, he knows how many modes of awareness there are. Like Merleu-Ponty, he talks about perceiving and believing and feeling, and then talks about each of us being the miracle of relationships. Both Elliot and I know Howard Gardner and we respect him a lot. Recently I had an opportunity to respond to Howard. He was going over his own life experiences and all the great Harvard professors he studied with. Howard really belongs to cognitive psychology. Elliot and I were talking and he told me that both he and Howard were at the institute at Stanford. He said if anybody made a real difference in education, it was Howard. That may be so, but I think Elliot probably has differences with Gardner, even though he likes the idea of multiple intelligences. But neither of us are psychologists.

I read an article in the paper about the attack on Descartes and Cartesianism. Some of that depends on a psychologist named Antonio Damasio, who wrote a book on Spinoza (*Looking for Spinoza: Joy, Sorrow, and the Feeling Brain*). People are beginning to say that that old hierarchal, technicist view is not supported, psychologically or otherwise. And Damasio puts a lot of emphasis on feelings and the feeling of experience in the mind. There's a lot of ongoing dialogue that I think Elliot is connected with, even though he did not read Damasio, and I've only read one book of his. He's a new cultural hero. He's going to be the main speaker at the Psychoanalytic Convention, and he was at AERA but wasn't yet recognized. I do think that despite the horror of our times, the pendulum is swinging toward us on some level.

Jonathan: Talking about the pendulum of the time, we have the National Standards, the national testing…

Maxine: I have to speak at a conference on assessment next month. I didn't want to do it. I refused to go. They told me they were going to give me an award and I said I don't want to be thought of as the Queen of Assessment. Now they're letting me write a paper of my own.

My own experience—and part of it is experience with artists I meet at Lincoln Center—is that a standard has to do with the way you reach outward to do something well. I go to Lincoln Center and meet a Balanchine dancer and she's still got her warmers on and she's been at the barre all morning, not because anybody told her she had to be. She knows if she's going to fulfill herself and belong to the Balanchine community, she must do that. And to me, you're each taught your own standard. It has to be something for me, that I create, that says I've got something. But I hate the idea of imposed standards. On the other hand, there's a wonderful little clip in one of the videos about Carnegie Hall and it shows Wynton Marsalis blowing his horn and a little boy is looking up at him. In his face is, "What do you have to do to be Wynton Marsalis?" Wynton Marsalis embodies something he longs for and becomes a kind of standard that the boy chooses. So, I look at it that way.

As far as assessment, I wish I knew the literature better than I do, but I'm very nervous about the uniform curriculum and pushing everything into one basket. I simply cannot believe that numbers can be applied to either art creation or art experience. You know, one of the hard things about teaching art is that you never know when somebody has an artistic aesthetic experience. How do you measure it if you don't even know if he has it? The kid says "Wow." Did you ever see the *Antiques Roadshow* on PBS? They bring in these antiques and these wonderful appraisers point out all the little details and end up saying, "Oh my goodness, you'll get $10,000 for this," and the owner says, "Wow." That's the standard. And it has to depend on what you see or what you feel. But, again, I don't think it should be imposed. And I can just see the school boards frowning.

Jonathan: When the folks who make these high-stakes decisions are relying on the standardized test, what happens to the arts and education, at that point, if it can't be assessed?

Maxine: It's hard. The school boards want the measurements; it's the only thing they understand, it seems. I think somehow or another, school boards have to find a way of protecting what we say about the work of art, its integrity, its impact, and so on. If the lines are crossed, I think we have to point that out every time we go to a school board meeting. When the Lincoln Center had its adventure with assessment, with Howard and Project Zero, it didn't work out. The things they tested were perception and language. But I don't believe in this high-stakes testing in art. This may seem surprising because I am in the field, but it's so incongruous to me to blacken the box for the Rembrandt portrait.

Jonathan: If you had to think about Elliot, what Elliot has done, what would you say has been his greatest contribution? What has he done that you think has been the most positive?

Maxine: Probably, the most positive is that he has done honest and elaborate work in curriculum and in the emerging curriculum in arts education. Also positive is his authority, when he talks about art experience. He talks about arts-based research, which I argue with him about. He already has authority as an educational thinker and even has a kind of nobility as somebody in the field. And therefore, when he talks about art, people listen, much more than they would if he were outside the field of education. He makes a practical difference in terms of continuity and context. And it's one reason, I think, that he's so famous. People know him for curriculum and for other things he's said about teaching and learning. Like in the NSSE yearbook he edited, that kind of thing has given him something that really makes people listen, even if it's in the field they're not in.

Bruce: What are your thoughts about his arts-based research?

Maxine: When he says "arts-based," I don't know what he means by art except, it's a theatre piece, for example. I never could understand why it's called art, that's why I said art with a small *a*. I accept it like that. I don't see that it is, in the last analysis, any better than any other qualitative research. It does capture qualities; it does capture nuances that quantitative research misses. But, I can't see a real important difference between that and qualitative research in general. And then I have all those problems about what they mean by art. They do collages and things like that and I think it's nice, but it's not what I would think of as art. Then, of course, I've always been in a tight spot, because art won't—in fact, can't—be defined. I know that.

There's a philosopher named Morris Weitz who writes about theories of art, the expressive theory, the mimetic theory, the formalist theory—all of them say something about the arts. And then he says at the end, nobody has a final definition that would apply to all the arts we haven't even seen yet. You should see what's at the Guggenheim here, a show about visual objects made of shellac or glue or snot, and images of totally naked women. That is what is being presented as a retrospective in the Guggenheim Museum. So, what the hell is all that? How do I define it?

Jonathan: Let's imagine that you're advising, as you probably do, doctoral students who are interested in issues connecting the arts and education. Where is the interesting work to be done now and in the next decade? Or in aesthetic education? Where do you see work needing to be done?

Maxine: In the *New York Times* the other day, there was an article about focus schools, where the principal is so committed to practicing the arts that they're present in the school all the time, where teaching artists play a very crucial role. I've seen some very good things happen. These schools create situations that are lively, and if the teacher participates and shows herself as a learner, say in dance or improvisation, the whole room seems to change. Another thing that people think works—and I've seen it work and I've seen it not work—is studio in the school. A visual artist is given a studio in a school and she's there a year and the studio is accessible to curriculum makers and to kids. Not everybody agrees with this. The Lincoln Center Institute works with teachers, in the summers usually, who work with professional artists. And in the winter, teachers whose budgets allow them can ask to have those artists and performers in their classrooms. That seems to work. And there's the Heritage School, which was founded by my colleague, Judy Burton, in a predominately Puerto Rican neighborhood. It depends a lot on community arts, using various Puerto Rican art centers and music.

Jonathan: These approaches all feature teaching artists in the schools?

Maxine: I have to say that Judy Burton, my colleague, doesn't like the idea of leaving art education up to unschooled artists, because she thinks that all artists, even very advanced painters or dancers, should take courses in art education. And I'm so cynical, in that I say, "No, leave them alone; don't bother teaching them pedagogical talk." I mean, I know that artists who go in the classroom should know the difference between a 4-year-old and a 12-year-old, but I don't think they have to be initiated into school methodologies. I prefer to leave them with their works of art. I see wonderful things happening even though they're unschooled in pedagogy. That makes me unpopular with my own colleagues. Though she likes my speeches, Judy doesn't like me to say that.

Epilogue

*W*hat can we make of the totality of what we find here? Our contributors' chapters covered the breadth of Eisner's scholarship and its implications for practice. They have extended his ideas and identified routes for future investigations. We end now with a few observations.

1. The great debt to Dewey's ideas has been acknowledged throughout. Although few, if any, writers have placed Eisner squarely in the pragmatic tradition, we contend that such a fit is appropriate. Eisner and his students would likely agree with philosopher Cornel West's statement: "American pragmatism is a diverse and heterogeneous tradition. But its common denominator consists of a future-oriented instrumentalism that tries to deploy thought as a weapon to enable more effective action" (West, 1989, p. 5).

Perhaps "weapon" is too strong of a term, but Eisner has always emphasized understanding and action. Moreover, according to West, John Dewey brought the philosophical ideas of pragmatism to a culmination. "After him, to be a pragmatist is to be a social critic, literary critic, or a poet—in short, a participant in cultural criticism and cultural creation" (West, 1989, p. 71). Eisner's aesthetically rooted reformations, as exemplified by his invention of educational criticism, situate him as a current proponent of the Deweyan project. In looking for further intellectual material, educators committed to Eisner's ideas would do well to explore other pragmatic writers, some of whom would include Thomas Alexander, Cornel West, Hilary Putnam, Richard Rorty, and Richard Shusterman, among others.

2. In the same way that Eisner has refined Dewey's ideas, we still need educators to refine Eisner's. Eisner has begun the larger project of applying aesthetic and artistic ideas, metaphors, and skills to curriculum, educational inquiry, arts education and teaching, teacher education, and school reform.

There are three avenues to be pursued for those interested in carrying on Eisner's work. First, some may wish to delve more deeply into areas that writers in this book have outlined. Concepts could be further developed, critiqued, and extended. Second, some educators may wish to extend Eisner's way of thinking to educational issues and concerns that have not been explored yet. This book has provided examples in museums, social studies, music, and dance, among others. Students of math, vocational education, or the natural sciences, for example, may wish to explore Eisner's ideas and their implications for these fields. Third, applications could be created from these concepts. Continuing work awaits those able to apply these ideas in specific, local contexts that will positively alter the schooling experiences of teachers and children.

3. As Donmoyer indicated, if the ideas of cognitive pluralism are to survive, we need curriculum writers to place Eisner's larger conceptual ideas into lesson plans and curriculum units. Teachers, curriculum writers, and administrators ought to consider these ideas and carry them forward. For example, how could teachers use a category such as *expressive outcomes* in lesson plans? Or, do we teach toward students' strengths in a form of representation or do we teach toward their weaknesses in order to strengthen their skills? Do we always try to provide a balance of forms of representation? Or, are there times in which some forms of representation are simply irrelevant? How do we assess nonlinguistic forms of representation?

4. A few writers have alluded to the fact that more work needs to be done with policy-makers and administrators. With the ever-increasing influence of state and national standards and assessments, those interested in advancing the Eisnerian agenda need to be involved in trying to influence their form. Admittedly, Eisner himself has long done extensive work with administrators, hosting meetings for both principals and superintendents. Still, with few exceptions, Eisner and like-minded scholars could do more to help administrators understand and implement cognitive pluralist ideas. Could administrators use educational criticism and connoisseurship to assess teachers? Could administrators create a school culture in which educational criticism and connoisseurship are part of the educational landscape? How might school time and space be conceptualized and partitioned to maximize cognitive pluralist ideas? In other words, what would it mean to think of classrooms with studio time and space? Similarly, more work ought to be done to meet with, understand, and influence policy-makers.

5. Because Elliot Eisner writes so eloquently and persuasively, one can richly experience him solely through the printed page. He cares tremendously about writing well. But for all his work on perfecting his words, Eisner's genius is more than good ideas clearly expressed. A large part of Eisner's genius is his personal dynamism, his ambition to make a difference, his unflagging energy and endurance, his joy in the discerning comment and interesting insight— from himself or from others—and the penetrating thrill that he experiences in the presence of the beautiful, the perceptive, the creative, and the wise.

How much do you care to make a difference for school children? How much can you give? How strong is your vision? How much are you willing to sacrifice yourself to try to fix what is broken in the schools? How much passion can you feel about what you claim is important to you? How completely can you express this passion to others? How much genuinely productive work can you accomplish in an hour, a day, a week? How little does fear keep you from doing what you know to be right? How easily do you succumb to fatigue?

Undeniably, it is the intellectual gifts that Elliot Eisner brings to bear that have enabled him to articulate his insights. However, without his personal dynamism, his enduring passion to communicate to others what he finds important, his impact would have been a fraction of what he has achieved.

The educational world desperately needs to hear the message that Elliot Eisner is communicating. This volume reveals that others are taking up the charge, carrying the good fight into the new century. While we hope that Eisner himself will lead this charge for many more years, our wish for those who resonate with his call is that they will continue to invigorate the message with similar passion and insight.

REFERENCES

West, Cornel. (1989). *The American evasion of philosophy: A genealogy of pragmatism.* Madison: The University of Wisconsin Press.

Essential Reading on Eisner

*T*he following is a list of Eisner's writings that we deem essential for those pursuing his ideas in the areas focused upon in this book. The criteria we have used are (1) the writing delineates Eisner's ideas, (2) the writing can be found in most libraries, and (3) the writing has historical significance. Note that some of the writings below could be placed in several categories, but we have included them only once.

ON EISNER'S LIFE AND INTELLECTUAL INFLUENCES

Barone, T. (2002). *Aesthetics, politics, and educational inquiry: Essays and examples*. New York: Peter Lang.

Eisner, E. W. (1998). *The kind of schools we need: Personal essays*. Portsmouth, NH: Heinemann.

Eisner, E. W. (2000). A trip to the moon on gossamer wings: My journey through academia. In Ralph Raunft (Ed.), *The Autobiographical Lectures of Some Prominent Art Educators*. Reston, VA: National Art Education Association.

Uhrmacher, P. B. (2001). Elliot Eisner, (1933–). Joy Palmer (Ed.), *Fifty Modern Thinkers on Eduation: From Piaget to the Present*. New York: Routledge.

CURRICULUM

Eisner, E. W. (1985). Educational objectives: Help or hindrance? *The art of educational evaluation: A personal view* (pp. 29–38). London: Falmer Press. (Original work published 1967)

Eisner, E. W. (1994). *Cognition and curriculum reconsidered*. New York: Teachers College Press. (Original edition *Cognition and curriculum: A basis for deciding what to teach*: Longman, 1982).

Eisner, E. W. (1994, May). Do American schools need standards? *School Administrator, 51*(5), 8–15.

Eisner, E. W. (1994). *The educational imagination: On the design and evaluation of school programs* (3rd ed.). New York: Macmillan.

Eisner, E. W. (1995). Standards in schools: Help or hindrance? *Phi Delta Kappan, 76*(10), 758–754.

ARTS EDUCATION

Eisner, E. W. (1965, May). Children's creativity in art: A study of types. *American Educational Research Journal, 2*(3), 125–136.

Eisner, E. W. (1972). *Educating artistic vision.* New York: Macmillan. Reprinted by the National Arts Educational Association, Reston, VA, 1997.

Eisner, E. W. (1973–1974). Examining some myths in art education, *Studies in Art Education, 15*(2), 7–16.

Eisner, E. W. (1981, September). The role of the arts in cognition and curriculum. *Phi Delta Kappan, 63*(1), 48–52.

Eisner, E. W. (1985). Aesthetic modes of knowing. In *Learning and teaching the ways of knowing*, 84th yearbook of the National Society for the Study of Education. Chicago: University of Chicago Press.

Eisner, E. W. (1991). What the arts taught me about education. In W. Schubert & G. Willis (Eds.), *Reflections from the heart of educational inquiry: Understanding curricula and teaching through the arts.* New York: SUNY Press.

Eisner, E. W. (1992, April). The misunderstood role of the arts in human development. *Phi Delta Kappan, 73*(8), 591–595.

Eisner, E. W. (2001, January). What does it mean to say a school is doing well? *Phi Delta Kappan, 82*(5), 367–372.

Eisner, E. W. (2002). *The arts and the creation of mind.* New Haven: Yale University Press.

Eisner, E. W. (2002). What can education learn from the arts about the practice of education? *Journal of Curriculum & Supervision, 18*(1), 4–16.

RESEARCH AND EVALUATION

Eisner, E. W. (1976). Educational connoisseurship and educational criticism: Their forms and functions in educational evaluation. *Journal of Aesthetic Education, 10*(3/4), Bicentennial Issue, 135–150.

Eisner, E. W. (1984, March). Can educational research inform educational practice? *Phi Delta Kappan, 65*(7), 447–452.

Eisner, E. W. (1985). *The art of educational evaluation: A personal view.* London: Falmer Press.

Eisner, E. W. (1988, June–July). The primacy of experience and the politics of method. *Educational Researcher, 17*(5), 15–20.

Eisner, E. W., & Peshkin, A. (Eds.). (1990). *Qualitative inquiry in education: The continuing debate.* New York: Teachers College Press.

Eisner, E. W. (1991). *The enlightened eye: Qualitative inquiry and the enhancement of educational practice*. New York: Macmillan.

Eisner, E. W. (1991). Taking a second look: Educational connoisseurship revisited. In D. Phillips & M. McLaughlin (Eds.), *Evaluation and education at quarter century*, National Society for the Study of Education Yearbook. Chicago: University of Chicago Press.

Eisner, E. W. (1992, Spring). Objectivity in educational research. *Curriculum Inquiry, 22*(1), 9–16.

Eisner, E. W. (1993, October). Forms of understanding and the future of educational research. *Educational Researcher, 22*(7), 5–11.

Eisner, E. W., & Barone, T. (1997). Arts-based educational research. In R. Jaeger (Ed.), *Complimentary methods of educational research*. New York: Macmillan.

SCHOOL REFORM, TEACHING, AND TEACHER EDUCATION

Eisner, E. W., & Vallance, E. (Eds.). (1974). *Conflicting conceptions of curriculum*. Berkeley, CA: McCutchan.

Eisner, E. W. (1983, January). The art and craft of teaching. *Educational Leadership, 40*(4), 4–13.

Eisner, E. W. (Ed.). (1985). *Learning and teaching the ways of knowing*, 84th yearbook of the National Society for the Study of Education. Chicago: University of Chicago Press.

Eisner, E. W. (1998). *The kind of schools we need*. Portsmouth, NH: Heinemann.

Eisner, E. W. (2002). From episteme to phronesis to artistry in the study and improvement of teaching. *Teaching & Teacher Education 18*(4), 375–385.

Author Index

Alexander, Thomas, 227
Allison, Brian, 97
American Association of Teaching and Curriculum (AATC), 153
American Educational Research Association (AERA), 156
Angelou, Maya, 176
Apple, Michael, 23
Archer, Bruce, 93
Arnheim, Rudolf, 93, 130

Bagley, C., 122
Bardwell, L. V., 82
Barkan, Manuel, 95
Barone, Tom, xv, 2; arts-based research, 22, 24, 25, 117–25; fiction and, 219; research, 139–40, 142, 146, 151
Bateson, Gregory, 159
Baynes, Ken, 93
Becker, Howard, 133
Berger, E., 192
Best, David, 99
Black, P., 203
Blake, William, 179
Bloom, B. S., 19, 135
Bobbit, Franklin, 49
Bogdan, R., 159
Boughton, Douglas, 81
Brooks, R., 142
Bruner, Jerome, 97, 99
Burke, T., 57
Burton, Judy, 226
Buttignol, M., 122

Callahan, R., 201
Cancienne, M. B., 122
Carroll, W. M., 22
Cassirer, Ernst, 130

Ceglowski, D., 122
Cherryholmes, C. H., 55
Cizek, Franz, 93
Clandinin, D. Jean, xvi, 81, 122, 163–72
Cohen, David, 157
Colwell, R. J., 108
Connelly, F. Michael, 81, 122, 164, 167, 169
Conroy, Pat, 176
Cox, W., 142
Cremin, L., 208
Cronbach, Lee, 21, 202
Cubberly, E. L., 201

Damasio, Antonio R., 223
Davis, Jessica Hoffman, 78, 122
Davis, O. L., Jr., 134
Denzin, N., 119, 159
Descartes, R., 223
Detels, C., 108
Dewey, John: arts, 19, 67, 70, 132; criticism, 71, 75, 132; educational reform, 203, 204, 205–9, 210–11; evaluation, 81; experience, 72, 78, 80, 83, 167, 219, 220; imagination, 35; impulses, xiv, 36; influence of, 93, 99, 117, 205–7, 216, 222; inquiry, 21; legacy of, 201–2; platform construction, 57; pragmatism, 227; progressivism, 185, 191; recreation, 37; sequential learning, 191; social studies, 184, 190; Thorndike and, xvi, 169, 198, 206–7; transactive knowledge, 130, 136; United Kingdom and, 93; vision of, 199–201

Subject Index

About the Authors

$\mathcal{T}$om **Barone** is Professor of Education at Arizona State University, where he teaches courses in curriculum studies and qualitative research methods. He is the author of *Aesthetics, Politics, and Educational Inquiry: Essays and Examples* (2000) and *Touching Eternity: The Enduring Outcomes of Teaching* (2001). Barone is coeditor of the on-line *International Journal of Education and the Arts*.

D. Jean Clandinin is Professor and Director of the Centre for Research for Teacher Education and Development at the University of Alberta. She is a former teacher, counselor, and psychologist. She is coauthor with Michael Connelly of four books and many chapters and articles. Their most recent book, *Narrative Inquiry*, was published in 2000. She is part of an ongoing inquiry into teacher knowledge and teachers' professional knowledge landscapes. She is past Vice President of Division B of AERA and is the 1993 winner of AERA's Early Career Award. She is the 1999 winner of the Canadian Education Association Whitworth Award for educational research. She was awarded the Division B Lifetime Achievement Award in 2002 from AERA.

Robert Donmoyer is currently a Professor of Leadership Studies at the University of San Diego. Prior to assuming his current position, he worked for 20 years as a faculty member and administrator at The Ohio State University. At Ohio State he served as Director of the School of Educational Policy and Leadership. He currently serves as a consultant on school reform and evaluation with a number of foundations and with school districts in Texas and California. He is the former features editor of the American Educational Research Association journal, *Educational Researcher*.

Kieran Egan is a Professor in the Faculty of Education at Simon Fraser University, British Columbia, Canada. He is the author of a number of books, including *The Educated Mind* (1998). He is a recipient of the Grawemeyer Award in Education and is a foreign associate member of the National Academy of Education.

David J. Flinders is an Associate Professor at Indiana University, Bloomington. He is the coeditor (with Stephen J. Thornton) of the *Curriculum Studies Reader* (1997), coeditor (with Geoffrey Mills) of *Theory and Concepts in Qualitative Research* (1993), and coauthor (with C. A. Bowers) of *Responsive Teaching* (1990). His research interests focus on curriculum and secondary education.

Howard Gardner is the John H. and Elisabeth A. Hobbs Professor of Cognition and Education, and a Senior Director of Project Zero, at the Harvard Graduate School of Education. He is the author of many books in psychology and education, including *Frames Of Mind* (1983) and *The Disciplined Mind* (2000). For more than 30 years, in loci all over the planet, he has enjoyed visiting, collaborating, and (on occasion) arguing with Elliot Eisner.

Maxine Greene is the emeritus, William F. Russell Professor in the Foundations of Education at Columbia University's Teachers College. For decades a Professor of Philosophy and Education at Teachers College, Greene continues to teach courses and serve as the founding director of TC's Center for Social Imagination, the Arts, and Education. She is also the Philosopher in Residence at the Lincoln Center Institute for the Arts in Education and the past president of the Philosophy of Education Society, the American Educational Studies Association, and the American Educational Research Association.

James Henderson is Professor of Curriculum Studies at Kent State University. His scholarship focuses on curriculum-based teaching. He has published a wide range of articles and books on the interrelated topics of reflective inquiry in teaching, transformative curriculum leadership, and democratic curriculum wisdom.

Sam M. Intrator is Assistant Professor of Education and Child Study at Smith College. He is a former high school teacher and administrator. His research inquires into what it takes for teachers and students to co-create intellectually vibrant and genuinely meaningful experiences in the classroom. He is the author of *Tuned In and Fired Up: How Teaching Can Inspire Real Learning in the Classroom* (2003) and is the editor of *Teaching With Fire: Poems That Sustain the Courage to Teach* (2003).

Philip W. Jackson is the David Lee Shillinglaw Distinguished Service Professor Emeritus in the Departments of Education and Psychology at the University of Chicago.

Jonathan Matthews received his Ph.D. in Education from Stanford University in 1994. His areas of interest include arts education, social studies education, and teacher education. He is currently an Associate Professor of Education, the Director of Student Teaching, and the Educator Licensure Officer at Carroll College in Helena, Montana.

Denise Clark Pope is a lecturer at Stanford University School of Education. Her research interests include curriculum studies, service learning, qualitative research methods, and adolescent academic stress. Her book *Doing School: How We Are Creating a Generation of Stressed Out, Materialistic, and Miseducated Students* (2001) was recently awarded Notable Book in Education by the American School Board Journal.

Bennett Reimer is the John W. Beattie Professor of Music Education Emeritus at Northwestern University, Evanston, Illinois. Author of *A Philosophy of Music Education* (1970, 1989, and 2003: Advancing the Vision), and author and editor of a dozen books and more than a hundred articles, chapters, and other pieces, he has lectured throughout the United States and the world, and has been inducted into the Music Educators Hall of Fame. A special issue of the *Journal of Aesthetic Education,* titled *Musings: Essays in Honor of Bennett Reimer*, was published in Winter 1999.

Janice Ross is a faculty member in the Department of Drama at Stanford University. Prior to that, for 10 years, she was staff dance and performance art critic for the *Oakland Tribune*. She has written for *Dancemagazine*, the *New York Times* and the *Los Angeles Times*, among other publications. Her book, *Moving Lessons: Margaret H'Doubler and the Beginning of Dance in American Education*, was published by the University of Wisconsin Press in 2000. She was a 2001–2002 fellow at the Stanford Humanities Center where she worked on a biography of Anna Halprin to be published by U. C. Press. She is a member of the Board of Directors of the Society of Dance History Scholars and is past president of the Dance Critics Association. She is the recipient of a 2001 Guggenheim Fellowship.

William H. Schubert is Professor and Chair of Curriculum and Instruction at the University of Illinois at Chicago. He has published about 200 articles and chapters and his books include *Curriculum: Perspective, Paradigm, and Possibility* (1986), *Turning Points in Curriculum* (1999), *Reflections From the Heart of Educational Inquiry* (1991), *Teacher Lore* (1992), *Curriculum Books: The First Hundred Years* (2002), and *The American Curriculum* (1994). He has been president of The Society for the Study of Curriculum History, the John Dewey Society, and the Society of Professors of Education, and vice president of the American Educational Research Association. One of his current interests is curriculum devised and perpetuated by collaborations among corporate, mass media, government, military, and other seedbeds of power.

John Steers was appointed General Secretary of the National Society for Art Education (now the National Society for Education in Art and Design) in 1981 after 14 years teaching art and design in secondary schools in London and Bristol. He was the 1993–96 President of the International Society for Education through Art and served on its executive committee in several capacities between 1983 and the present. He has served on many national committees and as a consultant to government agencies. He has published widely on curriculum, assessment and policy issues. He is a trustee of the Higher Education in Art and Design Trust and the Chair of the Trustees of the National Arts Education Archive, University of Leeds. He is also a visiting Senior Research Fellow at the University of Surrey Roehampton, London.

Daniel Tanner is Professor of Education in the Graduate School of Education at Rutgers University, where he directs the graduate program in Curriculum Theory and Development. He is a past president of the John Dewey Society and author of many books, including *Crusade for Democracy: Progressive Education at the Crossroads* (2002), and, with Laurel Tanner, *Curriculum Development: Theory Into Practice*, scheduled for its fourth edition in 2005, and *History of the School Curriculum* (1990). He has lectured at many universities in the United States and abroad, and has contributed articles to many leading national and international journals and periodicals, including the *Atlantic Monthly*, the *New York Times*, and the *Bulletin of the Atomic Scientists*.

Stephen J. Thornton is Associate Professor of Social Studies and Education at Teachers College, Columbia University. He is coeditor of the *Curriculum Studies Reader* (1997) and is currently working on a book about educating teachers to enact social studies curriculum, which is to be published by Teachers College Press.

P. Bruce Uhrmacher is Associate Professor of Education and Director of Curriculum and Instruction at the College of Education, University of Denver. He is the book review editor for the *International Journal of Leadership in Education* and a past president of the American Association for Teaching and Curriculum (AATC). His areas of interest include arts education, alternative education (e.g., Waldorf schools), curriculum studies, and qualitative research. He did his doctoral work with Elliot Eisner at Stanford (1985–91).

Elizabeth (Beau) Vallance is Associate Professor of Art Education at Northern Illinois University, coming there in Fall 2000 after 15 years as Director of Education at the Saint Louis Art Museum and a prior career in university administration. At NIU, she works with both undergraduate and graduate programs in museum studies. She has published extensively in the areas of aesthetic criticism and qualitative evaluation, the hidden curriculum, curriculum theory applied to the museum setting, and learning in museums. She did her doctoral work at Stanford with Elliot Eisner and coincidentally was Vice President of Division B (Curriculum Studies) of the American Educational Research Association while Eisner was President (1991–93). She is active in the American Association of Museums and the National Art Education Association.